C000065067

The Evolution of
Consciousness:
A New Science

Andrew Lohrey

"The Evolution of Consciousness: A New Science is a bravura achievement and a poke in the eye for uncompromising materialism and our current obsession with individuality. With this book Andrew Lohrey delivers a detailed explanation of consciousness and also what happens in observation. Drawing on an impressive array of sources, this courageous book bridges the physical sciences, philosophy, psychology and spirituality. For Lohrey consciousness is fundamental. I hope this life-affirming book will be widely read, because it will add to the peace, joy, empathy and love that our struggling species requires for our survival."

~ Larry Dossey, MD
Author: *One Mind: How Our Individual Mind Is Part of a Greater Consciousness and Why It Matters*

"This is a book about all that really matters – the truth underpinning all our life and all our words – the Truth beneath the truth, and you show us the one consciousness with a gentle courage so obviously a product of a life lived with great spiritual and intellectual maturity".

~ James Boyce, PhD, historian and Author: *Born Bad: Original Sin and the Making of the Western World*

"Your brilliant book is a fascinating read – very concise and clear – and a beautiful model of consciousness that makes absolute sense. It illuminates many aspects of social action, scientific thought and individual development, including:
- How to understand interconnectedness and nonlocality in quantum mechanics
- How elementary particles can exhibit consciousness

- How reductionism separates things that are actually unified and contributes to social fragmentation and individual alienation
- How it is possible to heal the binary division in Western culture between mind and brain.
- This book is recommended to everyone seeking to transform or transcend society and achieve wholeness through a collective wisdom that comes from comprehension and meaning. It is also a valuable resource for meditators."

~ Bruce Boreham, Professor of Physics/Head Department of Physics CQU, 1989–98

The Evolution of Consciousness:

A New Science

Andrew Lohrey

ICRL Press
Princeton, New Jersey

Now I a fourfold vision see
And a fourfold vision is given to me
Tis fourfold in my supreme delight
And three-fold in soft Beulah's night
And twofold Always.
May God us keep
From single vision & Newton's sleep.

—William Blake, 1802

Contents

Foreword

Andrew Lohrey makes some astounding observations in this remarkably clear book. There is great virtue in his clarity of expression, for we all know it is very hard to divorce form from content. In the process of reading it, you may have the experience, as I did, of gaining a sense of participation in the expanded and collective consciousness that he aims not to 'capture', 'explain' or 'describe', but to live through in a process of engagement. In that sense, Dr. Lohrey's mind is not at the origin of the thoughts he expresses, nor our individual minds its individual and piecemeal recipients. The language he uses, simply and clearly expressed, humbles itself before something much greater that aspires to universal relevance.

I join with him wholeheartedly in his rejection of the snake-oil salesmanship involved in much of the cognitive psychological approaches to mind and brain that dominate the fields of therapy, where patients are medicalised as individuals. Their brains, subject to chemical adjustment, are treated as 'command centres', organs in control of other organs, as if humans were structured like a corporation or army. But we are not alone, we are intensely social beings who live in movements of life-enhancement with other beings: human, animal, plant, spirits. It is cruel to isolate individuals and force them to identify with their symptoms.

The collective consciousness Andrew Lohrey is talking about has as its corollary the endlessly surprising unknowability of what we are in the habit of calling the Universe. Advances in quantum physics uncover as many mysteries as they appear to solve, as the infinitely small and the infinitely large seem to be without limits, yet with amazing internal resonance: what we think we know is known by virtue of, and only through, its shareability. Lohrey's embrace of relationality is not just his idea; it is found in the 'hardest' of sciences as well as contemporary theories of aesthetics. Language, the most familiar basis for human meaning-creation, is itself a relational thing. Its elements are structured differentially, or by way of on-going contrasts. It connects all of its speakers, decentring their individual brains, or linking them like nodes in a network. And yet we still don't know what language is! Perhaps this is because it is an on-going and open-ended process of participation, for whatever rules or certainties might emerge about phonetics, syntax or semantics, language's capacity to mean still depends on its rule-breaking capacities. And each time its forms delight and surprise us, we can glimpse that expanded and universalising consciousness that Andrew Lohrey is talking about.

The holistic approach that Andrew Lohrey has embraced (or been embraced by) is both very ancient and common to many non-Western knowledge systems. The atomisation of individuals I have discussed here is as recent an invention as the practice of the separation of the concepts of Nature and Culture, body and mind, subject and object. Those recent aberrations continue to serve their destructive and alienating purposes: turning non-human beings and things into materials feeding accelerated human (industrial) growth. Perhaps those wise traditions that Andrew Lohrey so eloquently joins us to, can forcefully combine, as we pay attention and attune ourselves to the multiple dimensions we necessarily inhabit. For reducing life to the mantra of objectivity, efficiency and profitability neglects other modes of existence: the moral, the spiritual, the aesthetic and the political, to name just a few. Yes, even politics, for those of us allied to

Andrew Lohrey's thinking have a fight on our hands. What we value as much as life itself will not be saved by withdrawing from the public sphere. But as he says, our participation can be both direct and indirect, explicit and implicit. This book is an invaluable guide to the enhancement of energies that hitch a ride through words, feelings and actions, energies that make each other grow as they weave and join.

Stephen Muecke, Jury Professor University of Adelaide, March 2018.

Preface

In 1997 the University of Michigan Press published *The Meaning of Consciousness*. My aim in that book was to argue for a more scientific treatment of consciousness through an analysis of signs and the role of language. This was a work in progress that I have come to realise is located within a broader cultural context or stream of thought. I refer here to the historical unification of Western and Eastern thought. While this movement has been going for over two thousand years there has been an increase in its energy and intensity over the last century.

The French intellectual and Nobel Laureate Romain Rolland (1866–1944) was fond of writing in the 1920s to his friends in India – Tagore, Gandhi, Nehru – about the necessity for Europe to profit from Asian thought and vice versa. He called the cultural distinctions that separate the West from the East the two hemispheres of the brain of mankind. This metaphor suggests that the Western left-brain scientific and technological thought processes need to be married to the more intuitive, joyful consciousness of right-brain Asian sensibilities. If the global culture of mankind is similar to an individual's mind (which I think it is) then this interlinking is a dire necessity for human survival. *The Evolution of Consciousness: A New Science* represents part of this historical unifying movement.

The capacities I bring to this book come from my training in the philosophy of communication and applied linguistics as well as the practical experience of working for some years as a clinical psychologist. What this training and experience have given me is a critical appreciation of how we make meaning through our use of language and how that usage constructs our thoughts and influences the way we perceive the world. No subject matter, whether religious or scientific, is free from the critical influence of the processes of meaning-making; no subject matter, therefore, will be free from consciousness, meaning and mind.

I began my studies into language, meaning and consciousness more than forty years ago from the standpoint of a secular materialist. Then in the early 1990s my secular view changed. Living in Sydney with my wife Amanda and daughter Cleo, I was persuaded against my better judgment to have a blessing from a visiting Indian saint: Mata Amritanandamayi, also known as Amma. At a free public program Cleo, who was then nine years old, asked me to take her up for a blessing. Amanda was busy – what harm could there be in this simple request? Amma took Cleo in her arms and as I looked at them I felt all the muscles in my body weaken. Then I was taken into Amma's embrace and with my head in her shoulder she held me tight.

I do not remember if anything was said. All I remember was the feeling. This was a baptism by *pneuma*, the kind Jesus was said to give. Outside I lay down under a gum tree, disoriented. I looked up at the midday sky and literally saw stars. I felt such strange happiness. That was it. No discussion, no discourse, just a hug. That year I was turning my PhD dissertation on consciousness and meaning into a book and for the first time I began to contextualise my writing by giving it some spiritual dimension. I had been a card-carrying materialist for years. I began to wonder if I was going soft in the head. However, the hug took the effect of broadening my horizon and slowly making me aware of the significance and omnipresence of the actual subject matter I had been working on: meaning. I began to realise that my atheist inclinations had kept me tied to the shadows of Plato's cave, a cave in which explicit, constituent features can appear dominant as if they could exist without any underlying context.

Then, in 2012, I trekked with my nephew Richard to the source of the river Ganges, a place called Gaumouk, high in the Indian Himalayas. I had come to Gaumouk thinking I was going to die. That thought was both liberating and fearful and at once physical and mental. The physical basis of the thought came from our terrifying jeep ride up from Rishikesh to Gangotri, the town from which we began our trek; the mental came from my long-held desire to bundle up all my fears and leave the package under a rock at Gaumouk.

For several days, I prayed for this to happen before we arrived at the source of the Ganges, for it seemed to me that this special spiritual place was the right place to leave my fears. I knew that if I lost my fears I would also lose my ego. In the event I didn't lose my ego but I did have some extraordinary spiritual experiences of unity along with a sense of my ascent to heaven (described in Chapter 17).

The spiritual experiences that came to me in India, along with my Western training in applied linguistics, have not turned this book into a confessional memoir or a theological discourse. Those readers who take the subject matter of meaning to be essentially theological will be disappointed. This book uses Western intellectual methods to articulate Eastern notions of consciousness and as a consequence, the meanings of a set of key terms will be slightly different from their traditional uses. For example, I use the term 'One Consciousness', with capitals, to mean the underlying ground or field of Meaning from which everything in the universe arises through a series of transformations. Sometimes the terms 'cosmic consciousness' or the 'meaning of Meaning' are used to refer to the same underlying ground. I have balked at using the word 'God' as it carries so many diverse meanings.

It is one aspect of my thesis that there are no terms more appropriate for the meaning of One Consciousness than *implicit-to-implicit* exchanges. This may sound dry and abstract but this term is explained with all its latent poetry in Chapters 3, 4 and 5. Broadly, this approach produced a seeding of ideas concerning the question of how science could deliberately include consciousness in the form of an evolution – an evolution that also involves the individual's spiritual evolution.

The Evolution of Consciousness: A New Science argues that the underlying reality of the universe, what David Bohm called the 'holomovement', is not information as most scientists think, but meaning – cosmic meaning. The distinction between information and meaning is significant. 'Information' is one of those closed icons used in standard mechanical scientific discourses, while 'meaning' is a more open, holistic and interconnecting term. Another consequence of the difference between these terms and approaches is the assumption that space and time are physical features of an independent universe. This mechanistic assumption is an illusion when consciousness is taken into account, for both are then seen to be features of consciousness.

This book argues that meaning and consciousness are content words for the same singular, unbroken, interconnected spiritual reality, which I call One Consciousness or the meaning of Meaning. One of the consequences of this focus on consciousness is the holographic nature of the individual's relationship to the whole of cosmic consciousness. 'Holographic' in this sense means that the whole inheres in the part (the individual's mind) while simultaneously, the individual's mind represents a local feature of cosmic consciousness.

A further consequence of this holistic approach is that humans have seven ways to see and make meaning of the world. Some of these ways are more reliable and meaningful than others but all have an internal bias, which means there is no objective and unbiased way of observing the world. The more trustworthy views make better meaning as they mirror the interconnecting structure of meaning more closely than do the confused shadows of more partial viewpoints.

Introduction

In *Mind and Cosmos: Why the Materialist Neo-Darwinian Conception of Nature Is Almost Entirely False*, Thomas Nagel proposes that science should take account of mind, meaning and value and should view them as being as fundamental as space-time. He writes: 'the current orthodoxy about the cosmic order is the product of governing assumptions that are unsupported, and that fly in the face of common sense' (Nagel 2012: 5).

Nagel criticises reductive neo-Darwinian accounts that see life as a result of a sequence of physical accidents. His comments have created a storm of criticism from mainstream materialists who castigate what they perceive to be his sympathy for intelligent design theory. Yet Nagel is a declared atheist who has attempted to occupy a sceptical position between the traditional theist, who proposes that God's intentional purpose has created life, and the reductive materialist orthodoxy that argues for the role of pure chance.

The space Nagel has selected is the 'hope for a transcendent self-understanding that is neither theist nor reductionist' (2012: 29). This is the space for his 'natural teleology', the idea that the universe has an internally coherent order. It's a place distinct from the conventional understanding of teleology, which is concerned with the intentional purposes of a supernatural God. Nagel's position represents a courageous standpoint for it is one that pleases neither creationists nor orthodox scientists.

Yet Nagel's stand on natural teleology is weakened somewhat

by his position on consciousness. On the one hand, he argues for a 'genuine alternative' to the reductionist program that would include 'an account of how mind and everything that goes with it is inherent in the universe' (2012: 15). On the other hand, he fails to put forward such a program, calling instead for a series of requirements that he sees as necessary to deliver this alternative.

The present book is an attempt to chart and extend Nagel's alternative of a transcendent self-understanding through mapping the contours of the evolution of consciousness. This program is neither theological, creationist nor materialist; rather, it is metaphysical. Being is the traditional subject matter of metaphysics, but mind, consciousness and meaning along with the concepts of order and disorder are also the rightful subject matter of metaphysical dialogue. Metaphysics deals with first principles and thus the order of the universe. Such principles provide us with a clear view of the 'flowing water' of consciousness, in contrast to those muddy streams of psychology based on biological instincts and drives (the approach taken by Sigmund Freud) or, more recently, the computations and brain states of neuroscience.

Consciousness and meaning function as metaphysical realities inherent in the order/disorder, structures and organisations of the universe. This book attempts to disclose those structures and functions through methods of investigation that rely upon critical distinctions, evidence and unifying models. This is a program that is not driven by adherence to a particular creed or narrative. What is important when confronted by the kind of ideological quandaries that surround Nagel's book (or this one) is not so much the question of whom we are to believe, but the more important and prior question of what kind of predispositions we bring to the subject matter of consciousness. In other words, what is the viewpoint we privilege? This basic question needs to be asked before any investigation begins, whether scientific, economic or religious.

The Evolution of Consciousness: A New Science details a range of supporting evidence for the proposition of one universal consciousness while also proposing seven ways in which humans are able to see and interpret the world. Seeing, or the more technical term 'observation', is a central feature of consciousness. Yet the practice of observation remains largely a mystery to mainstream science, and a few lines from Fritjof Capra's *The Turning Point* illustrate this:

> The crucial feature of quantum theory is that the observer is not only necessary to observe the properties of an atomic phenomenon, but it is necessary even to bring about these properties. My conscious decision about how to observe, say, an electron will determine the electron's properties to some extent. If I ask it a particle question, it will give me a particle answer; if I ask it a wave question, it will give me a wave answer. The electron does not *have* objective properties independent of my mind. (Capra 1982: 86–7)

Most of us take visual perception for granted as if it were a neutral act that plays no part in constructing the physical world or how we understand that world. Yet if observation can determine the properties of particles (the building blocks of the physical world) then the consciousness that is inherent in observation must have an agency that can order the world we see so that, as Capra says, 'we can never speak about nature without at the same time speaking about ourselves'.

The role of observation in science is recognised as central to doing science, yet the act of observation remains largely a mystery for both mechanical Newtonian science and quantum physics. It is a mystery because the reference frame of materialism says that the processes of observation do not influence the observed and these processes are limited personal actions that are independent of the real objective physical world. When there is clear evidence that this subject–object reference frame of materialism is inadequate, as in quantum physics, answers about observation become unresolved mysteries.

Most of us believe there is only one correct and 'real' way of seeing the world. Realist science uses the subject–object reference frame to tell us that the act of seeing comes from light entering the eyes and impacting the retina, rods and cone cells of the eye where it is then converted into patterns of electrical energy that travel along the neurons in the optic nerves to the brain's visual cortex at the back of the head and a visual experience is produced.

This mechanical explanation, with its exclusive focus on physical process, tells us little about our sense of seeing and suggests that consciousness is marginal or not involved. It also implies that there is only one real way to see. In my view these assumptions are mistaken: consciousness is not only involved in the processes of visual perception, it is the creator of them. In addition, I argue that there are at least seven ways of seeing, and when this diversity is taken into account the effect is to increase the possibility of understanding why others see the world differently from us.

Each of the seven ways of seeing has a bias, a predisposition, and several of these predispositions conflict with other ways of seeing. This means that there is no objective and unbiased way of observing the world, even for science. However, the seven ways of seeing are not separate from each other but fit together into an ordered framework that reveals the several dynamic steps of the evolution of consciousness.[1]

This evolving order means that some of these ways of seeing are more reliable than others. The difference between the trustworthy and the disorganised relates to how evolved and mature are the seeing practices we use. The most ordered is the most evolved way of seeing and this involves the practice of Self-seeing, which entails becoming aware of the *sight within our seeing.*

The present book is also an attempt to heal the historical rift between science and spirituality by focusing on the subject matter of meaning. To take meaning into account in any review of the world or mind is to begin to elucidate the structures and functions of what I am calling One Consciousness while also inviting context, connection, compassion and love into the debate. Such an invitation is a radical departure from mainstream materialist science.

I have begun, in Part I, by using a reference frame that is holistic. By holistic I mean something similar to what Capra argues, that we can never speak about nature without at the same time speaking about ourselves. This means that every observation, every proposition or statement we make or receive about the world will contain complementary implications about our preferences of interpretation – of seeing. It means that all knowledge, whether scientific or everyday thinking or experience, is dependent on consciousness and will have a bias in relation to the way we see and understand. This means that our view of any experiment or discourse will be constituted by the viewpoint we prefer to use. The important question is not how to strive after the fiction of objectivity, but to acknowledge and come to terms with the nature of the bias we privilege.

The holistic reference frame of this study is itself not neutral or 'objective' but values interconnection and the inclusion of consciousness and meaning within every observation, experiment or discourse. In order to appreciate the range of biases in the seven steps of human understanding my focus is on the underlying reality and power of One Consciousness – the omnipresent unity created by universal interconnections, which contain the preconditions that determine all mental and physical forms.

Teilhard de Chardin (1970: 76) tells us that 'In all things there is a Within, coextensive with their Without'. I call this Within and Without reality 'One Consciousness' rather than using a more traditional term such as Tao, God, Brahman, or *unus mundus*. If I were to use any of these terms I would be committed to a set of discourses and propositions that lead me away from a close reading and a forensic study of the metaphysical structures and evolutionary functions of One Consciousness. In the close reading I have embarked on here, meaning plays the key explanatory role, for as I see it, consciousness and meaning are two sides of the one coin.

In this examination I have focused on the metaphysical states, functions, relationships and structures of meaning, for these have greater explanatory powers than the computations of neuroscience, psychological terms, historical events or the analysis of myth. This use of meaning to explain consciousness offers a new framework for expanding our understanding of consciousness, our place in Nature and who we are. It also means that consciousness, meaning and mind have a central role to play in every scientific or mundane endeavour. Hence I am concerned to interrogate how meaning is made in the vocabularies of science, and specifically in theories of visual perception.

In order to deal with consciousness, mainstream science has tended to have two kinds of responses: i) meaning, mind and consciousness are simply deleted from any discussion of the physical world; ii) meaning is ignored as a subject matter, while mind and consciousness are devalued to an extent that renders them minor but necessary features difficult to analyse. Devaluing mind and consciousness is done most commonly by employing the doctrine of many minds. This doctrine, which is supported by absolutely no scientific evidence, says that each individual person has a separate individual mind. The doctrine of many minds is a key feature of the materialism of mainstream science and the kind of subject–object reference frame that tells us we live in two worlds: the dead physical one that is considered to be primary and devoid of life, and the subjective one that is mental, but secondary and of little relevance.

In the holistic approach I take here, observation stands as a bridge that connects the mental and the physical, and this connection contrasts with the materialist reference frame that separates these two. In order to understand this bridging function of observation it is necessary to discard all separating reference frames and replace them with a more holistic and integrated paradigm. Yet to discard the orthodox or what I call *separation seeing* is difficult and we can find evidence of this even with the Nobel Laureate Frances Crick, who in *The Astonishing Hypothesis* (1994) opted for this approach. Crick's astonishing hypothesis turns out to be nothing more than that the brain causes the mind and as a consequence, perception. In this and similar studies the mind and consciousness are poorly understood, and they are usually represented by bland descriptions of conscious deliberation that become almost add-ons to the intricacies of brain functions. Such common materialistic approaches tend to institutionalise the separating dogmas of materialism while telling us little about visual perception or what is going on with the transformations that turn light into visual images.

A prime example of the materialist approach to consciousness is found in neuroscience. Many experiments have shown how the human mind is closely linked to neurophysiological and biochemical processes in the brain, yet most of these studies rely upon detailed descriptions of brain functions in contrast to simple understandings of the mind. This approach has led to the belief that the brain can learn and relearn through processes that are called 'neuroplasticity', which I discuss in Chapter 1.

I argue in Chapter 2 in favour of the holistic proposition that says there is only one holographic consciousness that contains every mind. The basis of this unifying consciousness is not the politics of time, but rather, the politics of eternity,[2] by which I mean that the politics of time keeps us preoccupied with the details, forms and distinctions of the everyday physical world. While this focus is necessary for practical purposes, when we become hypnotised by this kind of engagement we will be blind to the underlying politics of eternity. The politics of eternity represents how we progress through the seven ways of seeing and these in turn constitute the various steps in the evolution of consciousness. In other words, the politics of eternity is concerned with our accord with, or resistance to, our own inevitable spiritual evolution. This evolution begins in a place of ignorance and disorder where patterns of identification tend to control and narrow our understanding and judgment. Then, through the internal momentum that innate learning brings, we gradually progress towards a broader, holistic understanding involving that eternal, implicit context that gives life deeper meaning.

In this holistic approach, there are no gaps or separations within the several physical and mental processes involved in perception or life. This is because the scope and force of One Consciousness encompasses the body, the environment and the wider universe and includes such universal functions as 'order' and 'disorder'. The argument for one universal consciousness is further developed in Chapter 3, 4 and 5 in terms of states, codes, relationships and structure of meaning. In Chapter 6 the limitations and confusion generated by information theory are examined and critiqued.

This book lays great stress on *relations* as the defining character of meaning and thus of consciousness. Since writing *The Meaning of Consciousness* I have come to appreciate that meaning can adequately represent the essential relations of intelligibility. As forms of intelligibility, relations of meaning can be understood as the forms referred to by Plato. Without relations of meaning there is no intelligibility. Plato's forms have always been somewhat mysterious to philosophers; nevertheless, they are generally understood to be eternal patterns of intelligibility, which come from a source that Plato called the Good.

From the perspective I am adopting, meaning is understood not simply as a by-product of signs or the effects of interpretation (the linguistic and semiotic view) but as the nature of beingness, that is, meaning has the same vital features as life and consciousness. As a consequence, meaning stands as the universal, eternal resource of intelligibility as well as manifesting locally within the individual's mind and through communication practices. Such practices are located both within the body and externally in society, as exchanges beyond the body. In other words, meaning is both the essence of intelligibility as well as carrying cultural and social intelligence by way of communication exchanges.

Hence the driving force of this study of consciousness comes from the metaphysical context of meaning. It is infinitely holistic in the sense that the relationships of meaning are present in every aspect, feature or point in nature, for they are omnipresent throughout the entire universe. It is, therefore, quite impossible to observe or analyse any aspect of the universe or society or mind without relying upon the eternal relations of meaning. The metaphysics of meaning also provide a way of comparing any human behaviour without resorting to the inevitable challenges that arise from employing the measuring sticks of cultural difference or linguistic formations.

Part II of this book is *First and Second Sight*. First sight represents our immediate visual experience of the environment, while second sight amounts to at least six ways we can interpret that first sight. First sight can be said to represent the 'isness' of Nature while second sight represents how we deal with that 'isness'. The distinction between first and second sight reflects what Susanna Siegel (2011) has called the difference between the content and the rich content view of visual perception. In Part II I examine the traditional arguments about visual perception and how these differ from my own approach, which relies upon the integrating and eternal context of One Consciousness.

The idea that there are different ways of seeing is not new. 'Ways of Seeing' was a successful four-part BBC television series that was adapted into a book of the same name (*Ways of Seeing* by John Berger, 1972). In the book and television series the authors John Berger and Mike Didd argue that we see differently when the social context changes: 'The way we see things is affected by what we *know or what we believe*' (Berger 1972: 8).

Perhaps the most celebrated text on ways of seeing comes from Plato (427–347 BC) as described in *The Republic,* circa 375 BC. Plato's parable of the cave of the mind presents a graphic image of how many of us see shadows, believing them to be reality, while missing the light of true knowledge. Plato asks us to imagine an underground chamber like a cave where men who have been there since they were children have their heads fixed so they can only look straight ahead at a curtain wall. On this curtain shadows appear like a puppet show. The shadows cast have a variety of forms that are created out of sight, behind the curtain.

Reality for these prisoners of the cave is the shadows cast on the curtain wall. As they live their entire life in a cave they are unable to look upon the outside light of the sun, which represents the 'light of the Good'. For Plato, the light of the Good is an eternal spiritual light of truth, beauty and justice and its glare will hurt the eyes of cave prisoners for their sight is only attuned to the darkness of shadows. We are told, however, that if a prisoner were to be removed from the cave it would take some time for him to grow accustomed to the light of the upper world outside the cave and, therefore, to see naturally. For Plato, our inability to see the light of the Good comes from a prolonged period of living in the darkness of a cave. I suggest that Plato's metaphor of the cave points us towards the current proposition that the spiritual reality of an evolving consciousness underlies the everyday life of time-consuming activity. His metaphor also suggests that of the seven ways in which we see the world, several take the shadows of separation to be real.

Today Plato's parable of the cave is generally unacceptable to the scientific community, many of whose members are content to live with the mystery of visual perception, a mystery that comes from the inexplicable gap between the mental and physical. A gap also appears to exist in the question of how the sun produces visual perception. There is no scientific response to this question.

Applying Plato's distinction between light and shadows to the seven ways of seeing, three of these ways can be called *shadow seeing*, and these are: *ego seeing, tribal seeing* and *separation seeing*, while *light seeing* is represented by *empathic seeing, clairvoyant seeing* and *Self seeing*. Each of the three shadow ways of seeing create the illusion of gaps and divisions in a world that is actually unified. These fictional gaps are created by various predispositions that have the common aim of producing a world of separations. The shadow ways of seeing represent the most common ways by which most of us see the world for most of the time.

Seeing, however, is not fixed into a single method, even in adults. Humans are able to change and have some control over their interpretations and predispositions, and therefore of the ways in which they see the world. In contrast to this freedom of choice is the first and fundamental way of seeing, which I call first sight. We have no control or freedom over its processes, for these are constructed by the eternal ordering potentials of One Consciousness. I also argue that these same potentials organise our autonomic nervous systems and link them to the environment through sensory and extrasensory perception.

In regard to first sight, when we open our eyes we have no control over seeing or not seeing. The only control mechanism we have is not to open our eyes or to look away. For materialists, the 'isness' of first sight creates the status of the independent physical world. This conflation of visual cortex images with an independent physical world occurs because meaning, mind and consciousness have been deleted from mainstream science to be replaced by the separating paradigm of subject versus object. From the holistic perspective, the isness of the physical world necessarily arises within the processes of perception and because of this dependency on consciousness the physical world cannot be regarded as primary, but simply as a secondary result of consciousness.

However, even though first sight is given, we retain the ability to evolve and change *shadow seeing* into *light seeing*. Such a change involves the six other ways of seeing that we have some influence over. How we see is greatly affected by the cultural milieu in which we live, and yet no culture determines these ways of seeing or the number of ways to see. Rather, all seven ways of seeing are transpersonal and transcultural for they arise out of the nature of meaning, that is, out of the evolutionary transformations of One Consciousness.

In Part III of this book, *Seeing the Light*, I provide a detailed description of the six ways of seeing. I argue that the movement from *ego seeing* to *Self seeing* represents an evolving path from the shadows of a fixed, isolated and narrow time-bound world of stress and pain into a broader, contextual and eternal landscape where equilibrium, peace and fulfilment are to be found.

Part I

The Frame

I

Many Minds

The reference frame through which we can study consciousness and visual perception (or anything else) is never a neutral platform; instead, it is always an active ingredient in determining what and how we see and understand. Because of this it is worth looking directly at the cultural reference frame used by almost all investigators into consciousness and visual perception, and as well to look at an alternative reference frame. This discussion covers the next seven chapters.

Since visual perception is an event that happens within consciousness we need to ask some questions about the connection between mind (incorporating perception) and consciousness. Broadly, this relationship is between a constituent and its context, and here consciousness represents the context in which the mind, the constituent, operates. Yet an immediate problem arises: all too often we tend to focus on the constituent data of the mind (perception and thought) and forget about the context of the larger consciousness that underlies it – One Consciousness. When this happens all kinds of problems are created such as the doctrine of many minds.

The doctrine of many minds is the most common reference frame used to either casually discuss or seriously study mind and perception. This is a doctrine that deletes the broader context of consciousness while overemphasising the constituent and explicit data of the mind. It tells us that each individual person has his or her own private and separate mind. There are many versions or models of this doctrine, from *laissez faire* economics to the cult of individualism to the belief that there is no such thing as society to the materialism of science, but they all agree on the central idea that the individual's autonomous being has a mind that is separate from other minds. The woof and weave of this doctrine has been woven on a thousand looms. This cultural drapery hangs on the walls of a million caves, convincing those who with fixed stares look upon the constituent marks and known boundaries of this fabric that they have a separate identity and that they die with their body.

In order to give a flavour of this doctrine I want to briefly discuss four of these models and then look at any evidence that could support this doctrine. The four models are: the neurological model; two norm-based models; the Christian model; and the physics model.

The neurological model is essentially a materialist model that says the individual's private mind arises from the brain. This model of the mind is fairly bland in that the mind is said to consist of the functions of conscious attention, volition and choice. There are none of the complications evident in psycho-analytic models such as unconscious repressed desires or redirected libidinal energy. Also in this model, there is no pre-reflective consciousness, no subconsciousness and no unrepressed unconscious. Here there is simply the one explicit category of conscious volitional (intentional) processes that on the scans of positron emission tomography (PET) show up as associated with increases in energy use within the frontal lobes of the brain.

Philosophers and neuroscientists who adhere to the doctrine of many minds interpret the correlation of brain and mind activity as the brain causing the mind. In addition, as mental activity is seen to consist of only explicit intentional action, these data of the mind (perception and thought) are reduced to become ancillary to the physical causes within the brain. With this binary interpretation, a variety of mind functions are commonly allocated to the brain and interpreted as brain functions. For example, the physical brain cannot learn or recognise things; it cannot encode or decode information; and it cannot differentiate, and so the terms 'neuroplasticity' and 'neurodifferentiation' are false.

Each of the following terms represents basic processes of mind: 'learning', 'differentiation', 'encoding', 'decoding' and 'recognition'. These are not and can never be brain processes. When neuroscientists call these mind functions 'brain functions', they are confused about which is which. When mind functions are allocated as brain functions it is usually because scientists and philosophers have a weak understanding of or interest in the mind and consciousness. Such interpretations also devalue the mind to such an extent that mind functions slip easily into oblivion and then seem to become part of a physical context.

This confusion and slippage has happened with neurological discussions about 'neuroplasticity'. Neuroplasticity is said to be the process in which the brain's neural pathways and synapses are altered permanently. The cause of this change is put down to the environment or behavioural or neuronal changes. Neuroscientists once thought that human adults had a hard-wired brain with fixed neural pathways. Such a view meant that rehabilitation for adults who had various kinds of brain damage was useless, an impossible dream. All that has now changed in the light of current research being conducted in North America and Europe.

Research in this area is now offering new hope to people with chronic pain, multiple sclerosis, strokes and Parkinson's, as well as with autism, attention deficits and sensory processing disorders. In his books, Norman Doidge describes this research in detail and tells the stories of a range of people who undergo treatment for what in the past has been largely seen as incurable conditions. Doidge's most recent book, *The Brain's Way of Healing* (2015), describes some remarkable recoveries from drug-free treatments without side effects. These are truly astonishing results unimagined by most in the medical profession even twenty years ago.

Yet while we applaud these new non-drug treatments and their extraordinary results, the analysis of neuroplasticity tends to fall back into the old reference frame that degrades the mental while separating it from the physical. Evidence of this view comes from the suggestion that neuroplasticity works on the basis of 'brain homeostasis as a new method of self-healing' (Doidge 2015: 267). The term 'brain homeostasis' excludes the mind yet it is the mind that learns, relearns and creates habits of behaviour as well as initiating the relearning of old habits. This is plasticity. The term 'neuroplasticity' is rhetoric and should be changed to something like 'mind-plasticity' or even 'psy-plasticity' to reflect more accurately what is actually going on.[3]

This materialist view is not unique to neuroscience but reflects the broad culture of science in its predisposition to separate what is essentially integrated while awarding honoured status to the physical and devaluing the mental. The predisposition of this reference frame I have called *separation seeing* because it creates separations by overvaluing differences in a manner that turns them into divisions. In relation to mind, *separation seeing* proposes that every person has a separate mind that is spoken about in terms of personal subjectivity, a state independent of and in opposition to the objectivity of the physical world. This belief is the doctrine of many minds.[4]

Norm-based models of mind. There are two models I want to discuss: the current psychiatric model and the older psychoanalytic model, both of which propose that individuals have separate minds. The American Psychiatric Association (APA) employs the doctrine of many minds when assessing and categorising mental illness, as published in their regular Diagnostic and Statistical Manuals of Mental Disorders (DSM). The APA approach to mental disorders compares the individual's mind and behaviour with the social and behavioural norms of North Americans.

One of the difficulties of this approach is its reliance on the character of the North American 'norm'. When making decisions through its committee structures on what constitutes mental disorder, members of the APA assess specific individual behaviour in relation to North American norms. One of the key features of the North American norm is a deeply held belief in the doctrine of many minds, a belief that is frequently articulated through the ideology of individualism and often in the more extreme forms of libertarianism. In other words, the North American norm that is taken to be the gold standard for 'normal' is by no means a neutral system or above the suspicion of having hidden cultural and economic biases.

As all social norms represent a series of community habits rather than clearly thought out social benchmarks, it means that when the APA uses norm-based assessments for mental disorders it is using a very crude tool for understanding the mind, consciousness or the causes of mental disorders. Closely associated with this norm-based approach to mental disorders is the traditional medical model that relies heavily on drugs to treat most mental conditions. While drugs clearly have a place in the treatment of a wide range of mental disorders, the medical model of mind leaves much to be desired when it comes to fully appreciating the role of mind in medicine. For example, the physician Karen Hitchcock offered the following statement in a column written for *The Monthly* magazine: 'Unfortunately, in medicine, in theory, in popular culture and society, we've disconnected the mind or psyche from the body and chucked the psyche part away' (June 2014: 17).

Hitchcock wrote about her experiences in a large Melbourne

hospital, and of an epidemic of patients (between 30% and 50%) who attend specialist clinics and present with 'functional' disorders, a functional disorder being one that has no organic cause. Hitchcock concluded: 'Don't blame medicine, for it is all of us who have decided that dreams are debris, that a symptom generated "in your head" is merely counterfeit and that sickness is always caused by a *thing*.' It seems that medical authorities feel compelled to deny the importance of mind while using their minds to do so.

The binary division between mind and brain that is evident in the neurological model is also present in the APA approach to mental disorders, while also acting to reinforce medical responses at the local level of the general practitioner. These models and approaches, based as they are on the doctrine of many minds, have a tendency to view the cause and remedy of mental illness as more likely to be physical. This kind of materialism represents one way of closing down questions about the role of mind, meaning and consciousness.

Different from the APA's view of mental disorders but still a norm-based approach to mental illness was Sigmund Freud's (1856–1939) view of mind. Approximately a hundred years ago Freud based his theories of mind and psyche on the doctrine of many minds. For Freud and almost every psychologist, psychiatrist, biologist and physicist in the twentieth century, the individual's mind represents a private territory that is separate from other minds as well as from nature, while pathology was seen as a condition that the individual's mind often manifests.

When Freud raised the question of neurosis and whether a community could be neurotic he admitted that here we are faced with a 'special difficulty'. This difficulty relates to the manner in which individual neuroses are diagnosed. He said, 'in an individual neurosis we take as our starting-point the contrast that distinguishes the patient from his environment, which is assumed to be "normal"' (Freud 1961: 91). Freud thought that one day someone might embark on diagnosing the pathology of society. For him, however, it was unnecessary to address this because he was concerned solely with the pathology of the individual's mind, which he assumed to be separate from anything that could be called a community or collective mind.

Freud was convinced that the impetus for all psychological states was essentially biological. It was, therefore, inevitable that he created a psycho-biological model of mind that had as its source the concept of a 'drive' or 'instinct'. The drive or instinct represents the physical agency that generates the movements of the individual's mind. Yet the term 'instinct' is confusing when used in relation to mental conditions because it fuses together mental with biological attributes in ways that are never explained. But this confusion did not prevent Freud from employing these terms in his theories. In particular, he asserted that he found human instincts embedded within hunger and love and also within love and discord.[5]

In essence, Freud's psychobiological model is too limiting and restrictive to truly represent a reflective human mind because it rests on the concept of animal instincts. It also overvalues the role of sexual and aggressive behaviour and excludes other more peaceful motivations. His approach was also limited by its reliance on the Western materialistic belief that the body contains the mind, specifically, a mind within the brain.

A **Christian model** of mind reflects to some degree the role that instincts play in Freud's theory of mind. The historian James Boyce makes this point in his history of the notion of original sin: *Born Bad: Original Sin and the Making of the Western World* (2014). Boyce suggests that the paradox for the twentieth-century secular West was that the old Christian idea of original sin would live on as a new scientific theory of mind. 'The most standout example of this was the work of the most influential exponent of the science of mind, Sigmund Freud' (Boyce 2014: 155).

While Freud had little time for religion, the instinctual role of his 'id' system reflects the role that St Augustine (358–430) ordained for original sin in Christian belief. This doctrine rests on the sure conviction that each of us has a mind that is unfortunately stained by evil. That mind, however, is private and capable of guilt but also separate from God. The Western concept of God has been of the Other. As Ken Wilber argues, this separation is not simply the separation of a psychological unconsciousness, or the separation of time, or a separation because of ignorance, but is an ontological separation, 'separate from us by nature, forever' (Wilber 1996: 5).

The separating metaphysics underpinning this kind of religious thought (separate minds separated from God) finds support in the doctrine of original sin. The guilt that comes from believing in this doctrine, or similar separating dogmas, continually produces a sense of personal failure and then alienation from others as well as from the Divine. Any institution that deals in the strategies and rhetoric of guilt (secular or religious) acts in a tribal manner to further its own institutional interests over those of its members.

The ideas of both the id and original sin have innately negative propensities with which we, the private individual must suffer. Both notions are associated with desires and sexual behaviour that we are told should be suppressed either by religious moral duty or, in terms of Freud's theories, by the 'superego' (our conscience). Both these ideas are dogmatic and demand acceptance without question, and both promote the illusion of many separate minds. However, neither the concepts of sexual desire (Freud's id system) nor original sin provide an adequate or compelling understanding of human behaviour, or the human mind, or the Divine.

The **physics model of mind** is often not well described because the subculture of physics dismisses or devalues mind in favour of a studied focus on physical processes. Yet the doctrine of many minds is an inherent part of classical Newtonian physics and Einstein's relativity theories. These practices contain the assumed binary separation of mind and matter and subject and object. The French philosopher Rene Descartes (1596–1650) thought that the world was like a machine and that each person had a unique immortal soul whose identity over time continued no matter what happened to the body.

Descartes first formulated the mind-body problem in the form in which it is known today. His dualism was based on the idea that the mechanical world of physical objects (*res extensa*) is independent and separate from the mind (*res cogitans*) of the observer. Amit Goswami states that, 'It was, however, Newton and his heirs going into the eighteenth century who solidly established materialism' (Goswami 1995: 15). Goswami tells us that to understand the Cartesian-Newtonian view of the world we should 'think of the universe as a big bunch of billiard balls' within a three-dimensional space. This was Descartes' view, a mechanical world that is independent of the mind.

Thus the role that mind plays in mechanical physics is that of an inferior category, which has little scientific interest. Nevertheless, I will argue that it is impossible to do any scientific work without also implying some model of mind. The model assumed by mainstream science posits a subjective, conscious mind that has few descriptive features except that it thinks, makes choices and is produced by the brain. One easy example of how the doctrine of many minds takes its place in the grounding assumptions of classical physics is the case of the rainbow and the question: 'is the rainbow real'? Everyone sees the same rainbow and we even have a consensus about it. Yet as the theoretical physicist David Bohm (1917–92) says:

But physics, which looks at things 'literally', says, "No, there is no rainbow. There are a lot of droplets of water, the sun is in back of you and it's being reflected and refracted off the water and forming colours. In seeing this each person is forming his own perception of a rainbow". (Bohm 2006: 67)

In this description we see the doctrine of many minds at work. It exists within the inference carried by the sentence 'In seeing this each person is forming his own perception of a rainbow'. Here is the hidden doctrine of separate minds that influences us in a logic that many minds must perceive many different rainbows, yet we assume they are all the same. The common consensus that we have of seeing the same rainbow happens with every single rainbow and every healthy person. Is this an illusion as physicists think? The physicist's response is that while we assume we see the same rainbow we never know for sure because we all have separate private minds. In other words, in the face of any evidence to the contrary the orthodoxy of separate minds produces the answer 'there is no rainbow'.

For the physicist, the rainbow is not real because the word 'real' can only be applied to an independent, objective physical world, and so cannot refer to mental activities. Yet I will argue that the doctrine of many minds is a fallacy, along with the separation of mind and matter. If this separating doctrine were true there would be no human society or community, only an aggregate of separate individuals who would have no common bonds or networks for exchanging meaning. It is the exchange of meaning in communication practices that create social and cultural networks, and hence if there was only an aggregate of separate minds there would be no communication and no shared, common underlying connections of meaning. Thus the end result of the logic of many minds is the impossibility of social and community intercourse. As we do live in societies where meaning is exchanged beyond the physical body the doctrine is clearly wrong.

When our tendency is to assume the reality of many minds

without question, this inhibits our understanding of science and also of many things about human behaviour. This doctrine also hinders our understanding of extrasensory perception, telepathy, precognition, clairvoyance and mystical sensations of oneness with the universe. Even though there is a vast array of scientific evidence for each of these transpersonal events, we will be inclined to dismiss all that evidence as so much 'anomalous phenomena'. This is what happens when we hold fast to the fiction of the doctrine of many minds.

Evidence

The fiction of many minds does not stand up to close scrutiny. For example, how do we determine the precise territory of the individual's separate mind? Where does the mind end and the environment or society begin? Where are these boundaries located and identified? It is extremely difficult if not impossible to show the precise boundary that separates one mind from another or even your body from the environment. For example, does the air you breathe become you once it is breathed in? And what about when you breathe out? Are you then losing yourself? The same questions can be asked about food and water. The body also represents millions of dynamic biological processes that are never separated from each other or from their environment. Like the problem of measuring the infinite length of the coast of Great Britain, it means the precise boundaries of any organism are impossible to determine.

If we were scientific about this question of a separate mind we would conduct a search of scientific experiments that showed support for the doctrine of many minds. Should we do this we will discover there is no actual scientific evidence that supports the idea of separate, private minds and therefore of private ownership. The closest we may come to finding supporting evidence for this doctrine of many minds is in the philosophy of Ludwig

Wittgenstein (1889–1951) and his famous proposal for the idea of a private language. The nonsense of a private language establishes itself through the limitation that you cannot use it to exchange meaning because as soon as you do it is no longer private. Like the idea of a private language, the idea of a private mind vanishes with its use.

Yet in the face of 'no supporting evidence' most physicists, along with most of the scientific community, continue to believe that the doctrine of many separate minds is secure and true. To understand why this widespread false belief is held we need to go back to Bohm's description of a rainbow. In that description, we see two overlapping assumptions in operation: i) the doctrine of many minds; and ii) the binary division that separates the subjective from an independent, objective world. These two doctrines are always interwoven and self-supporting: when one falls to the ground so does the other. Hence, in order to support the belief in an independent, objective world, which is the very foundation of mechanics, scientists are forced to take on board the other fiction of separate private minds.

In terms of visual perception, the doctrine of many minds lays before us two possibilities involving a private, subjective world and an objective, independent environment. The historical results of this binary division have limited our understanding of visual perception because we begin our studies based upon a lie. Either we say the objective world is unknowable, a position many philosophers have taken, and so perception is an entirely internal operation of the physical nervous system; or we propose that visual perception is an innocent act of mirroring an unknowable physical world. This last approach is called naïve realism, a position I come back to in Part II of this book. However, both these approaches are inherently problematic as well as leaving the processes of actually seeing an unexplained mystery.

In order to remove ourselves away from the shadows of this merry-go-round of many minds and the binary logic of subjective versus objective, we need to break the mould by assuming consciousness to be one whole integrated system. The down side of doing so is that we challenge not only the widespread belief in many minds, but also one of the basic tenets of materialistic science, which is the belief in the reality of an objective, independent world. I would like to have avoided these challenges if I could as it is always easier to be on the side of the mainstream, yet I see no other recourse than to actually speak of consciousness as one whole interconnected system. When we begin to use this holistic reference frame our viewpoint is immediately expanded and we gain a focus on the more important general evolving character of consciousness, of which visual perception is a part.

This holistic view of consciousness begins in the next chapter with the assertion that consciousness is one, and that the many individual minds of organisms are interesting but derived features of this singular, universal interconnected system.

2

One Consciousness

From the Stoic philosopher and Roman Emperor Marcus Aurelius (121–180) comes an early description of some of the features of the one universal consciousness that the present book proposes. In his *Meditations* he wrote:

> All things are interwoven with one another; a sacred bond unites them; there is scarcely one thing that is isolated from another. Everything is coordinated; everything works together in giving form to the one universe. The world-order is a unity made up of multiplicity. (Aurelius, Book 7, 9)

Meditations is a discourse on service, duty and how to establish equanimity within ourselves. It takes its philosophic base from Stoic thought, which conceives of the whole universe as only one substance: *Physis*. This one substance was considered to be reason, which in turn is God. Such ideas have now fallen out of favour not only with Christian thought but also with the materialism of Western science.

Ralph Waldo Emerson wrote the essay *Over-soul* in 1841. He describes the unity of the Over-soul this way: 'that Unity, that Over-soul, within which every man's particular being is contained and made one'. This is a description close to the proposal of this book: of one holographic consciousness in which every mind represents a local part. The Over-soul also has similarities with Carl Jung's (1875–1961) collective unconscious, which Jung considered to be the unconscious mind that all humans share. In the early part of the twentieth century, together with his physicist friend Nobel Laureate Wolfgang Pauli, Jung developed the theory of a unitary reality underlying all manifest things. Jung called it by the ancient term *unus mundus*, meaning unitary world.

The *unus mundus* is a 'cosmic order independent of choice and distinct from the world of phenomena' (Storr 1983: 334). As Pauli stated, it contains all the 'preconditions that determine the form of empirical phenomena, both mental and physical' (Hauke 2000: 249). In his book *Synchronicity: An Acausal Connecting Principle*, Jung (1973: 70) suggests that the nature of this underlying reality could be meaning. My view is that meaning and consciousness are two sides to the same coin and thus it follows that Jung and Pauli's unitary cosmic order (*unus mundus*) reflects the same reality that is discussed here as One Consciousness.

Also, early in the twentieth century a group of scientists became interested in the role that consciousness seemed to play in quantum physics. They had names like Bohr, Heisenberg, Schrödinger, De Broglie, Jeans, Pauli, and Sir Arthur Eddington. With the concerns of this group the long hiatus between Marcus Aurelius' thoughts and modern science began to close. Physics had begun to shift from ontology – learning about the identities of the physical world 'out there' – to epistemology – learning about what represents our knowledge of the world. Commenting on this change, Schwartz and Begley (2002: 273) tell us that 'Physical theory thus underwent a tectonic shift, from a theory about physical reality to a theory about our knowledge'.

With the change from classic Newtonian physics to quantum physics, the role of consciousness also changed from a marginal and inferior bit-part into the central starring role in the drama of science. This happened because of the increasingly important role observation – seeing – came to play in quantum physics, which began to reinforce an ancient Vedic understanding: the physical world only arises through the act of observing it. The theoretical physicist John Wheeler (1911–2008) was to tell us that 'No phenomenon is a real phenomenon until it is an observed phenomenon'.

This change from the realist perspective of Newtonian physics to the more inclusive but ambiguous view of quantum physics has not always been well accepted by scientists in the last century. This is especially the case for the role that consciousness plays generally in scientific endeavours. Early on in the twentieth century the astronomer Sir Arthur Eddington (1892–1944) summed up the difficulty that many scientists were having with consciousness and mind: 'It is difficult for the matter-of-fact physicist to accept the view that the substratum of everything is of a mental character. But no one can deny that mind is the first and most direct thing in our experience' (Wilber 1984: 187).

Eddington became famous for explaining Einstein's theory of general relativity and also for arguing that what we refer to as the physical reality of the universe is a mathematical skeleton scheme of symbols, and that this skeleton scheme is not the ground or base stuff of the universe. Rather, 'The stuff of the world is mind-stuff ... The mind-stuff of the world is, of course, something more general than our individual conscious minds' (Wilber 1984: 180).

The physicist and Nobel Laureate Erwin Schrödinger had similar ideas. In *What is Life* he wrote, 'consciousness is a singular of which the plural is unknown' (Schrödinger 1993: 89). He also refers to the arithmetical paradox of the one mind. Schrödinger suggests that the real world around us springs from the one source, which he calls the arithmetical paradox, that is, the paradox of how the many are one. This is the paradox of the many conscious minds 'from whose mental experiences the one world is concocted' (1993: 128).

One way to come to terms with Schrödinger's arithmetical paradox (of many minds being one) is through the model of the hologram. The hologram, for example, can act as an explanatory image that helps us understand how each individual mind is different from others, yet at the same time existing as an integrated part of the fundamental fabric that is universal consciousness.

A hologram is a three-dimensional image that can be imprinted onto a photographic plate. When a laser beam illuminates the plate, it reveals a three-dimensional image that is almost identical to the original object. When a small region of the plate is cut off and is illuminated again by a laser beam, what we see is not a piece of the image but the whole image in a diluted form. This is extraordinary for it means that the whole of the three-dimensional image has been recorded in every part of the plate.

The complex structure of a hologram is created by the exchange relationship of part-to-whole and whole-to-part, and it is these exchange relationships that give the hologram its undivided interconnectedness or wholeness. In addition, within the hologram is an asymmetric order in that the part arises from the whole and not the other way around. Together these functions of an exchange relationships and the inherent asymmetric order of the hologram provides a volume that is layered with interconnecting relationships.

Hence the hologram provides us with a general model for understanding what appears at first sight to be a multiplicity of separate and autonomous minds but which are wholly interconnected and integrated into the overall universal system of One Consciousness. Like the various visual patterns that make up the fabric of the holographic image, the unique patterns of individual minds create the interconnected fabric of society and culture, and these sets of distinctions are also part of One Consciousness.

The exchange relationship of part-to-whole and whole-to-part is a concept that goes back over three thousand years to the ancient scriptures called the Vedas, an example of which is the *Chandogya Upanishad*. Here it was written that within the city of Brahman there is the heart and within the heart there is a small house: 'This house has the shape of a lotus, and within it dwells that which is to be sought after, inquired about and realized' (Prabhavananda 1983: 119). What then dwells within this little house? 'As large as the universe outside, ever so large is the universe within the lotus of the heart. Within it are heaven and earth, the sun, the moon, the lightning, and all the stars. What is in the macrocosm is in the microcosm.'

In more recent times a number of scientists have used the hologram to explain various phenomena. In *The Holographic Universe* (1991) Michael Talbot lists the following people who have employed this model: the physicist David Bohm; the neurophysiologist Karl Pribram; the psychologist Kenneth Ring; the psychiatrist Stanislav Grof; and the physicist David F. Peat. Talbot also describes the 1982 landmark experiments led by Alain Aspect from the Institute of Theoretical and Applied Optics in Paris, which demonstrated that the universe 'possesses what appears to be an undeniable "holographic" property' (Talbot 1991: 3).

The holographic property that Talbot refers to is nonlocality. Locality is that quality of physical reality that is tied to a specific location in time and space and also to the direct actions of one object influencing others, like a billiard ball hitting other billiard balls. In contrast, nonlocality is the quality of wholeness in which the dimensions of time and space are missing and where there are instantaneous connections across the whole system. David Bohm referred to the quality of this wholeness as the 'quantum potential' and suggested that at this level discrete objects and locations cease to exist. Bohm's quantum potential is the scientific equivalent of the Vedic city of Brahman and, in relation to the current discussion, to one holographic consciousness.

Bohm thought that the entire universe operated like a hologram. Yet because he wanted to convey the dynamic and ever-active nature of the enfolding and unfolding movements that create the universe, he preferred to describe the universe not as a hologram but as a "holomovement" (Talbot 1991: 47). I argue that Bohm's holomovement represents the dynamics of One Consciousness.

In terms of psychology, Stanislav Grof made use of the holographic model in his book *The Holotropic Mind* (1993). Grof was one of the founders of the field of transpersonal psychology and made use of the idea of the hologram to discuss the many thousands of psychological sessions he conducted with individuals in the United States and Czechoslovakia. Grof defines transpersonal consciousness as infinite, and as 'stretching beyond the limits of time and space' (1993: 83). His mapping of this infinite consciousness involves three regions: i) consciousness within time and space; ii) consciousness beyond time and space; and iii) 'psychoide' experiences, a term taken from Jung to refer to archetypes of the collective unconscious. Grof drew on many of the examples of transpersonal consciousness that came out of therapeutic sessions.

* * *

From the holographic standpoint, the human being is not a single ontological entity with a separate, finite being. This is what is implied or stated by the many books and papers written about being and which usually assume the doctrine of many minds. Rather, the human being is composed of a trinity of relationships made up of an 'I', plus the collective 'us' and the universal 'That'. The universal 'That' represents the one nonlocal, holographic consciousness, while the individual' mind is a local feature of 'That' consciousness. In terms of meaning, the individual's mind is the sum of habitual exchanges that swirl around 'I' and 'us'. Within the local mind of the individual there are myriad social and cultural features. These have traditionally been seen to represent a separate domain from the individual. This conclusion is incorrect, for 'I' and 'us' are only distinctions within one holographic consciousness.

Within the trinity of being, 'I' and 'us' have an exchange relationship. In contrast, every local mind (comprising 'I' and 'us') has a holographic relationship to the whole of One Consciousness: 'That'. This holographic relationship represents the exchange involving the symmetry potentials of part-to-whole and whole-to-part. In other words, One Consciousness inheres in every individual mind, while individual minds represent the local, explicit, conscious and derived parts ('us') of the overall fabric of One Consciousness. Hence the trinity of being is always one, while the parts are distinctions within this quantum potential: this city of Brahman; this Kingdom of Heaven; this trinity of being. This three-part relationship of being can be roughly shown in diagrammatic form in the following manner:

The trinity of being

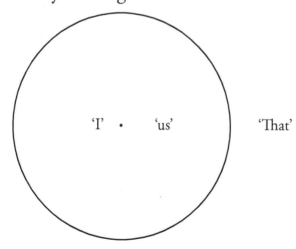

'I' • 'us'   'That'

The dot in the center of the circle represents the 'I' of the eye while the circle outside the dot represents a finite 'us' and the extended area outside the circle represents the infinity of One Consciousness. However, as the white background of this design continues through the circle of 'us and 'I', so too does the infinity of One Consciousness underpin these two features of being. This diagram indicates that the finite circle of 'us' represents an extension of 'I' and includes the ego, language, culture, communications, predispositions, subjective opinions and preferences. In addition, the potentials inherent in 'I' will always be part of 'us' because individuals are never separate entities from the cultural meanings propagated by 'us' and these in turn are always a part of the trinity of our being.[6]

The relationship between 'I' and 'us' is internal to the individual's mind and is supported by circular reinforcements through exchanges of meaning via different forms of communications. Also, the boundary of 'us' encloses not only our tribe, class, caste, skin colour, ethnicity or nation, which are only artificial divisions, but the cultural meanings of 'us' also include all cultural differences as well as the cultural exchanges of all sentient beings. Like drops of water, individuals are always part of a larger stream of 'us' that flows into the ocean of consciousness. As drops of water are not separate from the ocean neither are individuals separate from the social 'us' that spawns them or the hidden and infinite resources of 'That'.

In terms of the individual's mind, the two-way relationship between the intelligence of an individual mind (involving 'I' and 'us') and the intelligence of One Consciousness ('That') is not linear but complementary. This means that while the individual's mind ('I' and 'us') is a part of the whole of One Consciousness, the whole of One Consciousness inheres within every mind and provides the foundation context (the background) for the various explicit functions of the individual's mind. The individual mind is, therefore, not a separate and private entity having self-autonomy, but rather a secondary and what scientists may call an 'entangled' feature within One Consciousness. (I will be discussing these features more in Parts II and III.)

The relationship between 'I' and 'That' can be described as an insight path that manifests through exchanges of meaning occurring in intuitions, insights, revelations, epiphanies, synchronicities or visions. These holographic exchange patterns are overwhelmingly symmetrical in nature (part-to-whole and whole-to-part) and that means they are entangled to the degree that it is impossible to make clear distinctions or demarcation between 'I' or 'That'. This kind of exchange potentials may also arise in creative exercises when the ego gets out of the way and an activity appears to happen 'by itself'.

One of the important implications of a holographic model of One Consciousness for visual perception is the implication that the physical world is not separated from the 'That' of One Consciousness. Rather, as Sir Arthur Eddington suggests, 'mind-stuff' ('That') already exists within the whole universe. This means that we should expect that the 'mind-stuff' of One Consciousness would have a role to play in the processes of visual perception. In addition, the trinity of being ('I', 'us', 'That') logically demands that visual perception is not a play between two binary opposites such as an isolated finite being and an independent outside world, but rather represents a process that occurs wholly within the unifying confines of the trinity of being: ('I', 'us', 'That').

If the trinity of being is accepted it follows that our conscious mind represents both a local and secondary feature of consciousness and involves the capacity to be in sync or out of sync with that wider and deeper intelligence of One Consciousness: 'That'. This means that the small local mind can resonate or be discordant with the large mind of One Consciousness. In terms of order, it means that while our local conscious mind is a secondary manifestation of One Consciousness, it is nevertheless capable of mirroring the inherent order within the larger consciousness ('That'). However, such mirroring often does not occur. The reasons for this are complex but they generally relate to the seven ways of seeing described in Part III, which are the steps in the evolution of consciousness.

As a consequence of the unity within the trinity of being, the intelligence of perception, insight, realisation, intuition, awareness and clairvoyance does not represent a unique phenomenon that exists solely in the realm of a so-called private subjectivity. Rather, intelligence per se is the universal, metaphysical agency of life and being: the 'mind-stuff' of One Consciousness. In other words, it means that the colours of the rainbow have not been created by separate and private minds but are natural secondary features that have unfolded within healthy perceptual processes stimulated by the mind-like potentials of light particles: photons.

While this comment may seem speculative to some, Bohm has written that there is evidence that a 'mind-like quality is present even at the level of particle physics'. He went on to suggest that 'as we go to subtler levels, this mind-like quality becomes stronger and more developed' (Bohm & Hiley 1995: 386).

The trinity of being ('I', 'us', 'That') marks the major distinctions within the holographic One Consciousness. While the graphic above suggests a static model, this is not the case. Rather, the trinity of being is a *dynamic* model for explaining the unity of life and also visual perception, and as a consequence, how the rainbow can change from being categorised as an 'illusion' to a 'real' phenomenon. This is because in a holistic universe there are no binary divisions, no separate objective and subjective domains, hence the colours of the rainbow are real because they are features of one universe that has consciousness. This holographic model of consciousness also answers Schrödinger's paradox of how the many are one, for the multiplicity of different human beings represents that feature of the trinity of being, that is, the collective 'us', and this multiplicity in turn represents the prisms through which the intelligent light of the larger whole shines.

Evidence

The evolution of One Consciousness represents a challenge to those who believe that physics, chemistry, biology, neuroscience and mathematics are areas of study that should not include mind or meaning. Most of the arguments against One Consciousness are binary and assume a gap existing between subject and object, or between mind and matter. Yet Schrödinger has already noted that the dualism of object and subject is fallacious – subject and object are one. He went on to say, 'The material world has only been constructed at the price of taking the self, that is, mind, out of it' (Schrödinger 1993: 119). He went further by suggesting that mind has erected the objective outside world out of its own stuff (1993: 121).

What evidence is there of the one holographic, nonlocal consciousness that incorporates, as secondary and local agencies, the minds of individuals? One publication that supports and reiterates Schrödinger's view of one mind is *One Mind* (2013) by Larry Dossey. In this book Dossey cites a range of compelling research studies that offer evidence for the principle of one holographic consciousness. These studies include: shared thoughts, emotions, and physical sensations with distant individuals; communication between humans and animals; animal group behaviour that is instantaneously coordinated; and out-of-body experiences (OBEs).

In a more recent book, *What is Consciousness: Three Sages Look Behind the Veil* (2016), Ervin Laszlo, Jean Houston and Larry Dossey argue that consciousness is a basic reality of the universe. Each of these authors cites a range of compelling evidence as well as scientists who hold this holistic view.

The features of entanglement and nonlocal connections are important terms in quantum mechanics, yet they fit well into the holographic structure of One Consciousness. Nonlocality is the term that describes the ability of particles to know about each other's states even when separated by billions of light years. Schrödinger used the term 'entanglement' to refer to connections between apparently separated particles, which persist regardless of distance. In addition, these 'connections are instantaneous, operating "outside" the usual flow of time' (Radin 2006: 14). Both these features of entanglement and nonlocal connections suggest an intrinsic interconnected knowingness of all things in the universe – in other words, One Consciousness.

In his book *Entangled Minds*, Dean Radin (2006: 14) states that 'perhaps the most significant discovery is *entanglement*'. Schrödinger, who coined the term, said it was '*the* characteristic trait of quantum mechanics' (2006: 226). The entanglement of particles occurs when individual particles cannot be described as being separate or independent but must be described as a system or a whole. Entanglement appears to be something of a mystery for many who have been trained in the belief that the physical world is separate from mind and that objects can only be treated independently and separately.

The existence of connections that are beyond the conscious mind, a mind that involves space and time, indicate that the physical world made up of separate and isolated objects is only part of a much larger picture. Quantum physics points us to the conclusion that the whole of the universe is entangled and interconnected and that as a consequence, nothing exists in isolation and there are no special quarantined relations or isolated objects.

Radin quotes a review in the *New Scientist* (March 2004) of the developments on entanglement research: 'Physicists now believe that entanglement between particles exists everywhere, all the time, and have recently found shocking evidence that it affects the wider "macroscopic" world we inhabit' (Radin 2006: 14). If entanglement extends to everything in the universe then this conclusion agrees that the explicit, manifest universe that we perceive in all its separateness and diversity has underlying and interlinking relationships that are outside or beyond the boundaries of conscious perception, and that means beyond the boundaries of physical space and time. I suggest that this is the case and that nonlocal entangled connections are the common features of that large, non-explicit domain and that is the domain of infinite consciousness.

Extrasensory perception (ESP) is another area of science that implies the presence of one universal consciousness. Even though many thousands of experiments in (ESP) have demonstrated conclusively that the mind functions beyond the brain, those who believe in the materialist doctrine of many minds contest this evidence. In *The Roots of Coincidence* (1974), Arthur Koestler detailed the results of many of these early experiments and discussed some of the resistance to these results. He refers to Warren Weaver, one of the founders of modern communication theory, as saying 'I find this [ESP] a subject that is so intellectually uncomfortable as to be almost painful' (Koestler 1974: 19). Radin (2006: 7) found the same kind of resistance to the facts of mind beyond the brain and calls it the 'forbidden knowledge' of science.

Perhaps the most interesting contemporary work that demonstrates a global mind is the experiments carried out by the Princeton Engineering Anomalies Research (PEAR) program. Robert Jahn, then Dean of the School of Engineering and Applied Science, first began this thirty-year program in 1979. In *Consciousness and the Source of Reality: The PEAR Odyssey* (2011), Jahn and Brenda Dunne record these experiments and their results. Over the thirty-odd years since its inception, this unique program has involved a wide assortment of experiments in human-to-machine interactions that have consistently demonstrated the ability of human operators to affect the performance of machines in line with their intentions and/or resonance with the machines.

By resonance Jahn and Dunne mean some kind of emotional bond between the operator and the machine. They go on to tell us that these affects take place across the entire globe and within a global field of consciousness involving both the operator and the machine. Mainstream scientists call these results 'anomalous'. Yet the results of these many experiments point to the conclusion that consciousness is a universal field phenomenon that involves both human subjects and mechanical objects such as machines that generate random numbers. These results appear to be directly in line with the proposal of a single universal consciousness.

Vernon Neppe and Edward Close (2015) have also conducted some interesting research into universal consciousness. In their paper 'How some conundrums of reality can be solved by applying a finite 9-D spinning model' they use an inclusive approach to their mathematical descriptions of quantum particles. The mathematics they formulate took issue with the established view that all quantum physics should be thought of in terms of a four-dimensional space-time continuum. Neppe and Close argue that the mathematics of nine-dimensional particles produces the missing link of physics: consciousness:

> The key missing element is the involvement of a very specifically defined broader form of 'Consciousness' beginning at the level of the most basic quantal particles, or just possibly even sequentially, and proceeding to include a deeper understanding of the entire cosmos. (Morgart 2014)

Neppe and Close argue that the stability of atoms comes from the unity of three components: mass, energy and consciousness (which at times they call 'gimmel'). From their mathematical analysis they find, for example, that hydrogen, which is the most prevalent element in the universe and fundamental for living organisms, has the highest proportion of consciousness, which they calculate to be 0.893. Other elements essential to life such as carbon, oxygen, nitrogen, sulphur, phosphorus, calcium and magnesium also exhibit a similar ratio of consciousness at 0.762 (Neppe & Close 2015: 64–5).

Neppe and Close argue that that the stability of particles, and by extension the universe as a whole, is due to the role of consciousness; that is, a single unified consciousness that is immanent in everything at every level from particles to people to galaxies. This research is neither creationist nor materialist in its viewpoint, yet their mathematics locates a field of consciousness immanent in the whole universe.

The calculations by Neppe and Close also challenge the orthodox view that consciousness is restricted to living organisms that have nervous systems. From the holographic perspective, this orthodoxy is far too limited. The holographic view of consciousness may be of interest to researchers who, in recent developments in sensory ecology, are paying attention to the question of how plants use and extract meaning from their environment.[7]

That evidence indicates that plants can communicate with other plants despite not having a nervous system, which suggests that they have some form of consciousness.

In the next chapter, the relationship of meaning to consciousness is examined and from this the following definition of communication arises: *communication is any exchange of meaning*. Following the logic of this definition we can say that plants that can communicate will make meaningful exchanges and therefore have consciousness. Exchanges of meaning between plants is experimental evidence compatible with the calculations of Neppe and Close, that is, that consciousness is present not only within organisms that do have nervous systems, but also at the molecular level where there is no nervous system and down to the level of particle interactions. These mathematical calculations imply that the immanence of consciousness transcends the physical world.

One of the important features of mind (and therefore of consciousness) is agency. At the level of the individual this agency is often called 'intentionality' or, more traditionally, 'conscious will'. At the quantum level of particle interaction this ordering agency can be called causality. At the cosmic level, that is, at the level of the whole holographic universal system, this agency can be called the non-caused first cause. The contradiction of a 'non-caused first cause' is due to an intelligent agency that works both locally and nonlocally at the same time. In other words, a non-caused first cause (or Aristotle's unmoved mover) implies a universal agency that can only be spoken about in local terms. Such an agency arises from its immanence in everything as well as its transcendence over everything.

The term 'panentheistic' describes the concept of One Consciousness that is both immanent and transcendent and has the sense of being both inner and outer, and is close to the kind of Stoicism that Marcus Aurelius expressed in his *Meditations*. The traditional meaning of the term 'panentheistic' is of a universal spirit that is present everywhere, in everything and everyone, and is also present within time and space and yet transcends these four dimensions. The idea of a panentheistic consciousness stands apart from the doctrine of many minds and that means it is beyond the limited boundaries of a secular and mechanical world. A panentheistic approach is the current approach of this book.

3

Meaning

Every visual perception involves meaning. For example, I look at my watch. It is 8:30 a.m. I am late for work and for the presentation I am scheduled to make. The organisers will be annoyed – tension – apologies! All that meaning in the instant I look at my watch!

Understanding meaning is a good way to understand consciousness. Traditionally, consciousness has been discussed in psychological or philosophical terms. It has been my experience that such approaches have severe limitations and are unable to encompass the idea of consciousness as a whole. The problem with psychological approaches is that they begin by assuming that the mental is a local and private state of subjectivity, which can be discussed through its discrete parts (faculties). As a consequence, most psychological approaches produce a limited and fragmented view of consciousness while also reproducing the classic separation of subject from object, so essential to the doctrine of many minds.

My argument is that meaning is the metaphysical content of consciousness and by far the most useful explanatory tool we have when it comes to modelling its holistic nature. Hence I have found that the best method for analysing One Consciousness is to focus on the states, relationships and principles of meaning. This is a novel methodology and yet meaning is an excellent starting point because the act of making meaning is the self-known experience of intelligibility that cannot be denied by anyone. In addition, every meaning has structure, order and relationships, and these, I suggest, represent Plato's forms that can be analysed and traced back to their impersonal, universal roots through the holographic relationship of whole-to-part and part-to-whole.

To study meaning is to study intelligibility, a state that involves the consciousness of perception: seeing.[8] One of the benefits of using meaning as an explanatory tool is its intimate connection to consciousness. So close is that connection that we can say they are not two separate domains of activity but one. In other words, meaning represents the content of consciousness, and every feature of meaning is also a feature of consciousness. Consciousness and meaning represent two sides of the same coin and as a consequence they enable us to ask questions about meaning and get answers about states of mind.

Consciousness without meaning is akin to the idea of water flowing without motion.[9] 'Meaning' and 'consciousness' are terms with different histories, yet each nevertheless represents the same vital mental landscape. This implies that each feature of consciousness is also one of meaning, while each detail of meaning represents a micro feature of consciousness. Hence we are able to make meaning consciously, subconsciously, unconsciously, pre-consciously, self-reflectively, intuitively and clairvoyantly. Each of these terms represents a set of mental processes in which meanings are exchanged and/or transformed.

David Bohm believed that meaning was the essential nature of consciousness (Hiley & Peat 1991: 436). I fully agree. Because the terminology of meaning can fully represent the mental immaterial world it is the gold standard for discussing consciousness and mind. However, this integrated view is in direct opposition to the orthodoxies of language philosophy and psychology where meaning is seen as the separate discipline of semantics. The current approach also challenges formal linguistics where meaning is understood to be the product of language, specifically a product of interacting signs.

Essentially, meaning has been a mystery that most of us have avoided looking at directly. Even the great European linguist Emile Benveniste (1971: 106) once called meaning 'this Medusa's head'. In the Greek myth about Perseus the evil Gorgon called Medusa could turn to stone ordinary men who looked upon her face. So what did Benveniste mean by saying that meaning was Medusa's head? I can't be sure but the poet Percy Bysshe Shelley reminds us that grace as well as horror can stun. These lines are from his poem 'On the Medusa of Leonardo da Vinci in the Florentine Gallery':

Yet it is less the horror than the grace
Which turns the gazer's spirit into stone

Will we be so fascinated by meaning's grace and mysterious power that we are stunned into silence, unable to move? From my experience of daily meditation, I would say that if we are very lucky this might happen, but more than likely looking upon the face of meaning will produce little or no response. This is because linguists, psychologists, semioticians and philosophers have tended to look with *separating eyes* and thereby erase, dismiss or ignore meaning's relationship to consciousness.

While we have a range of ways to make meaning we do not have the freedom *not* to make meaning at all. Making meaning seems to be part of the reason for the embodiment we have in a physical body. In other words, meaning-making is natural and inherent in the state of being human. It is impossible to live without meaning because it is impossible to live without consciousness. In contrast to the compensation models of social psychology, problems arise within us not from a lack of meaning but because the meaning we are making is detrimental to our wellbeing.[10] Hence, while we can never stop making meaning, the choice of the kind of meaning we make is ours. We are free to make meaning that is confused, disorganised, fragmented, chaotic, limited, painful and detrimental to our health and well-being. We are also free to make meaning that is ordered, coherent and harmonious, and therefore beneficial.

Features

The normal mistake contained within the traditional subjects of linguistics, semiotics and semantics is to view meaning in a secondary role by assuming it to be a by-product of the more important and primary interaction of signs, language or symbols. This is a key reversal that simply creates confusion. It is not language that give life to meaning but the reverse: meaning gives life, vitality, agency and intelligibility to the interaction of signs and language. Language without meaning constitutes meaningless marks. A dead language represents meaningless smudges and spots that cannot be spoken because meanings have been lost. Speech is the practice of making meaning through the use of vocal language.

To appreciate the essentialism of meaning we need to understand something about its structures, functions, states and laws. To begin with, meaning is unlike a log of wood, so we are unable to speak of it in terms of local, spatial or even temporal coordinates, yet I suspect mathematicians could measure some of its attributes. The fundamental reality of meaning is neither external nor internal, neither subjective nor objective. It is prior to all categories and also prior to all forms, which are but explicit and secondary perceptual features of it.

In a positive sense, meaning has both local and nonlocal aspects. Local and nonlocal are complementary and work together through the minds of organisms such as the local conscious mind and the underlying but larger nonlocal realm of cosmic consciousness. Within this larger, infinite consciousness the relationships of meaning connect everything to everything else. From quantum science, we know that these relationships are entangled, which means they operate instantaneously across vast distances as well as being carriers of meaning.

Hence meaning is constituted by its two states: primary and secondary, generic and relative, given and constructed. As the ultimate *sine qua non*, meaning represents the ever-present vital background context of every explicit act, form, distinction or object. In addition, because meaning has the intelligent power to order or disorder, organise or disorganise, we can say that at this fundamental nonlocal level it represents the first or primary non-caused cause. This primary state of consciousness stands as the meaning of Meaning (see later comments). This state is outside the differences of time and thus has an eternal presence and cosmic wholeness and is immanent within every organism and transcendent over everything. From now on when referring to this kind of 'Meaning' I will use a capital 'M' to denote this universal, holistic ever-present, nonlocal intelligent awareness of One Consciousness.[11]

It is this holistic sense that is missing from all linguistic, semiotic and psychoanalytic analyses, for these disciplines have forgotten Meaning's primordial presence and have tended to concentrate on meaning's secondary, practical and everyday sense. We can speak of Meaning's secondary function as the meaning of everything *other* than Meaning. This secondary sense is the meaning we humans make by reference to forms, distinctions or objects (concrete or abstract) in our thinking, language, signs and expressions, or through the senses. These represent the data of our conscious mind. In this secondary sense, meaning is made and carried by signs and symbols and comes in the form of communication exchanges. Communication can thus be defined as any exchange of meaning. This secondary sense of meaning is signified by the concept of the 'relative' and can be denoted by the use of a lower-case 'm'.

David Bohm viewed meaning as having a universal application: 'If there is a generalized kind of meaning intrinsic to the universe, including our own bodies and minds, then the way may be opened to understanding the whole as self-referential through its "meaning for itself"' (Bohm 1994: 92). My understanding of the phrase 'meaning for itself' is a way of speaking about the meaning of Meaning.

With a nod towards the *Brihadaranyaka Upanishad*, some of the landscape of Meaning can be described in the following terms:

Meaning is constant, profound, and infinite.
It cannot be touched, but is the sensation of touch;
It cannot be seen, but is the sight within seeing;
It cannot be smelt, but is the aromas;
It cannot be heard, but is sound;
It cannot be tasted, but is taste.
The five senses are but the children of Meaning.

The meaning of Meaning is the Lord of the universe.
Every object runs on its power;
Yet it is not solid, liquid or gaseous.
It cannot be pierced by arrows, burnt by fire, or wet by water.
It is invisible, yet it is the nature of intelligibility;
It has the light of consciousness and the darkness of mind.

Yet Meaning can be felt;
In the tension of the muscles it is resistance;
In the pit of the stomach it is fear, and
In the lotus-house of the heart it is love.

* * *

There are a limited number of positive terms that can signify the generic features of the meaning of Meaning. In contrast, there is the very large vocabulary we use to describe the meanings and interpretations we make. Some of the generic terms that indicate the functions of Meaning are 'order' and 'disorder'. These are the terms that reflect what Thomas Nagel called a 'natural teleology' (discussed in Chapter 4). The terms 'order' and 'disorder' refer to the given states of a system in general and are not restricted or contained by any particular subject matter, theory or area of study even though every discipline uses or implies them when a system is being described or evaluated.

Related terms that imply order or disorder are 'organisation', 'disorganisation', 'equilibrium', 'balance', 'homeostasis', 'self-regulation', 'randomness' and 'chaos'. Each of these terms carries meaning about the Meaning of a system and hence they represent part of the generic vocabulary of the meaning of Meaning. This is the case irrespective of the particular kind of system, be that sensory, physical, chemical, biological, mathematical, economic or linguistic.

When order or disorder are stated or implied in any literature their use represents, as it were, the fingerprints of consciousness. This is particularly the case for disciplines like physics, chemistry, biology and mathematics, where the scope of enquiry is large enough to take in the entire universe. This means that even in those disciplines where consciousness, meaning and mind have been intentionally erased or ignored it has been impossible to eradicate every vestige of them, no matter how hard scientists may try.

The two states of meaning and Meaning are not binary and cannot be separated. For example, the process of making meaning by thinking, speaking or writing involves both primary and secondary states. When we think, speak, write or communicate these actions are like ripples on the surface of an ocean of being. Meaning represents the infinite being of beings, the primary resource that enables each of us to participate in the world through exchanges of meaning. The place in which each communication occurs represents the ever-present primordial ocean of Meaning. When we humans communicate we call on this infinite resource of Meaning in order to make and convey a secondary and relative set of ordered or disordered meanings through the use of language, signs and behaviour.

* * *

Apart from Meaning and meaning there is a further distinction we can make concerning the two cardinal functions of Meaning. These are the functions of implicit and explicit meaning. *Implicit* meaning represents the connections of meaning that are concealed or are concealing but are nevertheless also unifying. *Explicit* meaning is more tangible. This is the kind of meaning in which distinctions and differences are created and these always reveal meaning and occur within the conscious mind. Thus explicit meaning functions so as to reveal, and therefore it is meaning that is conscious, manifest, actual, differential and distinct. This is the meaning that forms the architectural relations of objects that appear differentially in space and can be measured through time or represented by language, measurements and discourse. Explicit meaning represents what the Australian poet Les Murray called 'the bars of our attention' (in the poem 'Equanimity'). These are the marks and the differential content of the human conscious mind, and this system has a relative agency in the form of intent or will.

Like fish that live in the ocean, we live within the ocean of One Consciousness, that is, within the universal and infinite sea of Meaning. According to Einstein's theories of relativity we live in the relativities of a space-time continuum. However, this space-time continuum is grounded in Meaning – implicit meaning – and we see this in the concepts of 'area' in terms of space, and 'duration' in terms of time. Both 'area' and 'duration' imply an ever-present background context or frame onto which the three dimensions of space and the many distinctions of past and future time are marked. This infinite and ever-present field of Meaning underlies every distinction of space and time while also being prior to all distinctions, which are but secondary and relative manifestations of consciousness.

Distinctions are the basis of logic and mathematics as well as being features of all forms, both abstract and perceptual. I look at this chair I sit in and without thinking any further I see it and myself and every object in the room as distinct and separate. Yet such a conclusion is mistaken. In his book *Laws of Form*, G. Spencer-Brown (1977: 1) begins to describe what constitutes forms by writing 'We take as given the idea of distinction'. His statement awards priority to distinctions, but this is not the order found in Meaning.

Distinctions are explicit, and so are features of the explicit world, and as a consequence they are derived from the underlying implicit meaning of One Consciousness. Therefore all distinctions are the secondary relations of meaning that arise out of the primary context of implicitness. While distinctions are given, as Brown says, we should not forget that they are given only as secondary and derivative formations. Because of their secondary status distinctions have the capacity to lead us astray (as they seem to have done with Spencer-Brown) when we assume they have a primacy they do not possess. The fifteenth-century Sufi mystic poet Kabir said something similar:

Behold but One in all things; it is the second that leads you astray. (Huxley 1970: 10)

Kabir's 'second' can be read as referring to the secondary status of distinctions. We are led astray when we assume that the distinctions of mathematics, logic or rationality are given so much value and weight that they seem to come before all else.

Thus the two functions of Meaning are not equal but have

an inherently asymmetrical order. That order runs from the one to the second; from implicit meaning to explicit meaning; from implicit context to explicit distinctions and constituents. When we violate that order by reversing it, as we so often do in language that values the second as if it were the first, we act against the order of Meaning. This inherent and universal order within One Consciousness provides a critique of materialism, positivism, rationalism and realism, for these 'isms' have led us astray, back into the cave of shadows to a place where we believe secondary distinctions and differences that appear on the curtains of perception and language are actually the true primary reality.

The two states of Meaning and meaning can be cross-referenced with implicit and explicit meaning in the following manner. When implicit meaning is associated with the secondary processes of communication it produces conscious thoughts, messages, language and signs, and in these forms we can speak about it as 'inferences', 'connotations' or 'implications'. Implications, therefore, contain those associated meanings that are yet to be revealed or made fully manifest through explicate processes that unfold their meaning. Therefore the ordinary conscious human mind is composed of unifying, implicit meaning as well as diversified, explicit distinctions. It is these two interconnected functions of Meaning that produce the two cardinal conditions of intelligibility: the principle of *unity within diversity*.

In contrast, when the function of implicit meaning is operating solely within the primary state of the meaning of Meaning, that is, within the infinite primordial domain of One Consciousness, it can be called implicitness. As a consequence, implicitness represents the function of the universal context of One Consciousness, and aligns with Plato's term 'the Good'. Within this domain there are no conscious, explicit distinctions, no signs or language, but instead overwhelming unity, connection and attraction without conscious and explicit distinction.

The implicitness of One Consciousness can never be fully transformed into explicit forms because all explicit marks, distinctions or bars of attention are but secondary to the foundation implicitness of One Consciousness. In religious discourses the word 'ineffable' is sometimes used to stand in for our inability to represent by explicit means that which is essentially implicit.

In relation to the trinity of being, the distinctions of 'I', 'us' and 'That' are cut through by the distinctions of implicit and explicit meaning. Thus my mind and the minds of others will have a structure where secondary distinctions are conscious, having arisen out of the universal implicit being of That. My relationship to others will therefore be horizontal and connected implicitly so that it is possible for us to communicate, that is, to exchange meanings that have both implicit and explicit features. It is the implicitness of That which provides the ground state as well as the conditions for any and all communications. Without this ground state of implicit meaning there would be no possibility of communication and therefore no life and no forms.

Because meaning and mind are two sides of the one coin, the functions of implicit and explicit meaning become two methods of knowing. As a consequence, we can know things explicitly, that is, by way of conscious and deliberate thought. We can also know things implicitly, that is, by intuition, realisation, insight and clairvoyance. Implicit knowing is a faster and a more complex way of knowing than knowing by conscious and deliberate thought. These two forms of knowing are available to us because the ordinary human mind is composed of both implicit unity and explicit diversity. Normally we do not experience explicit meaning simply as explicit meaning but rather as conscious thoughts, signs or perceptions.

Over the last three hundred years the revealing function of explicit meaning has been much prized by the rational Enlightenment of the West as well as today in school and tertiary education programs. Yet this is not the most important way of knowing. In contrast to the explicit emphasis by rational thought, we also have the capacity for a unified, implicit knowing that embodies an implicit awareness. The experience of implicit awareness represents a subtle, refined, sensitive and often clairvoyant method of knowing that comes with the concealed, the hidden, the resonant, the intuited and the unified. This kind of tacit knowing is extremely important for balance and perspective in judgments and choices, but it is so easy to ignore. Sometimes when we experience the subtlety of implicit awareness we call it a 'hunch', 'inspiration', 'revelation', 'intuition' or a 'gut feeling'.

Bohm's implicate and explicate orders

The two functions of implicit and explicit Meaning have a close resemblance to some of the work of David Bohm. Bohm spent a lifetime of research in physics and philosophy and his book *Wholeness and the Implicate Order* (1983) introduced what he called a new model of reality, which he described as the implicate and explicate orders. Bohm called the deeper, unified level of reality the implicate order because it conceals by enfolding within itself what he called 'information' as well as structures of the explicit physical universe. In Bohm's model, every manifest form that we perceive arises from an implicit unified background: the implicate order. In contrast, the revealed and explicit world is the explicate order, so called because it contains the unfolded, explicit diverse forms of a physical world we humans have come to know consciously through perception and conscious thought.

For Bohm, physical objects observed to be moving in the continuum of space and time represent the explicate order. Even though Bohm appears to have generally assumed the existence of an independent physical world, the relationship between his two orders is highly integrated in that the explicate order arises out of the implicate order. Within this hierarchy the potentials of the implicate order represent the prior causal forces that order and organise every motion and relationship associated with the manifest, explicit form in the universe. Bohm's examples of the implicate and explicate orders are almost entirely drawn from physics and mathematics and do not address directly the question of meaning, mind or consciousness.

However, what Bohm called the two universal orders of reality are almost entirely consonant with the structure and function of implicit and explicit meaning, and only in a weak capacity do they relate to the idea of a separate, independent physical universe. The unity of Meaning is reflected in Bohm's own hierarchical ordering within his universal interconnected system. We see that order in the relationship between his implicate and explicate orders. Bohm proposed that the explicate order consisting of all the diverse forms and objects of the physical universe arises from the primary and unifying implicate order.

For Bohm, the implicate and explicate orders were 'objective' orders of the universe which, in addition, related to human subjectivity. Unfortunately, Bohm seems to have implied the doctrine of many minds when describing these two orders in relation to subjectivity, and this has tended to produce a sense of separation within his unified model. Yet the idea of a separate and private subjectivity does not fit into Bohm's own descriptions of the implicate and explicate orders, for these are holistic, interconnected orders that embrace everything in the universe.

We see his view of a holistic, interconnected universe in the highly original book *The Undivided Universe* (1995) which he wrote with Basil Hiley. The thesis of this book is that everything in the universe is interconnected. An appreciation of the integrated structure and function of Meaning can add to Bohm and Hiley's view of interconnection by providing an answer to the question 'what' is it that is interconnected. The answer is that the fabric of an interconnected universe is constructed from the relationships of Meaning, implicit and explicit (discussed more fully in Chapter 5). When we take interconnection seriously, individual subjectivity cannot be a separate entity that is somehow split off or separated from this wholly interconnected system but must be an integrated feature of it.

An undivided universe demands that Bohm's two orders are universal orders of consciousness and not orders of an independent physical universe as is often assumed. When they are interpreted as orders of the physical universe this automatically creates a separating gap between mind and matter, between an independent physical world and a private subjectivity. Such gaps and separations do not, and cannot, exist in a wholly integrated, interconnected system. Rather, universal interconnection means that our individual thoughts and perceptions may often be unique, but they remain nevertheless as secondary features of the universal One Consciousness and as such they represent parts of the explicate order of the universe. Even though Bohm focused almost exclusively on physics and mathematics, his explicate order should not be interpreted as representing an independent physical world. If that were to happen Bohm's entire system of the implicate and explicate orders would be undermined by incoherence.

A separating view does not seem to have been countenanced by Bohm, and for these reasons I suggest that his explicate order represents nothing more than the differential contents of the conscious mind of individual organisms, made up of perceptions and, in humans, thoughts. In other words, Bohm's explicate order only comes into existence as a secondary reality of universal consciousness with the advent of conscious perception and thought. There is also nothing in Bohm and Hiley's approach that contradicts this position; in fact they associate the individual's mind with the implicate and explicate orders in the following manner: 'The implicate order is not only the ground of perception, but also of the actual process of thought' (Bohm & Hiley 1995: 383).

As a summary of this chapter, we can say that Meaning and One Consciousness are terms for the same metaphysical reality. This reality has two states: meaning and Meaning. It also has two functions: i) a resonant concealing and unifying movement involving all the interconnections of the universe; and ii) a smaller revealing, diversified movement involving an explicit, conscious, explicate order. Such explicit processes of the conscious mind represent secondary and derivative functions within the explicate order. These two functions of implicit and explicit meaning are the structural bases of Bohm's implicate and explicate orders; they are integrated to the extent that the explicate order arises from, and is a transformation of, the larger underlying implicate processes. Bohm's two orders provide a demonstration of the holographic relationship between the whole of One Consciousness and its many parts.

4

A Natural Teleology

Thomas Nagel (2012: 29) wrote about his hope for a transcendent self-understanding that is neither theist nor reductionist. He saw the possibilities of this self-understanding evolve out of an internally coherent order of the universe, which he described as a 'natural teleology'. If we accept the idea of a natural teleology, what would the patterns of this internally coherent order of the universe look like? Today such a question is controversial. The idea that the universe has an intrinsic order and purpose irrespective of use, survival potentials, opinion or laws of physics is one that has fallen into disfavour.

The pervasive culture of materialism tells us to see objects not as parts of a larger invisible event, but rather as independent, primary realities. Materialists believe it to be a waste of time looking for binding patterns of natural teleology that unify the universe because some day they expect to discover that physical 'Atlas that will hold all things together' – a materialist Theory of Everything.

From the perspective of Meaning, Plato and Aristotle along with Thomas Nagel were correct in their belief in a natural teleology. There is an inherently unifying and metaphysical order within the universe, a natural teleology that speaks to us about a coherent interconnected structural and functional order. This is not a postmodern 'grand narrative' but a universal order of

Meaning that organises and underpins – and is intrinsic to – all moving forms and objects in space and time. How can the patterns of this coherent order be described?

A coherent order

The *Tao Te Ching* names the invisible universal order as the Tao, which is often understood as the Way. The Way, like One Consciousness, is a singular, all-pervasive domain but which is not all and everywhere the same. In Chapter 42 of the *Tao Te Ching* we learn that the Tao has various general features:

> *The Tao begot one*
> *One begot two*
> *Two begot three*
> *And three begot the ten thousand things.*

The meaning of this verse may appear at first to be esoteric; however, as it is written here it indicates at least four levels or transformations that are ordered in a hierarchy and which run from the singular (Tao) to multiple diversities (ten thousand things). In addition, the word 'begot' signifies a causal relationship and so the hierarchy is one of causality that runs from unity to diversity.

It is possible to understand One Consciousness in a similar manner because it is an infinite, invisible field of awareness that is singular but not everywhere the same. There is, however, an important difference between Chapter 42 of the *Tao Te Ching* and the primordial awareness of One Consciousness: the causality in this verse suggests a linear set of relationships, whereas from the perspective of Meaning the causal order of One Consciousness is cyclical. What do I mean by a 'causal cyclic order'? An ordered cyclical flow represents a series of changes or transformations that ends up close to, or in the same place as where they began. (I have more to say about the circular nature of Meaning in Chapter 5.)

The cyclical nature of One Consciousness has five transformations and like verse 42 of the *Tao Te Ching* these broadly begin with the unity of a singularity then move to a state of multiple diversities. But then, unlike Chapter 42, this multiple diversity transforms back into the unity of One Consciousness. What then justifies the structure of this cycle from unity to diversity and back to unity? Since the functions of implicit and explicit Meaning are dynamic, their individual exchanges lead inevitably to the combination of four patterns as demonstrated below: 0, 1, 2, 3. The fifth transformation comes about because the relations of Meaning are cyclical rather than linear, and hence these exchange patterns begin and end with the 0 of *Implicit-to-Implicit* Meaning, as follows:

0   Implicit to Implicit
1   Implicit to explicit
2   explicit to explicit
3   explicit to Implicit
0   Implicit to Implicit.

What does this cyclical flow represent? First, it represents the politics of eternity, and by that I mean the underlying spiritual steps that provide the passion and motivation behind the politics of our transient everyday activities. This cyclical flow also represents the learning steps within the evolution of consciousness. Finally, it represents a similar set of relationships to those of Chapter 42. These are the relationships that are involved in every movement in the universe. That is, every mental as well as every physical form begins as a potential within the implicit singularity of One Consciousness, then transforms into something explicit and then unfolds into a multiplicity of explicit differences and then finally enfolds back into the 0 of

Implicit-to-Implicit Meaning. These five exchange patterns of Meaning provide a metaphysical outline of the ordering and organisation of all phenomena in the universe and that includes the evolution of the human mind.

The five exchange patterns also provide the pathway to a transcendent self-understanding along with an appreciation of the holographic interconnection of the human mind with One Consciousness. These are the five major exchanges in the life of every organism, from birth, to growth, to death, and in addition, these are the patterns that order the transient life of every physical and mental object in the universe. The five patterns signify the relationship between the unmanifest and the manifest, which is also the relationship between the transient (the transformations of 1, 2, 3) and the eternal and infinite (the 0 of *Implicit-to-Implicit* Meaning). Finally, I will be suggesting that the movement through these five exchange patterns has an evolving order that is inherent in both learning and maturation and, over a longer period of time, can be called the evolution of consciousness. (I discuss learning further in Chapter 12.)

The evolution of consciousness begins with the eternal, intrinsic awareness of 0 and then moves to the transient objects of 1, 2, and 3 and then returns to the unmanifest of 0. Within the 0 of *Implicit-to-Implicit* Meaning is the universal ocean of a priori awareness, which contains infinite hidden potentials but no explicit meaning or distinctions and no physical world. With the transformations of 1, some distinctions, movement, object or forms begin to emerge within an implicit space to become discernible.

With the exchange patterns of 2, mind develops from cosmic consciousness into a conscious awareness of exchanges between a multitude of physical or mental objects and forms (a galaxy or a language). As the body grows older, maturity develops so that thoughts evolve to the point where awareness can become aware of itself. This enfolding happens because differences and distinctions have become integrated into larger unifying and empathic systems. The final movement in this evolving cycle of consciousness is the return to 0. This happens with the death of the body, or more subtly when minds become unified with consciousness – that is, enlightened.

This five-step cycle can be observed within the cycle of birth, growth and death, and also within the manner that thoughts arise, persist for a period, then return to their original implicit state. In terms of the life cycle, before the embryo there is 0, or simply the intrinsic awareness of One Consciousness involving the potentials for conception and the birth of an identifiable 1. In infancy, the child learns to identify its body as distinct from the body of its mother. With childhood development we see the gradual growth in capacity to create and use distinctions and differences that over a period of years become more numerous, complex and abstract: 2. With developing maturity this language capacity, along with a repertoire of learnt behaviour, is integrated into systems of thought and action: 3. Thus as we grow older the importance of specific distinctions and differences becomes less, while there is a corresponding concern with unity and the bigger picture. Finally, when the body is dropped we return to the place from where we began, 0, the ocean of pure potentiality and intrinsic awareness of One Consciousness.

These five exchange patterns operate as an orderly evolving cycle that moves from a state of Implicitness through to explicit mind and then back to Implicit consciousness. These five exchange patterns of Meaning provide the framework for a natural teleology that orders and organises all phenomena in the universe, and that includes the human mind. These patterns also provide the pathway to a transcendent self-understanding along with an appreciation of the holographic interconnection of the human mind with One Consciousness.

A fuller description of these exchange patterns is provided in Chapter 12 as well as in Part III. How these patterns of exchange relate to brainwaves is described in Appendix A.

5

Relations of Meaning

In this chapter I want to focus on the structural characteristics of One Consciousness, which can be spoken about as relations. Relations, communication and meaning are linked in the following manner:

  i.   Communication is defined as any exchange of meaning.
  ii. Meaning is defined as any exchange of relationships.
  iii. Relationships are alive and have the structure and function of One Consciousness.

I begin by assuming that all relations are relations of Meaning and that there are no relations that do not have meaning. The negative of this proposition is that there are no relations devoid of Meaning. Proof that all relations are relations of Meaning rests on the fact that we are unable to offer evidence of a relationship that has no meaning. (Even random events have the meaning of a random event, while a distinction has the meaning of a difference or an asymmetrical relationship.)

The second feature of relations is they are omnipresent throughout the universe and they interconnect everything and tie the universe into a single holistic system. As a consequence, this single interconnected system can be understood as one of intelligence, Meaning and consciousness.

Relations have no mass and no measurable energy; they are entirely metaphysical and non-material and they stand as the universal mental forces of mind and consciousness. As such, relations are vital; they are alive and they carry Meaning, and they represent the integrated structural and field features of the one holographic consciousness. Both explicit and implicit relations are empty of physical objects for they cannot be measured directly by any technology. The emptiness of relations means that every object or form in the universe is full of the emptiness of relations. In addition, every object and form floats in an ocean of emptiness, that is, in a universe of relations.

Relations per se are given to us to use by One Consciousness and we make use of this resource through mind activity that is reflected in brainwaves. However, while relations are empty of physical attributes they are nevertheless the structural components of consciousness, that is, they provide the natural ordering capacity of consciousness. An ordering capacity is another way of speaking about agency. As already discussed, the agency of consciousness represents its causal potential, which creates stability or instability, order or disorder within the universe. This is the same intelligent faculty within the human mind that creates stability or instability, order or disorder.

The agency of relations that function within the human mind represents a set of secondary capacities that we call 'will', 'intention', 'attention', 'deliberation' or 'purpose', and these causal potentials derive from the cosmic potentials that are immanent within the universe, even down to the smallest particle. Scientists have known for some time now that every particle, as well as every galaxy, exists as a field of relations within larger fields of relations. If a particle can be described as a set of 'relationships that reach outward to other things', as Henry Stapp (1971) has said, then an outward-reaching relationship implies an intelligent capacity that can be demonstrated in the ability of relationships to create organised forms that interact in organised and regulated ways.

A form has a volume and can be solid, liquid, gaseous, abstract or symbolic. A form of any kind represents an expression of a certain regular pattern or assemblage of relations. Certain assemblages of relations create solid and concrete states of matter while others create the abstract forms of culture and symbols. Relations are the agents of organisation, order and stability and are omnipresent throughout the universe, within everything and surrounding everything. Relations operate as propagating, intelligent, organisational forces within and between every form in the universe.

The mathematical calculations of Neppe and Close (2015: 64) indicate that mass and energy without consciousness is impossible, and that consciousness provides the stability of particles, atoms, molecules and organisms on this planet and for the rest of the universe. These statements about relations mean that the component of consciousness found to be in particles and atoms can be spoken about as relations.

As Henry Stapp has said, if particles are composed of relations, and relations are the structural and holographic features of consciousness, it means that the calculations of Neppe and Close find confirmation in this understanding of relations. In support of this proposition, the relations that are essential in visual perception are those associated with light: the photon. Such relations contain and carry the complex meanings of our vision, and this ability to see is always a feature of consciousness. Visual perception would be impossible if photons of light did not carry meaning from the environment and had no component of consciousness. In other words, the photon's relations do carry meaning, and thus visual perception is possible.

The fingerprints of consciousness in the form of relations exist throughout the universe, and therefore we can conclude that there is an intrinsic awareness within and throughout the universe. This awareness is the result of unmeasurable *Implicit-to-Implicit* exchanges and these contain what are sometimes called symmetry potentials (discussed in Chapter 6).

Circularity

A further feature of all relations is that they tend towards being circular. Circularity is a condition that mainstream philosophy and science generally prefer to avoid. An argument that is considered circular is commonly seen to be adding nothing new, or worse, to be false. Be that as it may, circularity is a structural condition of our reflective capacity to know anything because it is a structural condition of the relations of Meaning. There is circularity inherent within wholes, in that the parts are derived from the whole and not the whole from the parts (Young 1999: 20). There is, therefore, circularity inherent in the volume of a hologram and it is this two-way circularity (part-to-whole and whole-to-part) that is innate in our holographic relationship to One Consciousness.

Whatever the kind of meaning we decide to make it will have the circular potentials of self-referral. These potentials can be consciously self-reflective, as in contemplation, or they can manifest as a habitual predisposition that reinforces the limited ways we view the world and ourselves. It is not too much to say that the universe is inherently circular, an idea that Arthur Young developed throughout his book *The Reflexive Universe*. The implication of these universal circular patterns is of a coherent singularity or oneness of Meaning beyond space or time. The concept of 'oneness' itself implies circularity.

Circularity is everywhere. It is seen in the planetary shapes that populate the universe. It is a biological function demonstrated by the processes of self-replication. It is inherent within chaos theory as iteration and self-similarity. Circularity is also a function of discourse as the reflexive tendency of language to refer back to itself. Ordinary mind circularity is created when we deliberately become involved in self-reflective thinking. On these occasions, we are mirroring the inherent circularity within the structure of Meaning itself. This is why inner self-reflective practices can lead us closer to the one universal consciousness.

Another circular organisational aspect of Meaning is the life-cycle of birth, growth and death to which every form in the universe is subjected. This life-cycle is the order of all transient things and is in agreement with the inherent order within the five exchange functions of Meaning (Chapter 4). In addition, the ordinary mind that deals with transient things is itself transient in that it also follows a circular path. The circularity of the ordinary mind can be extended so that we can think of it as the evolution of consciousness. The processes of a circular evolution of the ordinary mind may also be interpreted in spiritual terms as reincarnation, the belief that the soul may take many births before finally returning fully to the implicit and Divine context from which it arose.

An important consequence of the circularity of Meaning is that any linear sequences will always represent a partial picture within a larger circular context, a context that will refer back to the details of all linear sequences. This circularity indicates that within the universe there are no linear stand-alone sequences that have a beginning and an end. Thus within the principles of Meaning there are no beginnings or ends, only circular transformations or changes of meaning. One of the implications of this is that the universe is eternal, without beginning or end, and so raises questions about the theory of the Big Bang. On the level of the individual, death is often seen as an end, but in terms of Meaning this is not the case. Death is simply a transformational change in what can be seen as the evolution of a spiritual consciousness. Similarly, birth is not a beginning of life but a transformation of a life that has gone before.

To successfully argue against the circularity of Meaning one would have to demonstrate a stand-alone linear sequence that had a definite beginning or end and then show why these did not constitute continual transformations. The circularity of Meaning indicates there is no such thing as an individual object or set of objects existing on its own without an underlying ordering context. For example, there is no such thing as a separate and independent mind or an isolated organism that has the internal capacity for self-organisation. As for the ordinary mind, this is not a separate entity but a detail in the cosmic event called Meaning. Since no one to my knowledge has yet been able to demonstrate a stand-alone linear sequence, we can confidently assume that beginnings or ends are always qualified and conditional, and hence that linear sequences are simply limited visions of the unlimited and eternal circularity of Meaning.

When we pursue the consequences of circularity further we see that it implies a gestalt. A gestalt always has two exchange elements: i) a set of explicit details, objects or parts that represent the transient, relative and foreground features of ii) a more permanent holistic context. All meaning that is made has a gestalt structure involving an implicit background with an explicit foreground. In more conventional terms, this structure has the attributes of a relative and transient foreground on an infinite and absolute background.

We humans are led astray when we ignore or erase the implicit and infinite background while focusing exclusively on explicit, relative and transient foreground features. The cultural woof and weave of the twentieth century has been built on this fatal tendency that creates a partial and limited view. We see this in the widespread adherence to secularism; in Albert Einstein's theories of relativity; in the adherents of economic rationalism (now neoliberalism); in many of the practices of education and as well in postmodern theory. In science, economics, education and the arts we have been continually told that the 'marks and known boundaries' of explicit, relative details are the only reality of any value. This limited and partial view represents a cultural fabric that brooks no dissent.

Yet the gestalt of Meaning tells us that any object, form, mark, boundary or part represents only the explicit features of an otherwise whole event. These are the parts that are visible and that register in the conscious mind. But the major portion of all events is invisible, contextual and implicit, and within this implicate whole are the metaphysical attributes of intelligence, order, organisation and purpose.

Life, Meaning and consciousness come in wholes, quanta and events. They do not come in fractions, parts, dimensionless points or independent constituents. If we believe that it is possible for Meaning to come in such independent constituents it is because we have constructed a fiction by erasing most of Meaning, and that is the major part of the implicit context of Meaning.

A quantum is a whole unit that is constant. Arthur Young has argued that 'despite the tendency to refer to energy as quantized – a habit that even good physicists are given to – it is not energy but action that comes in wholes' (Young 1999: 19). He states that 'action is constant, energy is proportional to frequency'. This view of quanta suggests that Meaning is an action that comes in wholes and, in addition, that these wholes are composed of a gestalt involving a background context of implicit meaning as well as a foreground of transient explicit forms.

The circularity of Meaning arises when we speak directly about Meaning because the choices we make about the kind of meaning we make will produce the view we have of the world and of ourselves. In other words, there is a general circular relationship between the kind of meaning we make and the broadness or limitation of our perspective. This circularity indicates that the more we deal with whole actions, quanta and events the larger and more expansive will be our view and the broader our knowledge. This circularity also works in reverse so that the more we focus on explicit details, dimensionless points and/ or parts, the more we erase meaning and intelligence from our study, with the inevitable result that we produce a narrow view with limited and confused knowledge.

Hence a larger and more expansive vision is always created by the conscious use of exchange elements within this gestalt, that is, a conscious use of explicit foreground details that are integrated into implicit background contexts. When we attempt to destroy this gestalt by replacing it with a narrow-focused, linear stand-alone sequence or the mathematics of dimensionless points we also reduce ourselves as well as our vision of the world. In this way, *we come to see the world in the manner in which we make meaning.*

When we come across meaning that does not fit or reflect our predisposed expectations our first response is to dismiss, ignore or erase the evidence. This is the case in science just as much as it is in other aspects of life. For most activities, the kind of evidence that is normally dismissed, erased and ignored is the evidence provided by the implicit meaning of contexts. This is what has happened with the study of consciousness.

Traditionally, scientists have dismissed it from their consideration because the holistic context of consciousness cannot be adequately treated in parts but must be treated as a whole.

Wholes do not function as wholes when divided, and their order and organisational meaning is destroyed when we focus only on some of their parts. Yet mechanical science is dedicated to the study of parts and not wholes. In regard to Meaning, the parts (specific meanings) are derived from the whole of Meaning and not the other way round. This means that the whole of consciousness existed before the distinctions of its parts. As a consequence of the priority of the whole, we can say that consciousness is the singular whole that represents the first and circular cause of everything in the universe.

6

The Order of Symmetry, Non-symmetry and Asymmetry

In this chapter I look at the three ordering relations of symmetry, non-symmetry and asymmetry, which are important in understanding the role and scope of One Consciousness as well as of visual perception. The term 'order' is important in any proposition about agency or causality, especially when our focus is on relations.

When we focus on relations the effect will tend to produce a holistic mental universe, one in which the non-material interconnecting metaphysical structures of relations have agency. In contrast, when we take the materialist road and investigate the world with an exclusive focus on objects or forms, this approach will lead us astray in several ways. It will tend to blind us to the importance and nature of consciousness and to the distinction between implicit and explicit meaning, as well as to the differences between perception and conception. It will also blind us to the universal ordering capacity of relations, which will be seen as the by-product of physical causality.

The inevitable consequence of mainstream materialistic approaches is a world of separation, disconnection and disorder. The disorder of this separating approach contrasts with the interconnecting and ordered nature of Meaning, and so we can ask, 'how is it possible for separations to exist within a world of interconnecting relations'? Clearly it is not possible. They exist only as features of ordinary mind disorders, a subject I will return to in later chapters.

Order and disorder are interesting concepts that are used in physics and chemistry, and which as Schrödinger (1993: 4) says have laws that are 'statistical throughout'. Hence the ordinary laws of physics and chemistry are based upon the 'statistical tendency of matter to go over into disorder' (1993: 69). The statistical approach to order and disorder begins by awarding a priority to disorder (entropy) and is then followed by order (negative entropy). Hence for physics and chemistry disorder and statistical randomness represent the basis of the universe and from this chaotic state the miracle of order apparently arises.

However, when we are concerned with the processes of life then problems arise if we continue to use these statistical concepts. As Schrödinger says, 'The orderliness encountered in the unfolding of life springs from a different source' (1993: 80). This different source he calls the principle of 'order-from-order', which is distinct from the traditional statistical principle of 'order-from-disorder'. In terms of Meaning, the computations of statistics do not come first in the natural order of things, and therefore the statistical principle of 'order-from-disorder' is at best inapplicable to life and, at worst, simply incorrect. Rather, Schrödinger's principle of 'order-from-order' is the correct principle for Meaning, consciousness and life.

The terms 'order' and 'disorder' apply more appropriately to consciousness than they do to physical systems because they represent the way in which the various aspects of meaning and Meaning are structured. Physics and chemistry do not normally refer to Meaning or consciousness and this neglect has led to an unfounded faith in statistical probabilities in order to answer some difficult questions. To say that order and disorder are features of consciousness does not dispute the inherent order and stability within universal laws while also acknowledging the evidence of disorder. Order and disorder are everywhere about us, but what is the meaning of these terms and how do they relate more generally to the organisation inherent in the universe?

One example of how to treat the concept of order comes from Bohm and Hiley, who relate it to the idea of a hologram. They argue that the quality that determines the order of the points within the holographic image when illuminated is an order we can call implicit or enfolded. In this sense, the whole of the image is enfolded in each part of the hologram so that each part contains this implicit order (Chapter 2). They go on to state specifically 'that the order of the hologram is implicit' (Bohm & Hiley 1995: 354).

In contrast to this image, the order that Bohm and Hiley find within the object itself is unfolded 'and we shall call it *explicate*'. The process that conveys the order of the object to the hologram 'will be called *enfoldment or implication*', while the process 'in which the order of the hologram becomes manifest to the viewer in an image will be called *unfoldment or explication*' (1995: 354).

In this discussion, Bohm and Hiley have used the principle of 'order-from-order' when it refers to the two functions of meaning – implicit and explicit meaning. They also illustrate this question with a straight line divided into equal parts, and suggest that what characterises the order of this line is that the differences of successive segments remain similar (Bohm & Hiley 1995: 362). It is here that the terms 'similar' and 'different' are taken up by these authors to suggest further refinements of the order within 'similar differences' and 'different similarities of these differences'.

Such terminology, they suggest, may be called 'an order of order' and they go on to say: 'This treatment of order in terms of similar differences and different similarities appears to be broad enough not only to cover all orders found thus far in physics, but it seems to be valid in much broader areas of experience'

(1995: 363). I entirely agree with this conclusion and with the scope of their proposition but suggest it is possible to add to their 'order of order' still further by looking at the five exchange patterns discussed in Chapter 4 and relating them to the following three relations of Meaning.

Three relations of Meaning

There are three basic relations of Meaning that help us understand the processes of visual perception as well as the intrinsic order-from-order within One Consciousness. These are the relations of symmetry, non-symmetry and asymmetry. These three relations are important because they provide the metaphysical structure of the holographic order that is reflected throughout the entire universe. For example, they operate in my mind as they do in the collective mind of society and as well within One Consciousness.

The first thing that should be said about these three sets of relations is that they are not isolated or separated from one another but form a unified hierarchy, or what can be called an order of order. This is an irreversible hierarchy representing a continuum of consciousness. The ordinary minds of individuals represent the local part that has an *unfolded* and explicit character – a part in which the secondary and derivative relations of non-symmetry and asymmetry operate in that they have arisen out of the infinite potentials of symmetry to the extent that they form the conscious mind.

When we investigate the notion of symmetry we find that it is difficult to grasp at the outset because it is essentially a non-ordinary mind state. Its essential qualities are those that combine intelligent potentials with agency, awareness, beingness and Meaning. Arthur Young (1999: 40) describes symmetry as having complete freedom (uncertainty) and requiring measurement, but here I disagree with him. Symmetry can never be measured because its 0 – *Implicit-to-Implicit* exchanges operate prior to all explicit measurement. We can say that the being of symmetry is the kind of awareness found in the universal implicitness of space.

Symmetry is a relational description of *Implicit-to-Implicit* exchanges. In terms of the transformations of meaning, symmetry is the 0 of *Implicit-to-Implicit* exchanges. In addition, the relation of non-symmetry represents the singular and plural of 1 – *Implicit-to-explicit* and 2 – *explicit-to-explicit* exchanges of meaning. Finally, the relation of asymmetry represents in terms of the transformations of meaning 3 – *explicit-to-Implicit* complex and unified systems of thought. Thus these three relations of symmetry, non-symmetry and asymmetry provide us with another vocabulary with which to come to terms with the mystery of universal order and creation as well as with the processes of visual perception.

There is a common confusion surrounding the meaning of symmetry (0). Dictionary definitions of it tend to construct symmetry as an ordinary mind state, that is, as a passive by-product that is somehow mysteriously thrown up by the proximity or close association it has with similar shapes, sizes or forms. However, the intelligent potentials of symmetry represent much more than an interesting kind of one-dimensional similarity, correspondence or isomorphism. So-called measurements of symmetry are actually measurements of the degree of similarity or likeness that two or more distinctions have to each other. When there is perfect symmetry there is no explicit meaning and thus there are no distinctions to measure.

Strictly speaking, symmetry is not so much a relationship as the context in which the explicit relations of non-symmetry and asymmetry arise.[12] The implicit nature of symmetry (*Implicit-to-Implicit* exchanges) is a timeless and formless context that contains the potentials of connect-ability that become explicit as non-symmetrical and asymmetrical relations in the conscious mind, a mind that deals with myriad distinctions. Symmetry is the essential and implicit quality of the meaning of Meaning, that numinous and creative, mnemonic resonating and self-luminous force and intrinsic awareness out of which the conscious, explicit world is born.

Symmetry finds its fundamental character as the symmetry of space (in which everywhere in space is the same). Because the binary metaphysics of materialism makes us subjective observers of an external world, space is normally thought of as an external and physical state. This mechanical and separating view is a fallacy. There is no external domain beyond Meaning and as a consequence, everything in the universe represents an internal feature of the Meaning of One Consciousness. The symmetry of space is, therefore, an internal, non-separated feature of this one interconnected universe. For the materialist, this means that subjective perceptual space is the same as what is called 'physical space'.

The popular sceptic Lawrence Krauss tells us in his book *A Universe from Nothing* that 'Empty space … is a boiling brew of virtual particles that pop in and out of existence' (2012: 153). This is an interesting statement because it tells us that empty space is not empty, while he uses the word 'existence' without reference to the contexts of consciousness, perception or the conscious mind. Empty space has, in Krauss' language, 'non-zero energy associated with it' and also, 'something can arise from empty space *precisely* because [of] the energetics of empty space' (2012: 151). Even with the separating terms of mainstream science, empty space is anything but empty.

In order to describe the non-empty nature of empty space Krauss, along with most scientists, uses words like 'potential' and 'virtual' in relation to matter and particles. This is a typical materialistic focus on objects and not the kind of language I suggest is adequate to describe the fullness of the symmetry of space. We should note that the official mechanical doctrine that separates the mental world from the physical is reflected back and reinforced by this kind of materialistic language about objects. Perhaps the closest mechanical science comes to describing the nature of empty space is to say that the energy of nothing (empty space) is converted into the energy of something, for example a moving object in space. Yet this kind of vocabulary does not directly address the question of fullness and nor does it say anything about the processes of visual perception which are always implied when referring to space.

The scientist's view of empty space to some extent reflects something of the Zen view of emptiness. According to D.T. Suzuki, 'Zen emptiness is not the emptiness of nothingness, but the emptiness of fullness in which there is no gain, no loss, no increase, no decrease, in which this equation takes place: zero = infinity' (Merton 1968: 133–4). Yet it is this 'energetics of emptiness' which provides the ambiguity of this cosmic agency that mystifies all of us – including modern scientists as well as Zen Buddhists.

In terms of the relations of Meaning, the causal potentials of One Consciousness begin with symmetry potentials. The idea of empty space or emptiness is the concept that everywhere in space is the same (symmetry) without differentiation, that is, zero difference = infinity plus eternity. In contrast, objects moving through space are produced by the distinctions of non-symmetry and asymmetry, and together with the background symmetry of emptiness we find that these moving images are the features of all visual perceptions.

From the perspective of Meaning, physical space like Zen emptiness is the nature of my awareness and identical to the empty space that has been created by *Implicit-to-Implicit* exchanges of Meaning. Hence, this field can be understood, not as an independent and separate physical domain, but as a foundation feature of One Consciousness, an inner world in which we are participants. From this holistic view, the symmetry of space (or emptiness) is not empty, as everyone tells us, but full of the creative force of Meaning.

Within the integrating view of One Consciousness, the symmetry of space (*Implicit-to-Implicit* exchanges) represents the fundamental, unbegun beginning of consciousness. In other words, it is the infinite, eternal ground of all being. The materialistic world of mainstream science understands space as an external abstraction, external to ourselves with spatial relations external to each other. In contrast, within the integrating view of One Consciousness the symmetry of space represents a basic and internal feature of universal consciousness. In addition, the symmetry of space is an essential foundation feature of all visual images. For example, it would be impossible to have an image without the spaces between the forms and distinctions of the image.

The symmetry of One Consciousness is the eternal domain that contains the potentials for all distinctions (and movements), and these, operating within visual perception, become manifest through the agency of light. The symmetry of a hologram is evident in the interaction of whole-to-part and part-to-whole relationships. This holistic interaction is an essential and basic feature of light (the photon) that constructs the hologram. With visual perception, light creates all the distinctions (non-symmetrical and asymmetrical relations) that build a visual image, while the background symmetry of One Consciousness (from which these distinctions have arisen) creates the eternal moment NOW, as well as the spaces within all visual images. The symmetry of space is the essential given of perception and it represents that set of silent and subliminal exchanges of Meaning that precede the distinctions within an image as well as the distinctions of thought.

Symmetry may also be understood as the implicit intelligence of all nonlocal, entangled connections that have been discovered by scientific experiments. These intelligent potentials appear as the animate, omnipotent, immanent and transcendent creative forces that connect, construct, organise and regulate each and every form that is perceived or thought in the universe. This is the permanent background quality of the ocean of nonlocal, entangled interconnections.

In terms of Meaning, 'nonlocal' refers to that intelligent, infinite and internal interconnectedness: a state in which everything in the universe is connected to everything else, all of the time. What is usually erased from scientific discussions of the term 'nonlocal' is any reference to consciousness and meaning. When we deliberately focus on Meaning, the negative term 'nonlocal' transforms into the positive features of intelligent interconnectedness that underpin the ordinary mind distinctions and differences that are always foregrounded in the conscious mind.

Infinite interconnection is a description of an internal, cosmic domain that operates instantaneously across the whole universe. The empty space of this domain has consciousness because it contains exchange patterns of Meaning, that is, relationships. The scientific and negative term 'nonlocality' can, therefore, also represent a positive singular and quintessential intelligent force: a universal constant that holistically surrounds, connects and interpenetrates everything in the universe into one mind-at-large. The flexible nature of this universal constant comes from the quality of its implicit potentials, and its universal scope is captured by the idea of the one ambient ocean of cosmic consciousness.

The two secondary relations of non-symmetry and asymmetry are necessary features of the images of visual perception as well as the distinctions within the conscious mind, and they form a natural hierarchy. Differences, forms and parts are constructed within the conscious mind and always have a relational structure of non-symmetry and asymmetry. Differences, forms and parts are always secondary and derivative features within a broader contextual whole. Within the processes of visual perception as well as in thinking they represent the distinct and foreground constituent features of every visual or conceptual image. Differences, forms and parts are the explicit features of Bohm's explicate order, while the silent, unlighted symmetry of space is forever a primary, implicit context of One Consciousness.

We can say that the relations of non-symmetry carry the meaning of a distinction or a difference. These are the relations that play a prominent role in the thought processes of identification and/or recognition, and they have a structure provided by 1 – *Implicit-to-explicit* exchanges of meaning. In contrast, within the subliminal and autonomic processes of visual perception, patterns of distinctions (non-symmetry) automatically develop into coherent spatial asymmetrical images within the visual cortex. I discuss these processes more fully in Part II.

The story of these three relations is slightly different for conscious thought. When interpretative and deliberative thought makes meaning we have the relative freedom to choose how to think and make meaning. These choices relate to the two relations of non-symmetry and asymmetry as follows. Non-symmetry is a feature of the three exchange patterns of 1 – *Implicit-to-explicit*, 2 – *explicit-to-explicit*, and 3 – *explicit-to-Implicit*. In these exchanges, non-symmetry represents the 'explicit' and differential feature of each. In other words, in these three patterns of meaning-making, explicit meaning represents the foreground, differential and conscious features of the conscious mind.

In terms of asymmetry, such relations represent the contextualising of differences so that they fit within a larger spatial system or context. In deliberative and reflective thought, for example, this occurs in 3 – *explicit-to-Implicit* exchange patterns, where there is an awareness of context and even a degree of reflection and empathy. Hence when distinctions begin to appear relative and secondary they take on the added meaning of 'similarity' and so Bohm and Hiley's comments about the order of 'similar differences' and 'different similarities of these differences' provide a description of how such differences become ordered so they fit within deeper and broader contexts.

As a consequence, when we begin to look for similarities our focus will lead us inevitably to 3 – *explicit-to-Implicit* exchange patterns and to an asymmetrical contextual ordering within interconnected systems. In contrast, when we employ an excluding focus on differences or distinctions (2 – *explicit-to-explicit*), this emphasis will inevitably lead us into the separating forests so typical of the secular, materialistic worldview.

The architectural structure of these three relations provides an inherent order and stability for One Consciousness and also for the manner in which the ordinary human mind is a holographic part of that larger domain. These three relations, together with the five exchange patterns of implicit and explicit Meaning, provide an explanation for the possible chaos, disorder and randomness that is often seen to be part of the external world but which actually has arisen in the human mind. For example, the dark figures of disorder automatically arise if we neglect the meaning of broader context – contexts that are always primary and implicitly present. 'Do not neglect the context' sounds so simple, yet we forget it regularly whenever we are anxious, authoritarian, dogmatic, angry, depressed, selfish or egocentric. I will have more to say about our propensity to forget the context in later chapters.

The agency of these three relations of symmetry, non-symmetry and asymmetry provides an open yet infinite internal system in which the idea of separation or gaps or absolute vacuums is seen to be illusory. The order and architecture of the conscious mind is created by the relations of non-symmetry and asymmetry, and these we treat in a variety of similar and different ways depending on how we see the world.

In the next chapter I discuss the confusion that has arisen from the tendency to confuse 'information' with meaning.

7

Information Virus

The Claude E. Shannon Award is the highest honour in the field of information theory, named after the man regarded by some as the father of the information age. In 1948 his influential article 'A Mathematical Theory of Communication' (later made into a book) was first published and in it Shannon laid out the mechanical and mathematical bases of communication. His model involved a transmitter, channel and receiver, each of which reflected the then standard system within a Bell telephone exchange.

In Shannon's theory of communication, the transmitter produces a message that is sent through a channel or wire that alters the message in some way. The receiver then has to infer what would be the likely average information that was sent in the message. 'Information' is a highly abstract notion as it is based on a probabilistic model and defined as the negative of the logarithm of a probability distribution.

What is missing from Shannon's mathematical theory of communication, as well as from later quantum information theory, is the role of *meaning* in communication. And while the transmitter and receiver of his theory can be a person or a machine, the role of the agent, and in particular of mind, has been largely eliminated. As a result of these eliminations the calculated information content of the word 'coming' is mathematically considered to be the same as the non-word 'gnmioc'. Basil Hiley reminds us of this in his 2005 paper 'Process and the Implicate Order: Their relevance to quantum theory and mind'.[13] This inadequacy highlights the general problem of equating the negative and abstract equations of information content with what actually happens in communication exchanges.

A critical assessment of information theory tells us that meaning is essential to and for that theory. It is essential because it is impossible to exclude meaning from any discourse and that includes the various discourses of information theory. It is impossible because a discourse is defined in terms of exchanges of meaning. It is the meaning within a communication that represents the gold standard by which any discourse or communication is intelligible and is judged, and this applies to Shannon's information theory notwithstanding its reliance on mathematical 'probabilities'. To deliberately establish a meaningful theory that sets out to explicitly exclude meaning is to embark on a fantasy. This is a mathematical and technological fantasy that attempts to substitute the term 'information' for 'meaning'.

This fantasy is disseminated in almost every corner of science and popular culture and its circulation represents a widespread cultural malaise. Its nature can be gleaned from the following statements:

- Information is a real and effective feature of the universe.
- The universe is an interconnected network of information and energy.
- The primary currency of reality is information.

These statements have been used by various yet widely different investigators: Ervin Laszlo (2004); Peter Fraser, Harry Massey and Joan Wilcox (2008); and Robert Jahn and Brenda Dunne (2011). These statements and thousands more like them are false because when used to describe anything to do with communication or mind, the term 'information' is, as a lawyer might say, *unsafe* – unsafe because it creates shadows that are called on to stand in for reality.

These shadows conceal meaning by pretending to be something they are not. What is it that information theory pretends to be? The answer lies in a double bind: qualities of meaning and Meaning are ascribed to information discourses that deny having any association with meaning. What we are dealing with here is a language virus that, like a biological virus, needs a culture in which to grow. The culture in which the virus of information theory has grown is a reductive and simple-minded materialism and the outcome is a widespread use and application of information theory which has the effect of reinforcing the mainstream belief in an objective material world that is separate from mind and meaning.

In other words, the virus of information theory operates as a rhetorical device that functions to prop up the fiction of an objective world of local realism. This is how rhetorical devices work: by innocently presenting a portion of the picture as if it were the whole while they conceal critical elements through elision or occlusion. Shannon's information theory treats the vital dynamics of communication as if they are a set of mechanical devices. As a consequence, his theory confuses the exchanges of meaning in communication with electrical exchanges. His theory has also laid the foundation for 'communication' to be regarded as 'the imparting or exchange of information'. Communication is not and never will be the exchange or imparting of information. *Communication is an exchange of meaning.* Anything that can communicate and exchange meaning is alive and is not a machine. Machines like computers cannot communicate; all they do is to run on, and exchange, electrical charges.

Only one aspect of meaning's multilayered structure is formally recognised within information theory: the movement of *explicit-to-explicit* exchanges. These are the conscious exchanges of distinctions and differences that are so prized in mechanical models and mathematical calculations, yet they represent a minority of all the possible exchanges of meaning (see Chapter 4). This reliance on explicit distinctions and differences has meant that within information theory the mechanical 'noise' of a channel has been interpreted as no different from the natural uncertainty of implicit meaning contained and embedded in every message. What has this lack of distinction led to?

Shannon's theory is concerned with increasing efficiency and reducing ambiguity in communication. A channel is held to produce ambiguity in a message sent from a transmitter, yet the theory has nothing to say about the natural ambiguity that is involved in the layers of implicit meaning (cultural, linguistic, universal) that are a large and inherent portion of all messages. To confuse these two, one mechanical and the other a natural feature of all expressions, is to confuse a machine with an organism and in the process fuse together organic communication with mechanical exchanges. The outcome of this confusion leads us to believe that while computers can communicate, humans are by nature just less inefficient computers.

A further problem with information theory is that the theory assumes that the receiver recognises the 'information' of the message as a choice between known possibilities. This choice relies upon probability statistics as a substitute for the cultural, linguistic and individual richness that is inherent in the uncertainty of implicit meaning. In essence, this is an attempt to define implicit meaning as no more than a range of probable explicit meanings. This is a prime category mistake because the order inherent within Meaning mandates that the explicit will always arise from the implicit. Information theory reverses this order.

Further, it should be noted that it is impossible to delete the implicit meaning of contexts from any discourse, and that means from information theory. As a consequence, while information theory explicitly denies a role for meaning along with the agency of mind and consciousness, it covertly reinstates them as the intelligible feature of all its discourses, which are presumably meaningful to those who express or receive them or who give awards for 'information' excellence.

Every communication exchange, whether particle to particle, cell to cell, person to person, via touch or telepathy, by telephone, Skype or face to face, contains the generic factor of Meaning. Yet even scientists like John Wheeler have confused the role of information and meaning with the reductive formula 'it from bit'. How does the world (it) arise from the so-called substratum of a 'bit' of information? (Küng 2008: 72). This formula is actually nonsense because information in whatever form (bit or qubit) is a linguistic construct solely concerned with man-made measurements and computations.

Another recent example of the confusion of meaning and information comes from Giulio Tononi in his imaginative book *Phi*, where he writes: 'information integrated by the causal powers of a mechanism inside a system, from the system's "intrinsic" perspective, acquires meaning – in fact, it becomes meaning' (Tononi 2012: 145). This is not so much a covert statement that changes meaning into information as a confusion of the two, the effects of which undermine both information theory and a coherent understanding of Meaning. These kinds of comments fail to discern the distinction between a set of limited, man-made computations (information) and the essence of life and intelligibility.

To be fair I should add that to some degree almost every scientist has been infected with this language virus of information theory. Even David Bohm is not beyond using the term 'information' in a manner that retards our understanding of consciousness and communication. Take for example the following. At the end of their highly original book *The Undivided Universe*,

Bohm and Hiley refer to how consciousness relates to the subject matter of the book, which is quantum physics. The authors draw our attention to the suggestion that quantum mechanics and consciousness are closely related and that physicists should bring consciousness into quantum formalism. The authors then go on to qualify that by saying:

> Throughout this book it has been our position that the quantum theory itself can be understood without bringing in consciousness and that as far as research in physics is concerned, at least in the present period, this is probably the best approach. (Bohm & Hiley 1995: 381)

This would seem to be the established position of physicists in regard to consciousness. However, when these authors actually refer directly to consciousness they say that 'The implicate order is not only the ground of perception, but also of the actual processes of thought. For thought is based on information contained in the memory' (1995: 383). They then say that this information is active rather than passive.

While Bohm and Hiley argue that leaving consciousness aside is probably the best approach to quantum physics, they nevertheless incorporate many of its characteristics into their theory. They go on to say that 'active information' operates in thought in ways similar to how it operates in the actions of the quantum potential. While this is consistent with their theory it is a highly questionable statement, for 'information', whether active or passive, should not be seen to be part of mind or consciousness because these have already been deliberately excluded from the classical understanding of information theory.

This exclusion of mind and meaning from information theory leads to these very factors being arbitrarily imported back into the theory. Such reversals do damage to both the internal consistency of information theory and to an intelligent understanding of mind, consciousness and meaning. The outcome is confusion. Bohm himself was somewhat critical of the passive nature of classical information theory. He pointed out that within the quantum field, exchanges of information actively occur without our knowledge and so this kind of 'active information' is different from the 'passive' information associated with information theory (Bohm & Hiley 1995: 28–57).

According to Bohm, active information operates on its own and beyond our knowledge in a process that 'in-forms'. It does this by having a significant 'form' or pattern but very little energy. According to Bohm and Hiley, the form of the vibration enters into and directs a much greater energy force. This happens in a radio when the patterns carried by the radio wave give a form to the energy provided by the power plug through the amplifier. They write, 'we have seen that to obtain a powerful effect from a very weak field we need something like our concept of active information'. They go on to say that it is the form of the field and not the amplitude that 'in-forms' the self-movement of the particle (Bohm & Hiley 1995: 39).

'Form' is used here in a special way in order for us to understand how the idea of active information operates. Form is often interpreted as the peaks and troughs of a vibration or wave function and it is this kind of vibrational form that suggests the motion of particles. There are, however, several problems that arise out of using the terms 'forms' and 'form-forming' in this way.

First, the term 'active information' does not get over the inherent problem of reintroducing mind back into information theory when the theory excludes it. The word 'active' does not really help here, although it does provide a hint as to the vital agency within communication processes. Agency, however, does not fit with the mechanical elements of 'information'. Added to the confusion surrounding the use of 'active information' is the phrase a 'form that in-forms'. Yet only a *mind* can be 'informed' or 'uninformed' and such terms relate to the transformational processes of learning through education and by being conscious, all of which are mind conditions expressly excluded from the elements of classical 'information'.

The concept of a 'form' is as significant for physics as for chemistry, biology and linguistics, but forms are also important for Meaning. While forms appear universally, they only ever arise as explicit markers within the conscious mind of organisms and through the implicit processes of perception and conception. As such they represent the explicit features of the explicate order which has, in turn, arisen from the implicit potentials of Bohm's implicate order. Therefore, forms are not 'things-in-themselves', or in other words there are no 'objective' forms or objects that exist unsupported by processes of observation or a conscious perceiving mind. To believe this trick is possible is to deny the structure of Meaning while undermining the integrity of Bohm's concepts of the implicate and explicate orders.

So, what are Bohm and Hiley referring to when they write about active information, and what are researchers in neuroscience referring to when they write about 'brain information'? From the point of view of Meaning, it does not really matter – in relation to physics or biology – whether we use the term 'information' in a 'passive', 'active' or 'inactive' sense. The basic problem when 'information' is used to refer to communication is that it is embedded in assumptions that split subject from object and that separate explicit from implicit meaning. This separating function does not align with the reality of an interconnected universe that is structured by the relationships of consciousness.

I return to the point made earlier: the computations of 'information' are not 'meaning', and as a consequence it is impossible to communicate just information. As communication represents an exchange of meaning, in those instances where there is no meaning exchange there is no communication. A key example of where there is no meaning exchanged and so no communication is when computers interact with each other. In these interactions, there is no mind-to-mind communication and so these machine interactions do not involve 'understanding', 'realisation', 'insight', or even 'learning'; rather, the exchanges that occur within and between machines are a set of non-meaningful exchanges related to electrical circuits and charges.

The 'information' terminology used to represent these electrical patterns is often expressed in terms of mathematical computations. In terms of Meaning this is the language of *explicit-to-explicit* exchanges or of distinctions and differences. Because these mechanical and computational models (including Shannon's Mathematical Theory of Communication) have an almost exclusive focus on computations they are necessarily devoid of the subtle complexities of implicit meaning which is the main feature of human communication. Technicians and scientists may decide to call these electrical exchanges between machines 'information', but this vocabulary too easily slips into the confusion of mixing information with meaning and then calling this incoherent blend 'communication'.

This confusion is augmented by the literal rendering in which most discourses of information theory are expressed. The difference between a discourse that is rendered literally and one that is metaphoric – 'the ship of state' – has to do with layers of meaning. A metaphor deploys more than one meaning, while a qualified statement implies the possibility of other meanings. The discourses associated with 'adaptive systems', 'anticipatory systems', 'artificial intelligence', 'informatics' and 'machine learning', to take some random examples, are for the most part applied literally. A literal rendering also says something about truth. It says, 'the single meaning of this expression is unqualified and true'.

We should resist the temptation to be led astray by thinking that the shadows of information are contained in communication or that they constitute primary and universal givens. One example of the extraordinary confusion within science between meaning and information was demonstrated in the well-publicised comments made by the theoretical physicist Stephen Hawking, who was reported on BBC News to have said, 'The development of full artificial intelligence could spell the end of the human race.'[14] Such a view seriously fails to discriminate between the shadow and the real, that is, between the secondary computational languages of artificial intelligence and the infinitely complex, primary and vital intelligibility of Meaning.

Meaning exchanges do occur between different people and also, in general, between organisms and their environment, that is, between the whole and the parts as well as between the parts and the whole of One Consciousness. Thus what is absolutely necessary in any communication is an exchange of consciousness in the form of meaning. What is missing when we use this term 'information' to refer to communication is an appreciation of the difference between the skeleton computational language of information and the rich, ordered sensibilities of Meaning.

The question often asked about locating the much sought after mysterious universal 'information-generating process' can, therefore, be answered simply by studying the nature of One Consciousness. If in the future science should go down this track it will find that it will be looking for something like a meaning-generating process, that is, the symmetry potentials of One Consciousness: Plato's Good. Thus it is not information that is the primary substratum of the universe, but the Meaning of One Consciousness. To realise how we sometimes generalise and misuse the term 'information' we should try exchanging it for the specific phrase 'a telephone exchange'. For example, we could try saying, 'a telephone exchange is a real and effective feature of the universe', or even, 'the development of a highly efficient telephone exchange could spell the end of the human race'. Such statements may fit into the script of a Monty Python scene, by otherwise they are patently ridiculous.

As I decline to be led astray by calling the second the first, I will not be using the term 'information' to represent the communication exchanges within perception. Rather, in discussing perception I will be using the primary terms 'meaning', 'carriers of meaning' and 'Meaning'. While this terminology contests the objective rhetoric of those who have grown accustomed to using the term 'information', nevertheless this is the path I must pursue.

Part II

First and Second Sight

8

The Light of Sight

The six chapters in Part II of this book cover the holographic story of visual perception. I begin in Chapter 9 with a description of 'first sight' – our immediate visual experience – and how this is interrelated with but distinct from 'second sight' – our interpretation of what it is we experience: the 'isness' of Nature. There are six ways of seeing that can be bracketed within the category of second sight. These are described in Chapters 11–13, along with the influences that age and culture have on them. In this chapter I discuss some of the basic arguments related to how we can speak about visual perception.

When trying to explain the phenomena of visual perception we are usually confronted with a mystery. It is a mystery created by binary thinking. The processes of seeing necessarily involve a series of connections that link the environment to our conscious mind. These links become problematic when binary thinking continually tells us that mental and physical states are two separate domains. The mystery of visual perception thus relates to how the gap between the mental and the physical can be bridged.

There are ways of approaching this which relate to what I regard as the mistaken doctrine of many minds. In the first chapter of his book *Seeing Things as They are: A Theory of Perception* (2015), the philosopher John Searle wrote about the 'mistakes' of dualism, materialism, monism, functionalism, behaviourism, idealism and identity theory, classifying them all as mistakes of what he called 'conceptual dualism' (2015: 10). He went on say that there is yet another mistake, much bigger, that has overwhelmed philosophy since the seventeenth century: 'the mistake of supposing that we never directly perceive objects and states of affairs in the world, but directly perceive only our subjective experiences' (2015: 10).

Searle attributes this overwhelming mistake to an impressive list of thinkers: Descartes, Locke, Berkeley, Leibniz, Spinoza, Hume, Kant, Mill and Hegel. He sets about to argue that all these great philosophers were mistaken about visual perception because they 'thought the object of perception is the subjective experience itself' (Searle 2015: ch. 2). In contrast, he argues that what occurs in perception is that 'you are *directly* seeing objects and states of affairs, and these have an existence totally *independent* of your perception of them' (2015: 11). For Searle, his viewpoint represents the 'obvious facts' about perception and he called this stance Direct or Naïve Realism.

While Searle recognises conceptual dualism as a general mistake made by many, the effect of his naïve realism introduces another kind of thinking that I suggest is equally mistaken. This is the binary thinking associated with the doctrine of many minds and the assumption that a private mind has the capacity to visually record a world that is separate and independent from that mind. From this binary perspective of naïve realism, it is argued that we see an environment when the eyes receive stimulation (light), which in turn causes us to have a visual experience. The visual experience is subjective while the objects and light from the environment are objective and independent of us.

Yet the naïve realist argument goes further by suggesting that for normal vision not to be categorised as an hallucination, these two (the subjective experience and the objects of the physical world) have to be the same, or so close to being the same that it is impossible to tell them apart. This means that in order to have normal, healthy vision there has to be a one-to-one correlation between the outer, objective world of the environment and the inner subjective world of images. While Searle does not use the phrase 'one-to-one correspondence' this is the relationship implied in his 'directly seeing objects and states of affairs'. Yet how reliable is this approach of the naïve realist and is there any scientific evidence that challenges this stance? The answer to that is 'yes', there is some evidence from neuropsychology that undermines Searle's interpretation.[15]

Some well-documented evidence from Karl Pribram (1981) challenges the one-to-one correspondence implicit in naïve realism, that is, a correspondence between the outer objects of the environment and the inner images that occur within the visual cortex of the brain. Given almost a century of this kind of evidence, Searle seems surprisingly confident about his naïve realist approach.

Searle also argues that 'there must be a causal relation by which the objective reality causes the subjective experience' (2015: 11). He does not explain how it is possible for an independent, objective reality to cause the subjective experiences of perception, and, I may add, neither does anyone else. But he does suggest that when vision is biologically doing its job (by this he means when we are not hallucinating) the subjective experience of perception will be identical to the true objective facts of perception.

Putting Pribram's evidence aside for the moment (it is discussed later), is it possible to challenge Searle's approach directly? For example, it is impossible to verify or falsify the theory of naïve realism because the objective facts of perception can only ever be known through the subjective experiences of them. In other words, as there is no outside, objective mediator can we still appeal to an objective reality? It seems not. Alternatively, if we were to appeal to a common consensus, how do we know we are agreeing on the same reality if people really do have separate, private minds? Where does this leave us in terms of a workable framework from which to approach the problem of visual perception?

To answer that question, we need to look at those philosophers Searle criticises. To a large extent the strength of his naïve realist approach to perception rests negatively on his trenchant criticism of mistaken philosophers: Descartes, Locke, Berkeley, Leibniz, Spinoza, Hume, Kant, Mill and Hegel. While each of these philosophers has argued differently, they all generally adhere to the proposition that we can only ever know subjective experiences, variously called 'ideas', 'impressions' and recently, 'sense data'. Immanuel Kant (1724–1804) put the argument slightly differently when he proposed that we never directly know the independent physical world for 'things in themselves are unknowable'. The following sums up Searle's criticism of this group: 'Notice that the only reality that is accessible to us on this account is the subjective reality of our own private experiences. This makes it impossible to solve the sceptical problem: How, on the basis of perception, can we ever know facts about the real world?' (Searle 2015: 23).

In my view, Searle rightly concludes that this is an insoluble problem, because if we only ever know a world of private subjectivity we can never move out of that domain into what he calls the 'objective real world' that is not private. I agree with Searle's criticism of these philosophical arguments that refer to, or infer, exclusivity to 'our own private experiences'. But I cannot agree with his faith in naïve realism as being able to provide an acceptable alternative. Rather, I would argue that both positions have major faults: the subjectivists who say we can only ever know 'ideas', 'impressions' or 'sense data' and Searle's naïve realist position that holds with an independent universe. Both the subjectivist and the realist positions create and promote intractable difficulties that arise from their binary approaches that alternately focus on the 'subjective' or the 'objective'.

Both arguments have a common weakness in their understanding of the nature of mind. Each of the philosophers Searle mentions, as well as Searle himself, bases his argument on unquestioned assumptions about the mind. These assumptions relate to a conscious mind that belongs to a separate individual. Such views simply re-establish the problems inherent in assuming that each individual person has a private mind that is separate from other minds and also separate from an independent physical world.

This is the doctrine of many minds and it leads directly into binary conclusions which have exclusive implications that nullify the possibility of discovering bridging connections between the physical and the mental. In addition, binary arguments invariably give one side of the pair greater priority over the other. As a consequence, we see that naïve realism gives priority to the unverifiable 'obvious facts' of an independent environment, while those philosophers who have opted for perception being a subjective experience arrive at the point where things are in themselves unknowable. Both positions are inadequate to explain visual perception.

A related but important implication of the doctrine of many minds is its current disposition to view the private mind as an effect of the brain and then to locate the mind exclusively within the brain. Searle is quite specific about this when he says, 'All intentional states, without exception, are *caused* by brain processes and *realized* in the brain' (2015: 33). This is a position reflected in mainstream neuroscience. Searle defines intentionality in various ways but in general it consists of those psychological conditions that have content. The conscious, deliberate, intentional mind is, therefore, according to Searle, caused by the biology of the brain. But just how it is caused by the brain no one can say. Here in stark contrast is the unexplained, critical gap inherent in the doctrine of many minds.

The manifold difficulties that confront the investigator of visual perception when the starting point is the doctrine of many minds are overwhelming. The confusion that this doctrine brings to any approach to visual perception tends to narrow enquiry to a set of inconsequential and abstract debates about the role or status of such things as 'representation', 'object' and 'content'. Little else, it seems, is possible because the beginning point of these arguments is so profoundly flawed by the unquestioned acceptance of a separation within visual processes. What is needed is an entirely different approach.

A singular system

In contrast to the conventional approach, my starting point in discussing the processes of visual perception is to take account of the integrating relationships within one holographic consciousness and the mind of the individual. Specifically, consciousness is a singular and internal system in which the whole inheres in every part and the parts reciprocate in the patterned fabric that makes up the whole. From this integrated and holistic view the traditional gulf between mind and matter has already been closed by the acceptance that consciousness is an immanent feature within and surrounding everything, including the particles of light.

This is the conclusion supported by calculations performed by Neppe and Close (2014). The consciousness surrounding the relationships of particles offers an integrated foundation for an analysis of visual perception, for it means that mind-like characteristics of vision already exist within the larger holographic systems of our environment – specifically, surrounding particles/waves of light. As such, photons always already operate within the symmetry of space and so are features of consciousness that contain the sight potentials for visual perception in organisms.

Plato paid homage to the integrated relationship of light and sight two and half thousand years ago when he said, 'the sense of sight and the visibility of objects are yoked by a yoke a long way more precious than any other' (Plato 1986: 508). What I am arguing here is that the yoke to which Plato refers is the symmetry of space and the awareness of One Consciousness. These relations of space and sight surround as well as exist within particles/waves of light and are also contained within an organism's visual senses.

In more recent times the inventor and philosopher Arthur Young (1905–95) suggests that '*Light is pure action*, unattached to any object, like the smile without the cat (1999: 11). He goes on to say:

> This light energy is everywhere, filling the room, filling all space, connecting everything to everything else. It includes much more than the light we see by, for all exchanges of energy between atoms and molecules is some form of what used to be called electromagnetic energy, which extends over a vast spectrum and would be better named interaction. Visible light covers just one octave of that spectrum.

The visible light by which we see has some unique properties. It has no mass (no rest mass); it has no charge, and as Young said, 'as evidenced by the finding of relativity that clocks stop at the speed of light, it has no time' (1999: 10). If photons of light contain no mass, charge or time, what features do they contain, that is, apart from their magnetic fields characteristics and their wavelengths that create the colours of the rainbow? This is not a question about movement or speed, for we know that waves/particles have exceedingly fast speeds, calculated at 299,792.458 kilometres per second. This speed is said to be the ceiling speed within the universe, where nothing can go faster.

If photons of light have no mass, charge or time, does this mean that their behaviour transcends physics, a discipline that deals with the material world and the mechanics of moving objects? Of course, the question of what photons contain is critical to our

discussion of perception, and in a private correspondence with
Vernon Neppe and Ed Close (15 August 2015) I asked them this
question. They replied that the following results of the photon are
provisional but that their results come from careful mathematical
calculations. This is the formula they sent me:

Photon: mass-energy, like the electron, is 1;
consciousness is 105; total units 106.

How should we interpret this statement other than that the
calculations performed by Neppe and Close indicate that consciousness is not only associated with the photon, but over 99%
of the particle/wave is measured as the potentials and relationships
of consciousness? These are the symmetry potentials of space and
sight. From the calculations of Neppe and Close we could say
that photons are more accurately described as waves/particles
of consciousness than as waves/particles of matter or physics. I
understand this is a controversial statement to make, but in the
absence of any role for consciousness or meaning within mainstream physics the potentials of photons to produce visual images
within the processes of visual perception will remain a mystery.

It is interesting to note that apart from the calculations of
Neppe and Close in this century, Young had made a similar kind
of prediction about light in the 1970s. He suggested that light
presents a special kind of difficulty, like the difficulty of knowing about that which provides our knowledge. By this he meant
the kind of problem he encounters when repairing his glasses.
'Light is not like other things', he wrote. For example, it is not
like a snow crystal that can be photographed or seen by more
than one person. The photon, he said, *'can be seen only once*: its
detection is its annihilation' (Young 1999: 11). He elaborated
on that statement by stating: 'Light is not seen; it is a seeing'.

From these comments we can conclude that if the photon is a
seeing beyond time, what is seen by the individual organism (to

use Plato's phrase) are the moving images of eternity. The verb-phrase 'a seeing' is a compact way to describe the moving images of visual perception, and these have a gestalt of Meaning and meaning. Thus 'seeing' refers to a set of space and sight events that occur within the conscious mind of the individual and also within the infinite implicitness of One Consciousness.

At this point in Young's argument where he describes visible light as a *seeing*, we have lost the separating physics of a secular, materialistic world, along with the doctrine of many minds. With that change we have moved seamlessly into an internal but more integrated world where the space and sight of One Consciousness have become features of photons as well as visual perception. It is possible to draw the conclusion that Young in the 1970s was foreshadowing, four decades ahead, some of the work of Neppe and Close but without the benefit of their mathematics.

Young also tells us that the photons of light leave no physical residue in their work of transporting energy from one point to another in the universe. However, on the basis that visible light is 'a seeing' we can say that photons of light actually do leave residue in the moving visual images that constitute our seeing the environment. Given the agency of consciousness, such local images of eternity must be initiated and largely built from the symmetry of space and sight of One Consciousness, which we assume is an underlying part of the consciousness of photons. This conclusion follows quite naturally from the results of Neppe and Close's calculations and from Young's definition of light as a 'seeing'.

Three steps of perception

The character of visual phenomena, or the phenomenology of seeing, involves:

   i. A quantum of spatial and sight symmetry together with a range of distinctions carried by photons of light.

ii. This gestalt contains implicit and explicit relations that impact the pre-reflective consciousness already operating within the nervous system of the organism.

Thus there are two sets of conditions that make up the phenomenology of seeing. The first concerns the symmetry potentials of space, that is, the sight of seeing. This condition also contains a set of secondary explicit relations associated with light and movement. The second condition concerns how the derived distinctions of light interact with an eye, the optic nerves and the visual cortex of a live organism. The phenomenology of seeing thus represents a completely internal yet integrated system of interconnecting relations: beginning with cosmic consciousness and involving photons of light and finally, the construction of images seen.

Susanna Siegel has argued in *The Content of Visual Experience* (2011: intro.) that 'much of what we understand about the things we see is part of the visual phenomenology itself'. I agree, and while Siegel did not have in mind a set of interacting relations of consciousness that represent the phenomenology of seeing, she did stress that 'color, shape, illumination, motion and their co-instantiation in objects are taken to be represented in visual experience'. In other words, we can argue that the phenomenology of visual perception represents a complex series of contents that have a structure and an order and that involve both the photon's and the body's pre-reflective consciousness. That involvement is underpinned by the relations of One Consciousness, which constructs the symmetry of space and sight.

On the basis of Meaning being structured by relationships, I suggest that visual perception is carried out through a three-step integrated phenomenological process that involves three transformations:

i. the implicit symmetry of sight and space generated by One Consciousness

ii. photons of light that carry a complex set of distinctions

iii. the transformation by pre-reflective consciousness of those distinctions and then the integration of these into whole images.

The transformations that apply to these three steps involve the changes from symmetry to non-symmetry and then to asymmetry. The first transformation begins with symmetry potentials involving sight and space that are the background context to every photon's movement. These symmetry potentials have entangled, nonlocal connections that are found within the universe. Such instantaneous connections have been demonstrated in 1982 by Alain Aspect and his colleagues, and, in 1998, an even more conclusive series of tests by Nicholas Gisin's group at the University of Geneva (Radin 2006: 227).

The second transformation involves the complex set of distinctions related to the various light frequencies, a large range of colours, shapes and the movements of forms. The third transformation involves the processes of integrating this set of distinctions within the visual nervous system so that they form complete whole images that are consciously perceived as a set of moving images.

Thus the inherent order within the phenomenology of seeing runs from symmetry to non-symmetry to asymmetry. This is an irreversible order, with the final stage of seen moving images having a closure constructed from the asymmetrical integration of the many distinctions and differences of colour, shapes, motions, and luminous intensities that have in turn arisen from out of the symmetry potentials of space and sight that exist within One Consciousness. In this model, the symmetry of space and sight represents the nonlocal context from which the photon's contrasts construct the differences within any scene.

This focus on the three relations of consciousness – symmetry, non-symmetry and asymmetry – means that the phenomenology of vision can be understood as having holographic features; this is because these three general relations are also evident within physical holograms. We see this when the symmetry within the light of a laser beam is split by a beam splitter that creates two beams that then collide with each other, and the resulting interference patterns are recorded on film, producing a whole image. Thus the hologram contains symmetry potentials associated with light that transform into a series of non-symmetrical distinctions that have arisen from the beam splitter, the object and also from the interference patterns and finally the transformation of these various distinctions into a whole image.

A note of caution is in order here in regard to the claim that perception is a holographic process. This claim does not mean that perception reproduces the virtual reality of a hologram or that we live in a world of illusion. Holograms are produced by artificial, mechanical and explicit means of manipulating the phase differences of light. Such artificial means can produce the virtual reality of a hologram because they draw on and manage a range of existing visual potentials inherent within light. This also means that the phenomenological processes of visual perception, which carry a range of implicit meanings to us from One Consciousness, are entirely of another order than the explicitly calculated manipulations of the virtual reality of a hologram.

A second difference between perception and the physical hologram concerns singular and binary systems. The underlying assumption behind the materialistic worldview is that perception involves two objects: the objective facts of an independent world and the subjective experiences of that world. A similar case exists for the hologram, where a virtual object is constructed from a real object by interference patterns involving coherent light. In contrast, the natural process of perception contains no underlying binary pair and so there are never two separate objects involved in perception.

Visual perception represents the internal, holographic patterning involving nonlocal connections that are integrated into a singular reality of the scenes perceived. The journey of perception is, therefore, undertaken within the confines of a single consciousness and through symmetry potentials that are nonlocal. In general, this is a consciousness which is immanent in everything and which interacts with itself in a visual event that produces the images we see.

In relation to perception having holographic elements, Karl Pribram (1981: 142) has proposed the hypothesis that those brain functions involved in perception operate like a hologram.[16] While Pribram's hypothesis has some similarities to the approach here, there are several differences. Pribram uses the term 'information' throughout his book and does not refer to meaning or consciousness in any structural or phenomenological manner. He also conceives of the hologram of perception as essentially neurological, and so his approach is contained within the limits of a local nervous system. This limitation of the local tends to keep his study within the boundaries of the doctrine of many minds.

In contrast, my approach identifies perception as a nonlocal, cross-border and bridging event that encompasses the sight/space of One Consciousness together with photons of light and the mind of the individual. This integrated approach finds the phenomenology of visual perception arising within the relationships of consciousness, specifically within the three relations of symmetry, non-symmetry and asymmetry which give a structure to a consciousness that accompanies the photon's impact with the eye and nervous system in processes that structure visual images.

Partial truths

From the current standpoint of One Consciousness, there are partial truths in the naïve realist position as well as in those who argue that all we see is subjective sense data. First, the statement by naïve realists that we directly see objects and states of affairs is correct. It is true to the extent that the transformational, three-step process of perception directly delivers scenes and images – the 'isness' of perception. Our point of difference is that naïve realists believe that all external environmental objects and states of affairs have an independent existence, in the sense that they exist independently from our experiences of them. Yet because there is a built-in gap in the binary metaphysics of naïve realism it becomes impossible to bridge it if we totally rely upon this kind of metaphysics.

From the standpoint of One Consciousness, the environment is not independent of our experiences of it, even when our conscious experiences are limited to less than a thousandth of 1% of the spectrum of electromagnetic radiation; for example, to the narrow range of visible light. The logic that follows from an interconnected universe is that everywhere there are relations of Meaning and therefore of consciousness. As a consequence, our experiences of the environment are not independent of the environment, even when we do not have direct visible and conscious experiences of almost all of it. We are, however, continually connected to the unseen environment by connections of implicit Meaning, connections that are also the generative source of the sight within visual perception as well as the illumination of our thoughts.

From the standpoint of One Consciousness, those eminent philosophers who have argued that we are only in touch with the subjective, with 'ideas', 'impressions' or 'sense data', are correct in the sense that these terms stand for the scenes and images perceived. However, this traditional argument stops there and by so doing goes off the rails when it states either that our sense data (impressions or ideas) resemble real material objects, or alternatively, Kant's argument that things in themselves are unknowable. In both cases an independent material world has been re-created, a world that is independent of our experiences of it. Again, here is the binary metaphysics of the doctrine of many minds: the cul-de-sac that leads us to the contradiction involving an unknowable state of mind.

9

First Sight

First sight refers to those subliminal processes of Meaning that produce the seen images of vision. This set of processes exists prior to and distinct from our cultural-linguistic meanings or interpretation. The processes of first sight deliver our sense of location in space and time, yet the actual processes themselves do not have any specific location in time or space as they occur prior to the *beta* brainwaves that accompany vision (see Appendix A). From the point of view of the seer, these processes are nonlocal, which means they occupy several locations simultaneously, involving a whole set of instantaneously occurring operations.

From the seer's point of view there is no distinction in time or space between the conscious perception of a scene and the several visual processes that have gone into constructing it. A third-person measurement of the three steps of visual perception (involving the distinctions carried by light and a series of transformations that occur within the eye and optic nerve and their integration within the visual cortex) may well be able to indicate differences of time and space and hence a difference in physical locations of these steps, but such an exercise is irrelevant to the actual phenomenology of seeing.

In any case such a time scale is irrelevant because the conventional measurement of these processes only captures the physical and therefore local features of vision but fails to record the myriad relationships of consciousness that are involved in vision. In terms of Meaning, taking a measurement of any kind is a deliberate and explicit act of the conscious mind. The tools available for such conscious acts are overwhelmingly explicit. These explicit tools represent secondary features that arise out of an implicit integrated system of One Consciousness. In other words, it is impossible, even with a holographic approach, to use the crude, explicit tools of a conscious mind to measure the prior, nonlocal subtle quality of pre-conscious processes.

In all organisms that have visual perception there is only one consciousness involved. This one system includes a series of 'instantaneous' interconnections from the whole (of this consciousness) to the part (the image) as well as from the part to the whole. As a consequence, there are no borders, separations or cuts between the organism and its environment, and any attempt to impose one, as is immediately done by assuming the doctrine of many minds, produces ambiguity or confusion

A similar point was made by Arthur Young, who argued in *The Reflective Universe* that light is the beginning point in a chain of causation that runs from particles to atoms to molecules to plants to animals to humans. Young's model locates light as the first cause, that is, as self-caused or having causal potentials. Young's model has the following formula:

Light = quanta of action = wholes = first cause

This formula rests on the concept of 'action'. Young (1999: 19–20) argues that action is unqualified in that it can be counted but not divided. Actions come in wholes or quanta and as such, actions have a purpose that can be seen as a feature of the whole. As a consequence, action precedes the measurements of mass, length and time – the edifice upon which mechanical science is built.

While Young proposed that light is the first cause, his work does not explicitly take into account consciousness or meaning. In contrast, and as I have already argued, the order inherent within the universe proceeds from symmetry to non-symmetry to asymmetry, and therefore the first cause must be the symmetry potentials of One Consciousness. For visual perception, these are the symmetry potentials of space and sight. However, Young does imply that consciousness is evident in his formula of light through the proposal that inherent in light is purpose and purpose becomes apparent from the quanta of action, which is a whole.

The term 'purpose' is closely associated with 'meaning' and both are contents of consciousness. Young argues that purpose is always inherent within a whole, but if the whole is divided into parts then the meaning of the whole is lost. The same statement can be made about visual perception without loss of understanding, in that visual perception is a quantum of action. This is an action involving the organism and its environment that is not disrupted by any borders, separations, splits or cuts. The meaning of vision is discovered within the whole quantum of action and this is lost the minute we focus on the physical parts of the overall quantum of action. The purpose and meaning of vision is discovered in the communion that takes place in vision between One Consciousness and the individual.

While there are no splits within the nonlocal quantum of action of visual perception, there is, however, a margin that arises from the several transformations of Meaning. This is the invisible margin between the implicitness of One Consciousness and the conscious explicit mind of the individual. This is the margin that occurs within the processes of seeing between the implicit, holistic operations of One Consciousness and the end result of conscious moving images.

Only the results of the third step in visual perception (the seen moving images) register in the conscious mind of the individual; none of the processes of seeing do. The three-step process involving the symmetry potentials of space and sight, the various distinctions of light which are integrated into visual images, do not register in the conscious mind of the seer. It is not that we are unconscious of them (in the sense of them being repressed) but simply that like ultraviolet light and the rest of the electromagnetic spectrum their presence is not part of our perceptual apparatus and as a consequence these hidden processes can never be part of the explicit world of conscious perception.

This margin between One Consciousness and the conscious mind of an individual is a change in order and not a barrier, or a separation, or a division. It is a change from first-ness to second-ness within a series of processes. This means that the images of visual perception are secondary abstractions to the primary implicit and subliminal Meaning of One Consciousness. This margin between the implicitness of One Consciousness and explicit images is significant in the way we understand the quantum of action we call visual perception.

If we study visual perception from the habit of comprehending the universe in materialistic terms, we will mistakenly attribute a primacy to images that we will then call an independent physical world. This kind of approach tends to produce a schizoid world of separations, gaps and parts devoid of wholes. The mistake of this kind of approach is that a local world where distinctions and physical differences are treated as primary is an illusion, for this world is actually a limited, derived and secondary world. When we call this secondary world primary, this materialistic viewpoint can be said to be portraying the shadows in the cave of the mind and with it the reversal of the natural order of Meaning.

Yet when we accept the natural order of Meaning inherent within the quantum of visual perception it is possible to appreciate that the individual has no control over these steps of first sight because the conscious mind is excluded from them. These are operations that are subliminal and they involve space, sight, light and the operations of the autonomic nervous systems. In other words, these processes are pre-conscious and subliminal and therefore beyond our control in the sense that when we open our eyes we do not have a choice about seeing or not seeing; we see because the pre-reflective consciousness within our autonomic nervous system is working smoothly in coordination with the consciousness that accompanies light.

Sometimes we may see things we would rather not, and our only protection then is to turn our head aside or close our eyes. The pre-reflective and autonomic conditions of perception mean that this first seeing of an environment that has space, colour, movement, shapes and light intensities is unmediated by anything that is initiated, controlled or produced by the individual, that is, by our imagination, or by what John Searle calls intentionality and I would call the conscious mind. The consistency in the way the entire pre-reflective consciousness works along with our autonomic nervous system produces the stability or 'is-ness' of perception. This stability is essential in providing us with the certainty that 'we know what we saw' even in the face of distrust, cynicism or cross-examination.

From the standpoint of One Consciousness, the important question arises concerning first sight: who sees? The conventional wisdom of those who hold to the doctrine of many minds is to come down on the side of subjective experience and say that the identity of the seer, which is distinct from the seen, is the one that sees. This binary view imagines a private mind (the seer) seeing images on a screen-like mechanism in the visual cortex (the seen), not unlike the experience of watching a movie. Yet within the integrated principles of One Consciousness there is no separate, private mind that is the seer. Rather, this question of 'who sees?' can only be answered fully by reference to the holographic relationships between One Consciousness and the individual's conscious mind. Hence the sight within seeing comes from One Consciousness and not from the individual.

As One Consciousness initiates and is present in every step of visual perception, and as the pre-reflective consciousness of the autonomic system of the organism also contributes, we can say that all these processes are an interactive holographic event. The conscious, deliberating mind of the individual plays no part at all in these processes of first sight. As a consequence, there is no possibility that an individual organism on its own can generate visual perception or the sight within seeing. When we make statements that say or imply that it is 'the organism that sees' we erase the structural relationships within first sight while jumping to fictitious conclusions about the identity and the choice powers of the individual.

In addition, from this holistic approach, seeing is in general not a kind of projection from the brain out into the environment. Such a realist model assumes that the brain somehow causes perception to happen after being stimulated by the neutrality of light, and then the brain projects by psychological intention a set of images out onto an independent, external environment in order to see, among other things, how accurate these projected images are. From the perspective of One Consciousness there is no projection and nor is there any question of accuracy. As the conscious mind plays no part in the processes of perception there is no issue of accuracy, choice or control.

The concern for accuracy can only ever relate to those functions of choice performed within and by the conscious mind, and as a consequence accuracy is not a question related to first sight or to the functioning of pre-reflective autonomic systems that operate below *beta* brainwaves. The only qualification of this assertion concerns the health of the autonomic nervous system. For example, if we have taken hallucinogenic drugs what we see will be different from a nervous system that has not taken the drugs.

In terms of projection, unlike the bat we do not send out signals that bounce back from the environment to produce images of the environment in the visual cortex. Rather, humans represent relatively passive recipients that simply receive streams of visual meaning from their environment through the agencies of consciousness, light waves/particles that then become the moving images in the visual cortex. For the question 'who sees?', the ownership of this event of first sight must be awarded to One Consciousness rather than to the individual organism, whose conscious mind and intention has no role in the processes of visual perception.

To put it differently, the cause as well as the sight within seeing lies with the spatial symmetry potentials and their emanating patterns of relationships within One Consciousness, of which the photon's consciousness is a part. The only part the conscious mind of the individual plays is the results of these given processes. The ownership of first sight, therefore, cannot be awarded to a small, derivative explicit conscious mind, a mind that is in any case not in control of the autonomic processes of its own vision. Seeing is thus an event that is mostly implicit: carried out implicitly and containing a series of distinctions that are and remain subliminal, that is, operating below the level of the *beta* brainwaves of the conscious mind until they are received as complete images and can then be interpreted into a narrative to form part of the conscious response of the individual.

From the reference frame of One Consciousness, the actions of first sight necessarily unify the seer and the seen. The fruit of this union is the vision of first sight: an event that has a suchness and no mother other than One Consciousness. First sight is a process that brings the universe to us by creating it, while the purpose of this quantum of action is discovered within its holistic integration. First sight is a transformational, participatory event that simultaneously brings together some limited implications of the environment (visible light) for the benefit of the organism within an operation that results in a spatial, visual world to which each of us is a participating part.

The holistic reality of first sight represents a set of real causal processes beyond the control of the conscious mind of the individual. This acknowledgment of a causal world beyond the conscious mind is 'realistic', yet it is not the kind found in naïve realism, which is the kind of realism that promotes the separation of a private mind from an independent, external environment. Rather, this is the realism of Meaning where an explicit, conscious mind as well as its contents can never exist on its own in some detached formal state, but instead always functions as a set of secondary and derivative operations that have been transformed out of their implicit background wholeness. This is the holistic realism within the quantum of action called first sight.

The purpose of the quantum of first sight can be understood as the gift of a communion event. The exchanges within this communion are from One Consciousness to an individual's conscious mind. What are exchanged in this communion event are the many implicit meanings of vision, such as beauty, design, a whole variety of colours, shapes, forms, movements and light intensities. This complexity of first sight provides us, along with all other organisms that have vision, with the critically important location of NOW: the present moment. The present moment represents symmetry potentials of space and sight that are the ordered and stable base from which all our behaviour is oriented and conducted. Hence, NOW represents a stable place from which we orient our actions as well as our thoughts. The eternal moment NOW represents the implicitness of One Consciousness from which all our actions and behaviour flow.

Whenever this eternal location of NOW is ignored or erased or reduced in importance, as often happens through fatigue, anxiety, depression, drugs, or some religious or 'objective' orthodoxy, then our behaviour will become erratic and disorderly to the degree that we have lost touch with our fundamental base in the present moment. Being in the present moment is to be in communion with ourselves; with the implicitness of One Consciousness. Paying attention to the first seeing of NOW requires a lack of active thought but also a quiet and relaxed focus, though not necessarily a lack of physical activity.

Most of us do not realise, but the communion event of first sight is a gift that we are continually showered with and immersed in. This gift of vision provides the individual not only with an orientation base for his or her behaviour as well as an environment of beauty, space, colour and movement, but it is also an important bridge from the whole to the part. In other words, our first sight is the direct pathway from the immanence and transcendence of One Consciousness to us. Perhaps to fully appreciate the depth of implicit Meaning hidden within first sight requires a certain spiritual sensibility that is willing to embrace the symmetry, the no-thing of One Consciousness. This means going beyond the bars and marks that construct and separate the objects of a differential world into William Blake's fourfold vision where contextual meaning is dominant.

In summary, first sight is a quantum of action in which the seer and the seen are one. The purpose and meaning of first sight is a communion event from One Consciousness to the individual organism in order to produce the beauty of a visual world in which we humans are participating parts. The next step in this exploration of seeing is the distinction between first and second sight.

10

The Sign

In this chapter I explore further the distinction between 'first sight' and 'second sight' and do so by relating them to the structure of the Saussurian sign. This distinction between first and second sight should not be taken as a separation that exists anywhere within the invariant processes of visual perception. To appreciate the nature of this margin I need to make a few comments about the constitution of the conscious mind: the mind in which visual images register.

From the perspective of Meaning, the first and important characteristic of the conscious mind is its gestalt: its implicit/explicit structure. By this I mean that whenever the conscious mind is involved in the production of images, expressions, messages, signs, intentions, wilful actions or communications, the various contents associated with these actions will have an implicit/explicit structure. As these various contents of the conscious mind are never separate from its mental nature but, rather, constitute that mental nature, it follows that the work undertaken by the conscious mind has an implicit/explicit structure.

The significance of this integrated gestalt structure is that no content of the conscious mind can ever be fully conscious. That is, it can never be fully explicit because it will always have an underlying and intruding implicit foundation. For example, the visual reality of first sight contains a gestalt structure, a primary but hidden implicit background set of processes together with a series of secondary explicit foregrounded distinctions which make whole images. Because of this implicit/explicit gestalt structure the completeness of first sight can never be fully conscious and explicit.

The integrated gestalt structure of the conscious mind is difficult to represent by metaphor. It is not like the snow that sits on top of a mountain because it is far too dynamic for this static metaphor. And neither is it like one of the rooms in the house of the mind (the metaphor used by Freud). A similar and related metaphor is the Cartesian Theatre used by Daniel Dennett (1991: 107) to describe how conscious experiences sit in the brain. I would argue that both metaphors are inappropriate because the conscious and explicit part of the mind cannot exist on its own (in a room or a theatre) without its implicit surrounding foundations. Yet variations on the room metaphor have become popular and are often implied in discussions by neuroscientists, psychiatrists or philosophers like Dennett and Searle.

For these pundits, the room-of-the-mind metaphor becomes literal in that it sits somewhere in the prefrontal cortical regions of the brain-house. Within this mainstream approach the *beta* room (see Appendix A) of the conscious mind tends to be all there is to the individual's mind. Attending this *beta* room of the mind is the usual variety of little people (homunculi) who are the engineers that work the machinery of the conscious mind when it is engaged in any form of activity. As they all work together, the implication is that they all live in the same room of the *beta* brain-house. And in this manner the conscious mind becomes the poor cousin to the exciting work done by neuroscientists on neurotransmitters, or the diffusion of calcium ions, or the propagation of electrical impulses, and so on.

For descriptive purposes, it may not be necessary to find a good metaphor to describe the conscious mind; rather, perhaps, we should attempt to describe it in terms of the kinds of meaning it makes and its various predispositions. For example, a conscious mind predisposed towards separations will tend to view its *beta* self as the true self, walled off as an identity from other implicit mind features. Accompanying this predisposition will usually be a set of defence mechanisms that can reinforce the tendency to close itself off to the resonance of implicit meaning. Such a syndrome of separating tendencies can lead to a desire for certainty expressed through single meanings and 'black-letter' language.

In contrast to these separating predispositions, when we are able to sense the resonating influences of implicit meaning the conscious mind will be open to interconnection, unity and integration. A conscious mind predisposed towards open interconnection and unity will tend to view itself as a feature, a secondary and derived feature of a much larger and implicit One Consciousness. Even when viewed in terms of brainwaves, the conscious mind is just one *beta* part of a whole spectrum of brainwaves (see Appendix A). As such, conscious and explicit features will be seen not as the true self but simply as those foregrounded details within the general gestalt of mind. One of the important effects of this gestalt of mind is that we are never entirely conscious of anything we think, feel or see, which is simply a way of saying that learning is a permanent condition of embodied life.

In terms of the gestalt within visual perception, the margin between implicit processes and the seen explicit images represents the margin between the conscious mind and One Consciousness. While this gestalt within first sight contains this margin, there is a further closely related margin evident in the distinction between first sight and the next set of secondary perceptual processes that relate to how we conceptualise and interpret what we see. Thus first sight represents the dynamic, locational and spatial basement on which we build the various ways humans choose to interpret the seen world.

The distinction between the first sight and our various inter-pretative second sights is a distinction that has an echo in David Hume's (1711–76) difference between impressions and ideas. However, it is closer to Susanna Siegel's model when she writes about the differences between the 'content' and the 'rich content' view of perception. The content view of perception proposes that visual perceptions have spatial, colour, movement, shape and light intensity content, while the rich content view says that 'visual experience can be theory-laden, or influenced by other mental states through cognitive penetration' (Siegel 2011: intro.).

Siegel refers to the distinction between the content and rich content view of perception as a way of understanding what is going on with the disease of associative agnosia. A person who suffers from this cannot identify common objects they see, or even describe what the objects are used for. The associative agnosic thus sees objects that healthy people see but cannot name them or say what they are used for. But it is interesting to note that a sufferer can often identify objects and their use after they have touched them. This incapacity of associative agnosia highlights the margin between first sight and second sight where objects are identified, named, differentiated and integrated into the individual's cultural systems of thought.

This margin between the images of first sight and their lin-guistic/cultural identification is mirrored in the margin within the structure of Saussure's sign. One of the most influential and fertile approaches to language theory in the twentieth century was Ferdinand de Saussure's structuralist theory. Saussure's theo-ries and sign structure have been highly influential in the areas of semiotics, applied linguistics and cultural analyses, even though the Saussure sign 'floats', as it were, by itself, lacking explicit connection to a physical presence like a human body. However, that presence is implied through Saussure's description of the speaking circuit where he refers to speech – *parole* – as language in use (Saussure 1978: ch. 3).

Saussure's sign structure provides an important semiotic model that can be usefully employed in a new creative way to illustrate the margin between the essential meanings of first sight and the created linguistic and cultural meanings of various second sights. To illustrate this reinterpretation of Saussure's sign we need to look first at its dual structure:

Signifier | Signified

The margin within the sign structure may be represented by a line between signifiers and signified. For Saussure, the nature of this margin was complex. On the one hand, he implied that the two elements of the sign structure are necessarily linked together, while on the other he maintained that the connection is arbitrary (Saussure 1978: 67). In contrast, the French psychoanalyst Jacques Lacan (1901–81) described the margin between signifier and signified as a 'bar separating the two stages' and also as 'distinct orders separated initially by a barrier resisting signification' (Lacan 1985: 149).

If we leave Lacan's separating view aside for the moment, I find Saussure's comments about the complex nature of the margin between signifiers and signifieds interesting in relation to the various ways of seeing. I suggest that the margin that distinguishes first sight from the various second sights represents the margin between the signifier and signifieds. If this is the case the visual contents of first sight will be always be a series of signifiers containing the meanings of the environment. In contrast, the series of second sights represent signifieds, that is, the various ways we interpret the images (signifiers) we see. In Saussure's model signifieds are the meanings of concepts and this is exactly the meaning I wish to convey here.

With this in mind we can now say that the conscious images of visual perception represent signifiers. This is the case because these moving images carry meanings about and from the environment, for example related to the symmetry of space, movements, shapes, forms, colours, luminous intensities and the body's location within the environmental context. The next step in developing a meaningful response to these signifiers is to identify the seen images by subliminally connecting them to similar scenes in the past, and then to actually name and differentiate them in relation to the present context. This is both a necessary and arbitrary conceptualising process that in linguistics is called 'signification', while in psychology similar processes are called concept formation, or cognitive formations.

Within the sign structure the signifier–signified relationship is a necessary one in so far as it is a human necessity to identify, name and interpret the seen world; thus signifieds necessarily form in human minds in response to the given meanings contained within a set of signifiers. But this necessary relationship is also conditional in that there is never one set of interpretations or one particular concept that automatically follows on from a particular set of images (signifiers). Rather, the signifieds that necessarily follow are always open to a variety of possible identifications, cultural associations and interpretations and these will depend to a large extent upon our culture and predispositions for making conceptual meaning. Because of these possibilities of expressing a wide variety of concepts (signifieds) we can say that this necessary relationship is also arbitrary. Saussure is therefore correct when he says that the relationship between signifiers and signifieds is both necessary and arbitrary.

Hence the pathway for humans when they are involved in making meaning (signification) is one that will lead from a series of given signifiers to the formation of various cultural and linguistic concepts related to those signifiers of the environment. The only time these exchanges of meaning from signifiers to signifieds do not occur naturally in adults is when a person is suffering from the illness of associative agnosia and cannot identify the common objects he sees or even describe what the objects are used for. In these cases, the transition point or margin between signifiers and signifieds becomes a kind of barrier similar to that suggested by Lacan.

In normal behaviour, this margin between a set of given environmental signifiers and how we come to express and understand the environment represents a crossover point on a continuum of relationships of meaning that involves both given and constructed meanings, that is, between the implicitness of One Consciousness and the implicit/explicit gestalt of the conscious human mind. This crossover between signifier and signified is what Siegel calls the difference between the content and the rich content view of perception. As an aside, it also represents an important difference between Plato and Aristotle's philosophy. Plato's forms that consist of beauty and the Good are given and come first in his philosophy, while for Aristotle it is thinking itself: 'At the summit of the Aristotelian universe is not an Idea but a self-subsisting and eternal Act of thinking' (Gilson 2002: 33). In other words, Aristotle reversed the natural order of meaning in that he awards priority to the created meanings of signifieds before the implicit, given meanings of signifiers.

Traditionally in linguistics, signifiers and signifieds construct a sign, which is also known as a representation. A representation is a map to the territory that it stands for, or it can be described as the act of pointing to a something other than itself. A representation always embodies both the necessary and arbitrary features of the sign. Because of this complex embodiment a representation always has a dual structure made up of some revealing features, as well as some hidden concealing features of both signifiers and signifieds. But there is another important distinction within the mind related to the differences between signifiers and signifieds, namely that signifiers have visual contexts (arising from processes of perception) while signifieds cannot be perceived. In other words, the law of the sign tells us that no concept can be perceived. Only signifiers are visual and thus can be seen.

Because there is an asymmetrical order within the sign structure (first signifiers then signifieds) the non-sensory signifieds (concepts) always come *after* we have received a set of sensory signifiers. Only together do they construct a sign and hence a representation. A concept (signified) existing in isolation on its own, without expression, is no more than a potential musing. Signifieds must always be connected to some revealed features of perception. (This is the case even for the imaginary unicorn: it represents a composite image of a horse and a horn.) Second, a concept (signified) to be such must be connected to an expression or communication. In other words, for a concept to be a concept it has to be part of a sign and thus a feature of a communicated representation.

Similarly, signifiers on their own cannot be representations as they are only half of a representation, or half of the sign structure. When we experience signifiers on their own we are confronted with the implicit meanings of silence and peace devoid of communication or language. This is the moment of NOW. For some this essentially spiritual seeing can carry the 'intimations of immortality', to borrow a phrase from William Wordsworth. But most people are more at home with immediately identifying and interpreting the images they see, so the cosmic significance of first sight is quickly passed over, lost in the noise and chatter of thought and communication. (This also happens in linguistics when words are called signifiers when they are actually whole signs containing i) visible marks together with ii) a conventional order of letters of the alphabet that carry social meaning and so are signifieds.)

Hence, a communication happens when signifiers become representations, and this only occurs when they are connected to concepts (signifieds) in the formation of signs. When this happens the dual meanings (given and constructed) of signs are produced. This interconnection of signifiers with signifieds creates the necessary unity of signs and representations, and thus of language and discourse. Such unity occurs within ordinary healthy minds that use language and can identify and describe the world. This unity is one that involves second sight and that produces the six ways of seeing.

Where does the model of a sign structure lead us? I suggest it leads us to a description of the ways in which the conscious mind makes meaning. As a representation, the sign structure acts as the crossover communication mechanism that bridges the implicit meaning of One Consciousness (which come from the environment outside the body) with the meaning-makings of the conscious human mind. Language is composed of signs and therefore its use acts as a conscious representational map. From an integrated perspective, language and mind are not separated domains of study; rather, language constitutes the road maps of conscious thought. To analyse thought one can interrogate a text about both the content of the ostensible message and, more importantly, about the kind of meaning that is being made by the text. This book makes that approach explicit.

A specific instance of the way language is used in science, and one that relates directly to the bridging representation of first and second sight, is the proposition that space and time are the independent physical conditions of a space-time continuum. From the perspective of One Consciousness, there is no independent physical world and so space is not an objective physical condition that exists independently of observation or the observer. Rather, as I have suggested, the symmetry of space is the nature of my sight awareness and in addition, symmetry represents the given background conditions to my first sight. As Alan Watts has written, 'I cannot get away from the sense that space and my awareness of the universe are the same' (Watts 1975: 24).

In terms of Meaning, Watts is correct. They are the same because there is only one consciousness involved in first sight. The symmetry of space is a key implicit seeing potential of One

Consciousness as well as the central feature of visual perception. As such there is no division or separation regarding my participation in One Consciousness through vision. We can see only because One Consciousness has provided us with the sight within seeing. To use a famous phrase from Plato, what we see are the moving images of eternity.

Yet space can be also thought about and conceptualised as a three-dimensional construction. When this happens the symmetry of space does not disappear but has imposed on it the geometry of three dimensions. With the expression of a three-dimensional space we have created the sign structure of signifiers and signifieds, that is, a sight and space signifier register along with the added concept of three dimensions. To make this point about generating a set of concepts about the given nature of space we can go one step further and say (from the perspective of Meaning) that the curvature of space is an illusion created by a confusion.

In Albert Einstein's theory of general relativity (a theory that excludes the conditions of consciousness) space-time is said to be warped by the effects of large bodies of mass/energy. In other words, for space to curve there has to be some kind of motion, such as light moving through space and past large bodies of mass/energy (planets). The motion of photons of light creates images (signifiers) in the visual context, and then a related set of interpretative concepts can arise within the conscious mind of the scientist. When this happens, the scientist creates a proposition or theory about the seen events and in so doing, he or she is creating the sign structure of signifiers and signifieds.

Yet on these occasions, for the scientist who has erased consciousness from scientific consideration, something else occurs that results from a pernicious process of identification. With this kind of identification scientists tend to conclude that what they conceive to be the essential character of space (three dimensions and curvature) becomes for them the actual given feature of space. This is an illusion that has arisen from two orders of consciousness fused together as if they were one. For example, these characteristics (three dimensions and curvature) that science attributes to space are not the fundamental features of the symmetry of space or the awareness of One Consciousness.

These features are secondary and conceptual. For example, the symmetry of infinite space (*Implicit-to-Implicit* exchanges = 0) is of a prior order to the non-symmetrical and asymmetrical distinction produced by concepts and thoughts (1, 2 and 3). When we believe that curvature or three dimensions are quintessential feature of space we have renamed the transformations of 1, 2 and 3 as if they were the primary state of 0. In this manner scientists reverse the metaphysical order of Meaning and as a consequence they are led astray in the belief that their thoughts (involving 1, 2, and 3) are the objective features of a fictional, external world.

In addition, by ignoring the fundamental role of consciousness, mechanical science is handicapped in understanding the three process steps of visual perception. These are some of the cardinal distinctions of consciousness that were not made by Einstein in his theories of relativity; nor are they made by any scientist who, like Einstein, deletes consciousness from his theories. With the deletion of consciousness from mechanical science it becomes impossible to make these kinds of distinctions of consciousness. Yet once consciousness is included in scientific studies we will discover that there is no external world and in addition, that space and time are features of consciousness. We will also discover that everything in the universe is internal to the context of One Consciousness: everything is thus surrounded by the symmetry of space, which is at the same time the awareness of One Consciousness as well as a basic feature of our visual perception.

The conditions of consciousness in regard to time are different from those of space. From the holographic perspective, time is also a feature of consciousness and thus not an external, physical condition that is independent of the observer. Plato's conception of time as the moving images of eternity applies more to the signifiers of visual perception than to time. Space and time differ in terms of the order of relationships each occupies. Time is not a feature of perception and unlike space, which is a key feature of all visual signifiers, time is the conceptual result of human interpretative capacities. We create time by relating random environmental movements (signifiers) to a set of stable environmental movements (signifiers), and the ratio between the two represents the concepts (signifieds) of time. For example, the random changes of daily living are related to the stable changes of night and day and then later in history, to clocks. With this ratio, we produce the concept of time.

Other societies have created time by using the stable changes of the moon's phases or the changes of the seasons. Whatever method is employed, because it is a ratio time is a signified, a concept, and therefore a normal feature of second sight. This means that the commonly used metaphor of the 'arrow' of time is entirely false, for this metaphor can only ever be portrayed as a visual image and thus as a spatial formation. Yet time is not a visual signifier. (I might add that no concept can be a signifier.) Time is not so much the moving images of eternity as Plato suggested, but the moving thoughts of eternity.

The proposal that space and time are features of consciousness represents a contemporary rendering of an old debate about the nature of space and time. Kathleen Raine in her *Blake and Tradition* (1968, vol. 2: ch. 21) discusses this issue at some length. She refers to Blake's famous colour print of Newton on the sea floor of time and space and points to Newton having a white fabric (the loom of Locke) spreading from the scientist's head as he bends over his mathematical diagrams. (This is the image on the front cover of this book.) In this image Newton's diagrams represent the fixed points of his scaffolding by which he seeks to control the infinite sea of time and space. In terms of Meaning, the scaffolding of Locke's woof, that is, his 'Marks and known boundaries', represents his concept or signifieds associated with space and time, so they are not the given fundamentals of space or time but simply secondary constructed ideas of the philosopher and scientist.

The question of the integration of space and time into the physical continuum of space-time was a feature of Einstein's theories of relativity. The distinction I make here, however, in relation to their perceptual and conceptual differences is not made by secular materialist scientists because consciousness is deleted from their theories. What can we say about the relationship between space and time?

I have already discussed this relationship in relation to the Saussurian sign structure and have come to the conclusion that the relationship between signifiers and signifieds is at once necessary and arbitrary. These conditions must hold for the relationship between space and time because space is an important feature of all visual signifiers while time is definitely a signified. This means that Einstein's space-time continuum can be seen to operate within consciousness as a necessary but arbitrary connection for those individuals who do not suffer from associative agnosia.

A final point can be made about Einstein's theories of relativity and the question: 'what is the absolute and fundamental to which space and time are relative'? For many students of relativity this has been a vexed question. Einstein said the fundamental was the speed of light because nothing in the universe goes faster, and beyond that speed there is no time. From the point of view of consciousness, time is a ratio born from the womb of calculation and is therefore a concept, and so its status is very much a derivative and not a fundamental. In relation to the speed of light this is also a mathematical calculation and as all calculations are conceptual it means that this calculated speed is also a derivative and not a fundamental.

On the other hand, the consciousness that comes with light entails the causal features of visual perception. This function of light has a dominant role in creating the distinctions that relate to the intensities of light, motions, forms, colours and so on within every perceived image. Yet the consciousness that accompanies photons of light also contains the symmetry potentials of space and these, I have suggested, are the fundamentals of One Consciousness. Therefore the relativity of those distinctions within every image and also within every calculation of time or speed of light rest on the foundational base of the symmetry awareness of One Consciousness.

In summary, every sign represents a bridge from the meaningful contents of first sight to the meaningful contents of second sight: a bridge from passive reception to an active construction, from One Consciousness to the ordinary human mind. This bridging function represents our embeddedness in One Consciousness through the activities of first sight and the six varieties of second sight. The distinction between first and second sight represents the difference between signifiers and signifieds, that is, between the given, visually perceived images and the conceptually created response. This holographic interrelationship is both necessary and arbitrary.

11

Second Sight

'Second sight' refers to the way we humans identify, name, differentiate and understand the array of meanings contained within 'first sight'. First sight embraces all the meanings carried by light concerning space and the distinctions of movement, colour, forms, light intensities and how all these distinctions are unified into the final images that show the local reality of an ordered world. This is a real and local world but one limited and derived from the nonlocal, implicit background of One Consciousness.

This real but derived world is neither unstable nor illusory. The processes of perception are constant and invariant and have a stable unchanging order, and as a consequence what we first see is a set of real impersonal givens even though we are not fully aware of all the meanings contained within the manifold content of that reality. The stability of first sight comes from the stable order inherent in the transformations from consciousness to light and through to the conscious images that scientists mistakenly call 'the physical world'.

In contrast to the stability of first sight, second sight involves a set of cultural learning habits, practices and choices that lead to a variety of ways in which concepts are formed and therefore to a variety of ways in which we understand and see the world. In other words, the way we see and understand the world will depend on our culture, but more importantly, on our predisposition for making meaning. Concept formation represents one of the human organism's main practices for making meaning. We have no control over the content of meaning within first sight, but in second sight we have a choice about the content and how we make meaning and therefore how we see the world.

For almost a hundred years psychologists have been interested in concept formations. One of the early contributors was the Russian thinker Lev Vygotsky, who wrote *Thought and Language*. Like Jean Piaget, the Swiss child developmental psychologist, Vygotsky described concept formation in children as a function of maturation. His theory proposed that maturation begins in early childhood with concrete concepts associated with immediate sensations and perceptions. The maturing child then gradually develops mastery over more abstract concepts associated with an increased use of a linguistic system. Vygotsky saw every concept as a generalisation and thus the maturation change from concrete to abstract concepts was a change in the degree of generality of concept formation: 'The study of a child's concepts at each age level shows that the degree of generality (rose, flower, plant) is the basic psychological variable according to which they can be meaningfully ordered' (Vygotsky 1981: 111).

Childhood development can usefully be seen as a progression of degrees of generality by studying how a child can transfer concepts from one context into many. However, this linear developmental progression is inadequate for describing conceptual changes in adults. Because of this, or perhaps for some other reason, developmental theories that continue into adulthood have not been given much attention. Perhaps one of the reasons for the lack of an adult developmental theory is that psychologists have not taken up to any degree the subject of Meaning, along with different patterns of meaning-making. Yet by studying these patterns of meaning-making in adults we can arrive at a developmental progression in concept formations that is related to the way we see the world. This progression occurs because as we mature and become older our concepts change, along with the way we see the world.

Uexküll

Apart from the study of meaning-making, another approach to the proposal that the world can be seen in various ways is found in the theories of Estonian-born German biologist Jacob von Uexküll (1864–1944). Uexküll refined the term *Umwelt* to mean the various kinds of environment that different organisms perceive. For example, the bat will have an *Umwelt* that is different from the world of the honeybee, which will be different again from that of the wasp or the duck. Each *Umwelt* contains a series of meanings that represent the organism's model of the world. Uexküll viewed the organism's perceptions, communications and purposeful behaviours as part of the wider purpose of nature, and as a consequence his biological analyses parallel some of the features of my approach, mainly in the view that the mind and the world are inseparable.

Uexküll was convinced that non-human organisms were not machines and can be accounted for in terms of their varying perceptual models of the world: their *Umwelten*. His general approach held that each organism creates and reshapes its own world when it interacts with it. This view has now fallen out of favour with most biologists, perhaps due to Uexküll's insistence that natural selection was inadequate to explain the orientation and purpose of an organism's behaviour. Dorion Sagan writes in the Introduction to Uexküll's *A Foray into the Worlds of Animals and Humans* (2010): 'Uexküll may be right. Natural selection is an editor, not a creator'.

Uexküll's theories and his emphasis on meaning and purpose did, however, influence semiotic discourses in the United States and especially Thomas A. Sebeok and his Zoosemiotics, which is part of the larger field of biosemiotics. This influence appears to have come from the fact that Uexküll located meaning as the causal factor in the creation of the various *Umwelten* for creatures like ticks, sea urchins, jellyfish, bats and sea worms. He believed that the question of meaning must have priority in all living beings (Uexküll 2010). I agree entirely with this statement.

However, Uexküll's theory of meaning tended to be limited in some respects by the strong value he placed on exclusive distinctions. An illustration of these is his closed worlds of *Umwelten*: 'Each environment forms a self-enclosed unit, which is governed in all parts by its meaning for the subject' (Uexküll 2010). Yet he was also concerned with the connection of the subject to the carriers of environmental meanings, and writes of this connection as 'a functional cycle'. To translate a functional cycle into human terms I suggest it can be understood as the sign structure where environmental signifiers are connected to the subject's naming and interpreting what is seen (signifieds). As a biologist Uexküll was most interested in the functional cycles that involved such biological features as nourishment, the enemy and sexual activity. Yet he also thought that meaning and music were closely aligned: 'Meaning in the natural score takes the place of harmony in the musical score' (Uexküll 2010).

Uexküll related his concept of *Umwelt* to humans and it was this development that caused consternation in some European philosophical anthropologists who, while accepting the animal portion of his theory, denied that humans have *Umwelten*. Some of Uexküll's human *Umwelten* were nations, regions, gender and professions. Critiques of the human *Umwelt* have been varied and while I do not intend to discuss them here, in general these arguments boil down to the notion that humans have reason and this allows us to live in more than one *Umwelt*.

Human *Umwelten?*

Do humans live in the kind of sealed-off world that Uexküll describes for other organisms? Humans are greatly influenced by social contexts and also by how these contexts provide a focus for some of the features that Uexküll describes: nation, region, gender and profession. One only has to reflect on how accents develop in different regions of a country like the UK to appreciate that our behaviour is strongly influenced by our immediate social context. But do such social influences produce in humans the kind of species-specific closed-bubble view of the world that is implied by Uexküll's *Umwelten?*

While the social context and social norms of behaviour exert a great influence over our behaviour and in many ways guide and promote our meaning-making capacities from the time we are infants, the nature of the social has within it a large arbitrary component. The biological focus Uexküll brought to bear on his analysis of organisms like ticks and sea worms would appear to be inappropriate as a way of explaining the arbitrary nature of social and cultural behaviour in humans.

In order to come to grips with the arbitrary nature of the social it is first necessary to comprehend the status of the social. From our discussion of the sign structure and the nature of representation it is clear that the social is an inherent feature of signifieds, that is, of concept-formation. The kind of signifieds we create will influence the way we see and comprehend the world, and so these secondary meaning-making capacities are essentially social. The status of the social is, therefore, a second-order derivative one, and so to fully comprehend the arbitrary nature of social signifieds we must first recognise this natural hierarchy of Meaning. With both the given implicitness within signifiers and the created explicit meanings of signifieds we are dealing essentially with the relationships of Meaning and meaning.

This focus on the relationships of Meaning gives us a

fundamental way of speaking about the various ways we see the world and in so doing prevents us from falling into the trap of looking at second-order constructions as if they were fundamental. The possibility of reversing the order of Meaning happens automatically when we assume that social relations and social norms are paramount in the way we see the world, or in the case of biology, by attempting to extend Uexküll's biological *Umwelt* directly to humans. As I am concerned to avoid that kind of reversal I intend to focus not on the idea of *Umwelten* but on the relations of Meaning in order to map the various ways in which humans see the world.

If a biological approach to the various ways of seeing is inappropriate for mapping the social activities of humans, what other models might be used to map the territory of the six ways of seeing in second sight?

The conventional criticism of Uexküll's human *Umwelt* is to suggest that we are saved from a species-specific view of the world by our ability to reason. This suggestion has not prevented a range of contemporary writers from proposing that we humans do actually see the world in a variety of ways. For example, David Bohm has written about the way we see and interpret the world without the need to refer to Uexküll's human *Umwelt*. In Bohm's view, many of the problems of society as well as of science come from us breaking things up that are not really separate.

Bohm suggested that this tendency to break things up creates a sense of social and personal fragmentation. Fragmentation results in a 'world of nations, economies, religions, value systems, and "selves" that are fundamentally at odds with one another' (Bohm 2006: xvii). Bohm's utopian solution to this modern culture of alienation and disconnection was his suggestion that people should form dialogue groups that could, over time, meet together and transform not only the participants but also the nature of consciousness in which these relationships arise.

The psychologist Lawrence LeShan has provided another approach to ways of seeing. In his *Clairvoyant Reality: Towards a General Theory of the Paranormal* (1980), LeShan argues the case for extrasensory perception (ESP), which involves precognition, telepathy and clairvoyance. LeShan maintains that ESP is a different way of seeing from our ordinary everyday sensory perception. He draws on the work of scientists as well as mystics and 'sensitives' to show how these two ways of seeing are quite distinct from each other. ESP has had a history of being much maligned by mainstream scientists who reject the suggestion that perception could occur outside the five senses.

The territory of second sight, that is, the six ways of seeing, involves the way we make meaning; it is distinct from a biological approach, and neither does it have an exclusive linguistic focus that tends to credit the social with an absolute arbitrary nature. How we make meaning through interpreting the seen world relates to our dispositions, which comes back to the question of the kinds of meaning we make.

This question of the ways in which we make meaning is not a question about the consistency of any specific argument or the content or truth of any text or discourse. Questions of content, or truth, or opinion are always secondary to the more fundamental question of what are the organising predispositions we bring to bear on the interpretations we make. The six (second sight) ways we have to see and understand the world are discussed in the next chapter.

12

Ways of Seeing

Humans have at least seven ways of seeing. These seven ways are made up of two brackets: i) first sight and ii) six ways of second sight. First sight is constituted by One Consciousness without any input from the individual. As for second sight, the individual conscious mind becomes involved through the processes of interpreting the meanings of first sight. The act of interpreting involves identifying, naming and forming concepts, and these actions will be largely carried out on the basis of our experiences of past similar environments.

The process of using the past to understand the present without reflection represents the conditions that construct our habits and predispositions of mind. It means that how we see will often reinforce older patterns of seeing, that is, old predispositions. Such predispositions operate below the level of *beta* brainwaves and will often act as subliminal drivers for our current behaviour. Hence, when I write about 'the six ways of second sight', I am initially concerned with a set of habits and predispositions that have already been laid down within the pre-conscious mind and that operate below 8 Hz. (The relationships between brainwaves and mind are discussed in Appendix A.)

We should remember, however, that visual perception begins at the point of *beta* brainwaves (12–38 Hz). Thus two operations are involved simultaneously in most visual perceptions:

i) subliminal predispositions operating below the level of the conscious mind (below 8 Hz); and ii) conscious awareness of the current environment operating within the bandwidth of 12–38 Hz. This bandwidth tells us that the processes of intellectual interpretation are actively engaged in most of the six ways we see. While this layering of meaning is evident in all ways of seeing, in those areas where there is resistance to learning or an unwillingness to change old habits it becomes welded together into identification formations. These formations are largely hidden from conscious view and are unconscious (in the Freudian sense of being repressed). With these few cursory remarks, I want to turn now to the differences and distinctions that mark off the six second-sight ways of seeing.

I have used two models to arrive at these six ways of seeing. The first model that I discuss now draws on the features of Schrödinger's arithmetical paradox (of many minds being one). These are the features within the concept of unity within diversity. When the values of these two features (unity and diversity) are cross-referenced they produce four dispositions for making meaning. These are:

i.   Unity is overvalued while distinctions and diversity are devalued or ignored.

ii. Unity is seen to be separate from the differences of diversity.

iii. Differences are overvalued while the connections of unity are ignored.

iv. Unity and diversity are integrated as in the principle of unity within diversity and also within the hologram.

The first disposition occurs when we overvalue unity and devalue or ignore differences and diversity. The politics that goes with this strategy commonly relates to those activities that centre narrowly on the ego's self-interests and its defences. The predisposition to ignore or erase differences is reflected in those cases when the different interests of others are judged as having value only when they fit into the overvalued self-interest of the ego.

The second disposition that separates unity from differences tends to create a group unity that is seen as separate from other groups who are different and often seen as foreign. This is a tribal disposition that can produce prejudicial social reactions that lack tolerance towards various forms of differences. For example, racial, ethnic, age, gender, regional and sexual preference are common differences that tend to be suppressed or excluded from orthodox institutions or tribal groupings that make meanings with the underlying binary values of them/us.

The third disposition, in which diversity and differences are overvalued while the connections of unity are ignored, is a strategy that has a broad secular appeal and focuses on intellectual, rational and symbolic forms and displays. This third strategy represents among other things the politics of mechanical science where a schizoid worldview is produced, a world in which the scientist's mind is deleted from all theories and experiments related to an independent world.

The fourth disposition has a focus on holistic integration with a tendency to concentrate on relationships, interconnections and the integration of differences and distinctions. The human responses that are associated with this interpretative strategy are those of inclusion, compassion and empathy.

These four predispositions provide the possibility of four second-sight ways of seeing. They also provide four views of the self, of who we are. In summary, these four predispositions have a focus on:

i. me
ii. my group or tribe
iii. secular, objective reason and logic
iv. holistic integration and empathic responses.

The second more comprehensive model I have used overlaps

and cross-references these four ways and provides for another two. This second model comes from the five major exchanges of Meaning referred to in Chapter 4 and also in Appendix A. This model allows for the complex layering of meaning-making when privileging past predispositions in order to see the world and then justifying such views by reasoned argument. This model involves the two cardinal functions of implicit and explicit meaning and the associated movements of consciousness and mind that lead inevitably to the combination of five flowing patterns: 0, 1, 2, 3, 0, as follows:

0	Implicit to Implicit	intrinsic awareness
1	Implicit to explicit	pre-conscious awareness
2	explicit to explicit	awareness of abstract forms
3	explicit to Implicit	awareness of awareness
0	Implicit to Implicit	intrinsic awareness.

This five-step cycle indicates how individual minds are created out of One Consciousness, but it also demonstrates the methods by which we make meaning through concept formation (2, 3). In addition, if we treat this five-step cycle as one whole quantum of action, its underlying purpose of learning becomes evident. In other words, the innate bias within this whole system of meaning transfer is for the individual to mature through a series of learning steps. Yet whenever one or more of the five parts of this quantum of action are split off for some reason, or ignored, the overall purpose disappears and the resulting separation affects our view of the world as well as our will to learn and to mature. Hence the cyclic flow of 0, 1, 2, 3, 0, among other things, represents the structural cycle of learning and maturation. This learning and maturation structure also underpins the various ways we see the world.

In other words, the concepts we construct and use to interpret the world are learned from society, yet such learning is not wholly idiosyncratic but follows a precise patterned order: 0, 1, 2, 3, 0. In order to clarify the learning content of these numerals we need to relate the meaning exchanges of each of these steps to their predominant learning patterns. Thus the five patterns of meaning exchange produce the following patterns of human learning:

0	Implicit to Implicit	–	mnemonic resonance
1	Implicit to explicit	–	identification
2	explicit to explicit	–	differentiation
3	explicit to Implicit	–	integration
0	Implicit to Implicit	–	mnemonic resonance

These five exchange patterns of learning suggest that learning any activity and becoming proficient in it represents a movement through a circle involving a series of predictable changes and transformation. Learning anything involves the transformation of Meaning and meaning and will, therefore, contain the exchange patterns above. The following image emphasises the cyclic nature of learning:

The circle of learning

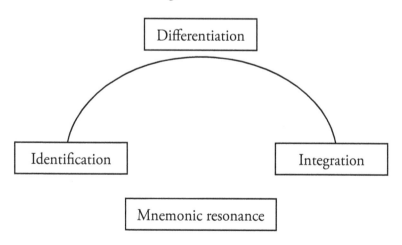

Conscious and deliberate learning is primarily concerned with the progress of the patterns *identification, differentiation and integration* (steps 1, 2, 3) and these three steps sit in the middle of the *Implicit-to-Implicit* resonance of One Consciousness. Hence formal and deliberate learning does not operate in a vacuum but always within an immediate ocean of implicit consciousness, which has a resonance that is mnemonic. In addition, all human learning entails pre-conscious awareness, with an awareness of abstract forms and then an awareness of awareness itself.

The word 'mnemonics' concerns memory, and mnemonic systems usually refer to those special techniques used to improve memory. Such techniques rely upon the idea of association, which can be interpreted as those kinds of connections related to *Implicit-to-Implicit* exchanges of Meaning. As for the term 'resonance', this occurs in all types of vibrations or waves, while resonant systems can be used to create vibrations of a specific frequency such as those created by musical instruments.

The resonances created by *Implicit-to-Implicit* exchanges are innate to One Consciousness and are not created by any deliberate action of the human mind or by any technological system. Rather, they exist as the continuous background context of the ordinary human mind by which we identify, differentiate, deliberate and integrate meaning. The term 'mnemonic resonance' thus refers to a universal and infinite state of innate unmeasurable vibrations of Meaning: a metaphysical field beyond sensory perception but one that involves memory, which operates within and between the ordinary mind of individuals as well as within the cosmic surround called One Consciousness. Exchanges of intelligent awareness in this medium are instantaneous and nonlocal.

During our lifetime, we will learn many things; some things we learn quickly, others take a long time. This is the case from the small circles of learning (how to tie your shoelace) to the larger circles (how to get on with your neighbour). Different-sized learning circles also have different names. The smaller circles of formal education tend to be called learning programs. Larger circles that extend over many years tend to be called periods of development or maturation. All learning occurs in cycles that are repeated over and over again. A very important feature of learning anything is our disposition towards or against learning itself. In other words, how are we predisposed towards the three patterns of *identification, differentiation and integration*?

Deliberate learning usually has a focus on the processes of identification, involving memory (1), that arise from the exchanges of *Implicit-to-explicit* meaning. For example, the flow of implicit content within first sight creates the explicit, seen images (signifiers). Our first creative step in this semiotic process of learning is to identify these explicit images in terms of some cultural and linguistic forms (signifieds). This may be when the infant first says the words, 'Mum' or 'Dad'. The next learning step (2) comes from discovering more complex distinctions or differentiations associated with the ordering of concepts within a sentence. This is achieved through *explicit-to-explicit* exchanges.

The final step of learning does not stop at the explicit meaning of a name or an object or even a complex of discourses but involves the integration of a series of distinctions by way of *explicit-to-Implicit* exchanges (3). For the infant, this final learning step may take the form of settling back into the security of the implicit background field that surrounds and binds together mother and child. For the adult, the final learning step will always involve the integration and contextualisation of intellectual and abstract forms and practices into some practical application. Integration also occurs when we positively value and promote different kinds of contextual meaning.

Progress through this cycle of learning (0, 1, 2, 3, 0) is inevitable in order to master, for example, a musical instrument, a second language, a sport, social and emotional competence and, in the long run, a spiritual life. While we can choose individual learning programs during our formal education as well as a variety of activities that produce our informal education, we are unable to choose *not* to learn anything so that our mental development and maturation cease. While we are unable to prevent ourselves from learning anything, however, we can choose to close off our mind to learning so as to inhibit the processes of maturation. Choosing not to learn is a feature of several predispositions that create the shadow ways of seeing that are described below.

When the model involving Schrödinger's paradox of many minds is cross-referenced with the five major exchanges of Meaning the following six ways of seeing arise:

0   Implicit to implicit – mnemonic resonance – Self seeing
1   Implicit to explicit – identification – ego seeing
1   Implicit to explicit – identification – tribal seeing
2   Explicit to explicit – differentiation – separation seeing
3   Explicit to implicit – integration – empathic seeing
0   Implicit to implicit – mnemonic resonance – clairvoyant seeing

Four of these ways (ego, tribal, separation and empathic) involve the conceptual features of the sign structure where signified (concepts) relate in some manner to environmental signifiers.

The first on the list, *Self seeing*, involves undertaking some deliberate action in order to become aware of the universe's awareness. The capital S in *Self seeing* denotes the primary status of this cosmic awareness, which is exemplified on a local level by the sight within our seeing. Self seeing is a holographic state in which the local and the nonlocal are unified; where the sight within visual perception is understood as the sight and light of One Consciousness. These practices are discussed more fully in Chapter 20.

Each of these six ways of seeing is discussed fully in Part III of this book. What follows is a short summary of ego, tribal, separation, empathic and clairvoyant seeing.

Ego seeing

The first learning step of identification and recognition involves relating given signifiers to constructed signifieds. These transformations occur in relation to all sense perceptions, not just in visual perception, and they lead on to the construction of thought and the formation of concepts. While this first learning step of identification and recognition is absolutely necessary for learning anything, it can become a problem if the processes of identification are not conceptually transformed by increases in differentiation. This means that if the steps of learning do not progress much beyond the first step of identification the learning cycle itself will be inhibited and truncated.

How can inhibition to learning occur? This situation often arises in childhood when a learning environment is accompanied by fear, anxiety, pain, humiliation, shame, or other negative conditions. In these situations, the first step of identification can easily slide into more complex patterns of identification, in which identifications build on other identifications to produce syndromes of negative and inhibited behaviour.

The result of multiple identifications is a closed formation of knotted relationships that are more hidden than disclosed. These formations or syndromes exert considerable (concealed) influence over childhood learning, responses and behaviour. In addition, when such identification formations solidify in adults into self-reinforcing and self-justifying systems they produce patterns of damaging behaviour that are habitual and entrenched. Our ego and the desires that flow from it are usually constructed from these kinds of self-reinforcing and self-justifying closed and knotted formations.

Tribal seeing

In adolescence ego patterns of identification often become attached to peer groups so as to fulfil desires for social recognition and acceptance. While this development is a natural part of adolescent life, the process of bonding the ego into a group also represents a normal part of most adults' worldview. Most people understand they belong to a group, and such groups can be cultural, linguistic, national, religious, sexual, sporting, regional and so on. Problems begin with this form of social bonding when the identification patterns of bonding turn into some form of defensive behaviour in order to promote and/or defend 'my group'.

When this happens, a pathological response occurs when our ego's defences are extended to include the group's activities so that when we defend the group's behaviour we feel that we are actually defending ourselves. When this happens, we become predisposed to see a world in terms of them and us. This kind of binary seeing is essentially tribal. A tribe does not have to live in mud huts and carry spears. A tribe can be a private school, a cricket club, a religion, a political party, a nation-state or some form of scientific or religious orthodoxy. A tribe is not a series of physical conditions or a particular social formation; rather, a tribe is an unhealthy state of mind, a shadow way of seeing the world.

Ego and tribal seeing are closely related in that both are stuck in the learning patterns of identification. The difference between ego and tribal seeing will become apparent when I discuss examples, but ego seeing does not recognise differences as seriously important. Ego seeing is essentially a seeing that only recognises those kinds of differences that may possibly become an integral part of the self-interested desires of the ego. In this sense, the unity of the ego takes precedence over all differences.

In tribal seeing, differences are actually recognised as

differences but they are then devalued by being treated as superficial and at the same time as threatening. Tribal seeing represents a small step away from ego seeing because it can at least recognise differences as differences. For this way of seeing, unity is overvalued while differences are seen to be separate from this unity.

Separation seeing

The next learning pattern involves an emphasis on differences and distinctions mainly associated with abstract symbols. Here there is an unfolding of greater levels of differentiation that can give rise to an increased complexity of abstract thought. These are the thoughts produced by *explicit-to-explicit* exchanges and are characteristic of all complex formal systems. This kind of intellectual meaning-making is essential for useful language exchanges, for scientific measurements and rational debates and therefore for human survival.

Yet like the learning step of identification we can become stuck in this mode of thought and fail to progress to the next learning step of integration. This happens when the processes of *explicit-to-explicit* exchanges become iterative, and then the result is overabundance or a turbulence of differentiation. When differences pile on differences, disorganised complexity occurs and the usual outcome is a sense of fragmentation and chaos. When we make generalisations about the world based on a turbulence of differentiation the usual conceptual result is a belief in an underlying randomness.

Separation seeing tends to be blind to links, connections and unity. The common strategy employed to justify this kind of seeing is based on the disposition to ignore, erase or devalue implicit, contextual meaning. Contextual meaning is always implicit meaning, and implicit meaning connects, links and unifies. When we choose to ignore connective, implicit meaning all that is left are the separating explicit differences of a mechanical, dead and superficial universe.

Inherent within implicit meaning is uncertainty. When we are confronted by innate uncertainties we have two options: i) to accept the ungraspable nature of implicitness and come to terms with the uncertainties of consciousness. This acceptance will take us to the next learning step of integration and into the knowledge of holistic systems. Alternatively, we can ii) choose to resist the uncertainties of implicit meaning and fall back into a comfort zone by simply deleting them from our understanding. Such a blinkered view is commonly expressed in the forgetting that is associated with orthodox dogmas and doctrines.

Empathic seeing

The third deliberative pattern of learning (3) involves exchanges of *explicit-to-Implicit* meaning. These exchanges begin to enfold the explicit differences created by earlier learning patterns so that they are valued not as ends in themselves but because of their similarities as well as their links and connections within larger systems and contexts. This is the learning process of empathy and integration and its method is to fit any and all distinctions and differences within the contexts of a larger system(s). Empathy involves love and compassion and the possibility of a transcendent self-understanding. These feelings arise from meaning exchange where the connections of implicit meaning have become primary and dominant and where explicit meaning in the form of differences and distinctions has a secondary or derivative role.

The result of this kind of contextual ordering produces complexities that are organised into asymmetrical systems. As a consequence, this holistic ordering of empathy stands in contrast to earlier disorganised patterns created by *explicit-to-explicit* exchanges which produce separation seeing.

Clairvoyant seeing

For the ordinary mind the subtle vibrations of *Implicit-to-Implicit* exchanges represent the foundation of our thoughts, of our conceptual mind. These subliminal exchanges convey to us intuitions, insights, realisations and joy. Such are the non-perceptual pathways that link the cosmic mind of One Consciousness to the ordinary mind of the individual. These implicit exchanges also function between individuals and other organisms, and in this manner they are usually called extrasensory perception. Such exchanges of mnemonic resonances also act as the basis for all learning regardless of the age of the learner or the predispositions that the learner has towards each of the other learning steps.

Exchanges of *Implicit-to-Implicit* Meaning are essentially non-symbolic, non-verbal and extrasensory, that is, they operate outside the boundaries of conscious thought and the ordinary everyday mind and thus beyond the conscious content of sensory perceptions. As these exchanges contain no deliberate and conscious markers of time or space they are essentially infinite and eternal. In addition, such *Implicit-to-Implicit* exchanges contain no conscious conceptual forms and they have no arbitrary or social content and cannot be fully represented by any sign or representation. They are therefore beyond or prior to any measurement or computation and also beyond the terms of similarity and difference, which are part of our ordinary conscious mind. Exchanges of *Implicit-to-Implicit* Meaning are the symmetry exchanges within the several features of One Consciousness.

While there are six ways we can choose to make meaning and thus see the world, the choices we make are for many determined by the cultural pressures that come from the 'us' of a wider society. These influences are discussed in the next chapter.

13

Contexts of Age and Culture

In terms of the six ways of second sight, each of us lives, thinks and acts as organised or disorganised individuals within the implicit background harmony of One Consciousness. As such, the way we see our relationship to others and to nature as well as to One Consciousness will be determined by the manner in which we are predisposed to make meaning. Our predispositions for meaning-making will be influenced by two key contexts: our age and the cultural norms that guide our behaviour. In this chapter I discuss these influences in relation to predispositions to make meaning and see the world.

Carl Jung considered that maturation did not end with adolescence. For Jung, childhood represented one period of what he called 'psychic growth' and a second period began around forty years of age. About this age it is common for individuals to have feelings of anxiety and perhaps to experience a mid-life crisis and/or depression. The conventional view of these disorienting emotional feelings relates to career success or failure or to sexual or childbearing problems. Jung was impatient with such 'simpleminded' views and 'stressed that the human organism was simply preparing itself for death' (McLynn 1997: 301).

Jung's view is interesting as it implies that the common mid-life crisis is not due to social success or failure, lack of children, war or even illness, all of which are but outward signs of internal and essentially spiritual change that is taking place. In terms of meaning-making, we can see these underlying spiritual changes as an aspect of the evolution of consciousness. On the positive side, Jung believed that when we finally emerge from these difficult crises, which he saw as necessary for psychic growth, we would have more mature personalities. Jung's second stage of psychic growth he called 'individuation'. Both his stages of psychic growth related to the age of the individual.

The general proposition that all humans pass through stages of maturation related to age is not new. Within the Hindu scriptures there are four houses (*ashramas*) that signify the four ages of an ideal spiritual life for an individual. Another view of long-term psychic evolution comes from Owen Barfield (1898–1997), who proposed that there are three stages in the evolution of consciousness: *original participation; non-participation; and final participation* (Barfield 1988). While Barfield's theory was not age-related he did view these three stages as historical and that they move humanity slowly towards the final goal of communion with nature.

The connection between the age of our body and how we make meaning (think and see) is clear in the sense that at fifteen our thinking and social responses are going to be different from what they will be at thirty, fifty and seventy. Yet while the body's age relates to the way we make meaning, our incarnate body also acts as our anchor and orientation point throughout life for it provides us with a sense of place and the present moment. The body locates us through an array of autonomic processes involving, among others, the systems of perception and sensation. This orientation function comes with a sense of the present moment NOW, which is so decisive in producing healthy responses.

Hence the incarnate body has complex functions even though its organisational role is secondary. By this I mean that the physical body occupies a place secondary to the primacy of Meaning and One Consciousness. Its secondary status tells us that the body does not organise its own birth, patterns of growth, development or death, even though these stages affect the way we see. The body's secondary status may be likened to a flute in the hands of the master flute player. Because of this dependency the question can be asked, 'what does a flute know about music'?[17] Or, a similar question from the point of view of science: 'what do the cells know about the overall blueprint that arranges and creates the body's form, its morphogenesis'? On this question Rupert Sheldrake (1987: ch. 16) has argued that while our DNA can make the protein bricks that build the body, the body's master plan is not contained in these bricks. Thus from this perspective these protein bricks are only a set of useful resources in the hands of the master builder and musician: One Consciousness.

The body's secondary status also implies that the conscious mind of the individual has only a relative autonomy that comes from its ability to learn and create signifieds, that is, to identify, differentiate and integrate conceptual meaning. We may like to understand the body and conscious mind's secondary status metaphorically as the relationship between the musician and the flute, in that the body, like a flute, does not create music (meaning) but simply plays a variety of tunes that are best suited to the physical structure of the instrument. As a complex instrument the body and the conscious mind can play essentially two kinds of tunes: i) songs of dissonance and disorganisation; or ii) songs of harmony, order, compassion and love.

Most of the songs of dissonance begin with patterns of identification associated with the body. These are the ego, tribal or separating tunes that in effect begin by singing: 'I am the body and I need protection.' As a consequence, we think of ourselves as alive when the body continues to be active and then expect to be no more when the body dies. Such songs confound us about who we are and what is in our best interests. These songs contribute to misery, hatred, jealousy, envy, greed, war and often difficult deaths. Some short-term pleasures may result from these songs, which can fulfil immediate desires and our need for protection, but this kind of singing usually comes with a good deal of grief and suffering.

Alternatively, the songs of harmony and love are sung by using the full range of notes, for these songs are about the holistic integration of connection, joy and empathy. They tell stories about lifelong learning and they embody uncertain and incomplete pictures that have no final closure or solution. They are sustained by intuitive connections that underpin all discrete appearances and by big visions of a larger self that is beyond the ego and also beyond the ordinary mind. People who sing these songs, even badly, are likely to experience some degree of communion and a level of joy and satisfaction that sustains them through the vicissitudes of life and also through the processes of dying.

With these comments about the songs we sing I am suggesting that dying need not be the miserable event of the five stages of grief described by Elisabeth Kübler-Ross in her seminal book *On Death and Dying* (1997). Rather, dying may involve a final learning stage when a dying patient feels connection, love and equanimity. Kübler-Ross even refers to this kind of response when describing the reactions by one student who was upset by a dying patient's 'calmness and equanimity'. The student thought the patient was 'faking' it 'because it was inconceivable to him that anyone could face such a crisis with so much dignity' (Kübler-Ross 1997: 40–1).

Yet I have also observed a similar state of equanimity in my brother in the face of death. He was at his home and I was leaving after a weekly visit. I touched his shoulder and said 'see you in a couple of weeks', when I would drive down again from the east coast to Hobart. He seemed in a particularly buoyant mood and as I walked across the room to the door for what would be the last time, he said to me, more as a declaration than a question, 'Do you know that big river?' I was at a loss. I thought of the Derwent River running out to the sea a block from his house. That is a big river. Without waiting for my reply, he said more quietly, 'I'll see you on the other side of it'. He died the next week.

Maturation ages

I now want to address the idea of stages of maturation.

Waves of vital light flow continuously through the body's autonomic systems, making it pulsate with life. During the body's lifetime, these waves organise its growth and development, and then its decline and death. These normal developmental changes affect our perspectives and the way we respond to the world generally. Yet in the words of the Zen Buddhist Thich Nhat Hanh (1974: 104), 'things do not have their own nature', which for the body means that it does not have its own self-caused nature.

The body's nature has been given by an ordered set of procedures that are not isolated but stretch back through molecules, atoms and particles to the organisation inherent in light, and beyond, to the symmetry potentials of One Consciousness. The incarnate body is best seen as an organic apparatus through which Meaning is transformed, channelled and made. The age of the incarnate body is thus germane to how we think, to the kinds of meaning we make and hence to the way we see the world.

The question then arises: are there two, three or four ages/ stages related to how we construct signifieds and therefore think and see? Taking a cue from the structure of meaning, and in particular the three deliberate learning stages of *identification, differentiation and integration*, it can be suggested that there are three stages of maturation. Hence these three learning stages can also represent the three maturation stages that extend over the lifetime of a human.

If we roughly follow the timeline laid down in the Hindu scriptures for ideal spiritual development, the first maturation period associated with identification will span approximately the first twenty to twenty-five years of life. The second (associated with differentiation) covers the next twenty-five years and the maturation period of integration accounts for the rest of life. By bringing together the three steps of learning into a correspondence with lifelong maturation stages, the following matrix is produced:

identification	–	the first 20–25 years
differentiation	–	from 20 to 45 years
integration	–	from 45 years onward.

These three maturation stages represent a learning bias related to age. In the first twenty years of life we begin our long maturation journey towards a more mature consciousness. Identification is the beginning step in all learning, no matter how old we are. In the first twenty-five years, however, we will often mistakenly take this first learning step to be the final and mature conclusion of things. When this happens, we will jump to all kinds of premature conclusions about a variety of life's problems, but especially about who we are and how to act, as well as our likes and our links to groups. The bias in this first period of twenty to twenty-five years will normally be towards patterns of identification associated with the ego and its desires and these are often idealised, romanticised or sentimentalised.

The next maturation stage involving the bias of differentiation spans approximately the next twenty-five years. It is in this period many of us may begin to master the social and cultural differentiations that for twenty years we have slowly been moving towards. This can be a period of high performance and expertise in our chosen field. The end of this stage coincides with Jung's second stage of psychic growth, and so a mid-life crisis may bring this stage to an end through a painful reassessment of the way we generally think and act and see the world.

The third and final stage of maturation is biased towards integration and an increased sense of connection and empathy. When we reach mid-life the mode of our thinking will generally turn naturally towards integrating the values of an earlier life into a bigger picture that comes with feelings of social integration, harmony and empathy. This turn of events can often cause a crisis for a life that has grown used to all the division and separations that a finely tuned intellect can create in a modern technological society. The mid-life crisis that eventually ends in a more integrated, mature and harmonious life is a common feature in contemporary society.

From the perspective of Meaning, the three maturation stages represent those extended periods in life when there is an innate stress on each one of the three learning functions. As there is an order in these learning steps that moves from identification through differentiation to integration, so this order is repeated in the order of our maturation. Growing older, we slowly mature through a greater appreciation of the connections and integration that the experience of empathy brings. In latter years life will be more congenial if lived in a spiritual manner where we experience a sense of integration into the implicit context of the whole universe.

To what degree will these three maturation contexts exert an influence on the way we create signifieds, the way we think and see the world? For most of us the influence of these three stages will be of a background nature, as we will also be affected by the intensity of our thoughts as well as the intensity of the cultural norms by which we live. For example, if we live in a highly competitive society that reinforces the doctrine of many minds and promotes ego seeing, then these values, and not learning or maturation, will be the magnets around which many of us will organise our life. In addition, on reaching mid-life, we may seek to resist the inevitable movements of growing older by attempts to reinvigorate a youthful ego through the use of drugs or cosmetic surgery. By middle age these earlier patterns of thought have passed their use-by date and so indulging in them represents a sadness that inhibits maturing.

Cultural influences

I turn now to the prominent cultural norms that guide our thinking and behaviour. As everyone is a member of a cultural group we share with others all kinds of unspoken and implicit agreements about what is important and how to live our lives. Contrary to common belief, culture is not a set of external manifestations or forms separate from our mind. We only have to visit a foreign country to realise we have brought our culture with us in the form of language, accent, dress style, food preferences, social manners, rituals, interpretative habits and so on.

This brings me back to the trinity of being ('I', 'us' and 'That') discussed in Chapter 2. The trinity of being is a dynamic model of the integrated, holographic three parts to our being. Thus the human being is never a singular, private entity separate from other beings or the cosmos; rather, human beings represent a trinity of 'I', 'us' and 'That'.

In terms of cultural influence, we can ask the direct question, what are the relationships between 'I' and 'us'? The model of the trinity of being (below) indicates something of the nature of these relationships. The 'I' part of the trinity represents the dot in the middle of the circle: 'us', which can be understood as representing the cultural influences of our interpretations. Hence the 'I' of the trinity of being is not a private space (or individual entity) but simply a local expression of the universal sight of That.

The trinity of being

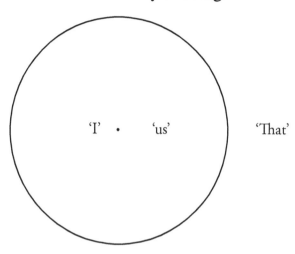

The circle outside the dot represents the cultural influences of 'us', which means that this cultural circle is a pretty busy place made up of shared understandings and shared concept formations as well as including all our predispositions, subjective opinions and preferences. As the potentials of 'I' (signifiers) are closely related to the cultural meanings of 'us' (signifieds), it means that we are never separate from others but instead are always a part of each other because others constitute the cultural meanings of 'us'.

As I have stated in Chapter 2, the relationships between 'I' and 'us' comes from exchanges of meaning in the forms of symbolic communications or clairvoyant exchanges. In cultural studies the term 'culture' is often left undefined, but in terms of Meaning it can be defined as that social context in which shared meanings are exchanged. All significations, discourses and symbolic exchanges happen within a cultural context (the circle of 'us'), whether with a member of our culture or a foreigner. These exchanges include the subjective opinions of the everyday as well as the so-called 'objective' truths of science, as these are the consensus truths that groups of scientists have agreed upon.

An analysis of communication exchanges indicates that every exchange of meaning within the circle of 'us' will be simultaneously revealing and concealing (see Appendix B). Whether with a member of our own family, tribe, society, or a foreigner, these communications represent exchanges that both reveal and conceal meaning. Exchanges of meaning that are concealing have two overlapping faces. The first is the kind of meaning we do not wish to reveal because we would feel overwhelmed, ashamed, fearful, guilty or stressed. This kind of concealment is related to our ego defences and desires.

The second kind of concealment represents the implicit aspect of Meaning that occurs naturally and below the *alpha* bandwidth of 8–12 Hz (see Appendix A). In relation to cultural exchanges this kind of concealment can be called our 'swarm intelligence'. The distinction between these two is that ego defences and desires conceal meaning through implications which may be exposed by self-reflection but which are usually mostly repressed or suppressed. On the other hand, swarm intelligence represents the natural concealment within coordinated social actions that are devoid of explicit communications strategies or forms. 'Swarm intelligence' is a term often used to describe the in-flight manoeuvres of birds or the coordinated activities in beehives or termite mounds. As the mind is made entirely of relations of meaning and these are essentially interactive and communal, there is a strong natural force working within every community, and that includes human communities, to respond and react spontaneously in a coordinated and collective manner.

However, unlike animals or termites, every individual has a choice as to how they respond to concealed cultural meanings. That choice involves the decisions we make to either ignore or challenge the cultural values and habits that influence our thoughts and behaviour. If, like most people, we largely ignore the dominant cultural values, habits and assumptions that rule our life and accept them without question, our thoughts and the meanings we make will be based largely on a kind of social unconsciousness and we will then act as if we have no choice.

In contrast, should we question and challenge the underlying cultural habits and values, such questioning will put in train a process of explication, that is, a self-reflective learning that alerts us to the import of our cultural assumptions and ego defences by making them more explicit and thereby increasing our knowledge of their relative influences. Hence, in order to be tolerant and understanding of other cultures we first need to understand our own, especially those concealed cultural assumptions that are so much part of our habitual responses to the world.

* * *

The circle of culture (us) also has a relative agency. By this I mean that its influences, while often appearing dominant and extremely influential, especially in a social crisis, are actually only relative to a specific time and place. Owen Barfield (1988: 20) has argued that our collective cultural representations tend to constitute 'the world we all accept as real'. The 'real' is what we consider to be the norm: the predictable and acceptable world in which social behaviour is judged, rewarded or punished. This kind of real world is largely constituted by our ignorance or denial of the relative nature of our culture. The cultural context is relative and because of this relativity this context of 'us' cannot answer to the absolute demands of 'the real'. Being relative, the realities that we construct by our norms of behaviour are also relative. To believe otherwise is to believe blindly in the illusion that you and your cultural practices are universal, exceptional or superior to all others.

The linguist Benjamin Lee Whorf (1897–1941) had a similar view of culture. Whorf was famous in the twentieth century for his principle of 'linguistic relativity'. He studied the language habits of Native Americans, such as the Hopi and Shawnee, and compared these with Indo-European habits or those of what he called the Standard Average European (SAE). What Whorf meant by the principle of linguistic relativity was that 'all observers are not led by the same physical evidence to the same picture of the universe, unless their linguistic backgrounds are similar, or can in some way be calibrated' (Whorf 1979: 214); in other words, the way we construct concepts (signifieds) and thus see the world will vary according to our cultural and linguistic habits.

This principle of linguistic and cultural relativity means that no one, not even physicists or mathematicians, are free from partiality in their descriptions and measurements of the universe. Different cultures have different language habits and so they view the world differently, and this difference will also depend on the predisposition and habits that underpin our culture, or subculture, and how we choose to respond to those predispositions and habits. Whorf's principle of linguistic relativity assumes that cultural and linguistic values play back into the way we see the world so that we will see in the manner we have been taught, either formally or informally. An example is the contemporary cultural habits of users of Indo-European languages that tend to describe a mechanical world by using those linguistic habits that value nouns over verbs.

This linguistic predisposition means that objects tend to become conceived as isolated and more important than the underlying event that gave rise to them. In other words, the linguistic habits of SAEs have tended to create a literalism along with an objectification of the physical world. An objective literalism finds expressions in statements that focus on discrete parts, separations and divisions while ignoring broader connecting contexts. Whorf gives an example of an American Indian model of the universe by stating that 'the Hopi language contains no reference to "time", either explicit or implicit'. Yet 'the Hopi language is capable of accounting for and describing correctly, in a pragmatic or operational sense, all observable phenomena of the universe' (Whorf 1979: 58). To the Western literal, objectifying mind, how could this be possible? Whorf gives the reply that the Hopi language and culture conceals a metaphysics, just as our view of space and time contains a concealed metaphysics.

While modern SAE metaphysics is different from the Hopi's, so too are our language habits that are formed by our metaphysics. When a society's linguistic norms of expression rest upon linguistic habits that value nouns over verbs (thus tending to increasing abstraction), these kinds of practices produce something like our contemporary culture with its master narrative of a mechanical universe. The metaphysics of mechanical science is overwhelmingly concerned with the constricted values of the conscious and the explicit while tending to ignore or erase the larger implicit and contextual picture. As a consequence, meaning and consciousness are normally erased from the narrow realism that has become a cultural standard for science, technology and mass culture.

The current globalised world culture places a value on parts and differences to such a degree that the discrete part or difference becomes a way of seeing: *separation seeing*. When differences are overvalued they multiply and turn into separations that divide. A cultural orthodoxy based upon divisions and separations is one that fragments our knowledge, alienates individuals from their group and works against developing easy social interactions while promoting the dogmas of individualism, materialism, rationalism, realism or positivism.

Within our modern globalised culture of mainstream materialism people believe they are their bodies which have a private mind that is separate from the mind of others. This cultural metaphysics has also produced a 'real' material world that appears independent from subjective processes of observation. Hence these collective habits represent our collective forgetting. We tend to forget that culture is relative. Like the fiction writer who tells a story from the omniscient point of view, the reductive materialist scientist has tended to assume an omniscient point of view. Unlike most fiction writers, scientists do not normally take into account their own language, their cultural habits, meaning or consciousness in their investigations. Yet such scientists cannot escape the relativity of their cultural responses simply by assuming that their theories and experiments are beyond the culture in which they work.

Barfield refers to this kind of cultural forgetting as the making of idols. An idol is made when the relative status of a representation is forgotten and it becomes instead a solid and unqualified reality. This is also a description of an illusion. Cultures that create a 'real' world of idols through the literalism of objects suffer from idolatry. Idolatry always involves a collective forgetting. But a collective forgetting is a state of mind that not only refers to some primitive forms of religious worship; it also describes many common aspects of scientific and economic thought and practice today.

In terms of meaning-making, a tribe is a culture group based largely upon the learning processes of identification and having a culture where members share the normative values of 'in' and 'out' groups. When we identify with a modern-day tribal culture this double identification involving 'them' and 'us' creates customs and norms of behaviour that carry exclusive values and serious threats of excommunication or worse for those who fall outside the norms of the tribe. This is a culture of stress, anxiety and pain.

In general, tribal cultures tend to produce *tribal seeing*. Yet we can also find evidence of this practice within secular societies where mainstream responses are predisposed towards erasing the integration of the bigger picture and the larger context while all the time overvaluing superficial distinctions and differences through calls to scepticism. The effect of this kind of meaning-making in the modern globalised community is to create separation seeing.

Then there is a culture of empathy. While empathy has not

yet become a widespread collective response in many places, there are many individuals in every society whose way of life and mode of thought are predominantly empathic. What is real for the person of empathy is compassion and the integration of diversity. What is important for this person are the connections he/she has with others and with the cosmic foundation of his/her mind. For the empathic person, interpersonal relationships are more real and more important than tribal rules and pronouncements, which tend to divide the world. For the empathic person, the importance of interpersonal relationships often represents the daily feature of a real spiritual life that is focused on the present moment or the Spirit within.

An empathic culture uses language, not in a black-letter literal manner, but as symbolic pointers and representations where signs 'stand in' for wider, broader non-symbolic contexts. Some appreciation of language's representational nature is necessary in order to appreciate metaphor, allegory, parable, irony and satire. This empathic predisposition to the reality of multiple levels of meaning is quite distinct from the disorder of a literal reading and of an either/or tribal view and also different from the complex disorganisation of *ego seeing*. An empathic response takes its own cultural practices as relative to other cultural perspectives and habits of behaviour, and in this manner makes meaning by fitting complex distinctions into their wider cultural contexts.

In summary, our ways of seeing will be influenced by the age of our body and also by the culture in which we live. If we accept without question the hidden metaphysics of our secular and materialistic culture then cave shadows will become our reality and we will live largely in ignorance of who we are and where we fit in a wider, brighter, more meaningful future. To 'know thyself' does not come from looking down a microscope. It comes from seeking the Self within, an experience that incorporates a broader vision involving our cultural relationships as well as the insight path from 'I' to the 'That' of One Consciousness.

Part III

Seeing the Light

14

Ego Seeing

In this third Part I will be discussing in detail the six ways of seeing. The first to be discussed is ego seeing, together with its reactive mode of desire. Ego seeing is always overwhelmingly ignorant. It produces disorganisation because it is blind to most of the meanings in which it is engaged. It is blind to other people's worldviews, their preferences and their interests. When we become infatuated with another we do not see their penchants or predilections very well, for all we tend to see is an extension of our own ego. A life lived by continually looking at these shadows is full of reactions, fears, disappointments, blame and misery.

There are perhaps three levels of intensity of ego seeing, which can be called *normal, neurotic* and *extreme*. The difference between them relates to how complex is the degree of identification complexity at each level. The first level of *normal* has patterns of identification that are relatively direct and associated with some out-of-control behaviour that is undertaken to confirm the ego's needs for support and attention. One historical example of a normal ego seeing was St Augustine's 'disease of lust' that as a young man he wanted to satisfy rather than extinguish (Augustine 1960: 8, 7). His famous prayer to God was, 'give me chastity and continence, but not yet'.

This kind of ego behaviour is relatively direct and uncomplicated and can be markedly different from an individual's work patterns or political activity. Hence the level of intensity in *normal* ego seeing allows for other expressions, including empathic responses and values outside the narrow confines of the ego. And so in this often contradictory manner the *normal* ego seeing in the mature person is sometimes called an aberration that we hope he can grow out of and that contrasts with his broader, more stable approaches to the world.

Ego seeing that is more *neurotic* has an intensity that comes from a series of complex knots of identification. These patterns can be enlarged and intensified by some kind of supporting cultural ideology. Such reactive identification patterns tend to restrict our vision so it narrows into that long corridor of self-justification or continuous monologues about 'me'. 'Me' and my self-interest represent the central focus of ego seeing that is neurotic. In some, the hoped-for fulfilment of desires comes from the accumulation of material wealth. This kind of ego seeing is neurotic and produces a miserable life dominated by the shadows of the mind. Here is one possible example of *neurotic* ego seeing:

> The wife (Doris) does not work; the husband (Troy) is a currency speculator with a merchant bank. They live in a large, well-appointed five-bedroom house in one of the leafy suburbs of Melbourne. Their 7-year-old son (Bruce) is a fulltime boarder in an exclusive private school ten minutes away by car. He comes home on long weekends and holidays. This domestic arrangement suits Doris who suffers from chronic fatigue, which would make her daily 10 km run difficult. Troy tends to work long hours at his office or spend time at his exclusive club after work. Troy is on speaking terms with Cabinet ministers and in his spare time promotes investment opportunities in Australia for Chinese businessmen. On the few occasions they eat together, Doris and Troy like to drive in the latest model Mercedes to the latest fashionable restaurant. They

are both apprehensive about the future and in particular about Muslims and those refugees coming to Australia in boats. Neither Doris nor Troy has any sense of the spiritual but they do attend their local church for family funerals and weddings.

Here are lives lived through the screen of conformity that aligns with the ideals of neoliberal success within a culture saturated with the beliefs of individualism. Success within this materialistic culture can represent an accumulation of material wealth along with the false sense of personal control, autonomy and the fulfilment of all desires.

In contrast, in *extreme* cases of ego seeing our sight can be like looking through a miasma of pain, loss, alienation, failure or shame. The *extreme* ego seeing occurs with individuals whose patterns of centripetal thought about themselves are so dominant that they have lost touch with the realities that come with first sight. So intense are these patterns of identification that the mind's orientation loses its hold on the present moment and becomes unlocated in a cloud of competing thoughts containing high levels of anxiety, fear and/or depression. Sometimes a self-inflicted death appears as the only logical answer to this impossible situation.

Sometimes there is a tendency for *extreme* ego seeing to be reinforced by a capacity to use language, language being the most abstract and at times the most separating form of meaning-making. It is not surprising then that we should find hospitalised cases of young women with high IQs and a superior facility with language suffering from extreme ego seeing in the form of anorexia nervosa. Here are several different sketches of *extreme* ego seeing:

Natalie is 16 years old and has been hospitalised for her anorexia nervosa. She is down to 35 kilos and thinks she is still too fat. When she looks into the mirror at her stick arms and her skinny body the imperfection of her physical shape overwhelms her. At school, she was good at athletics. In her bedroom at home there is a clothes drawer that has a handful of $50 notes in it. These are her mother's bribes to try and motivate her to win at sport. She has now given up fighting the nurses who feed her and plans to wait for a future time when she can again control her life and restrict her intake of food.

Dick is a 55-year-old sovereign citizen who is totally focused on his liberty and independence. He does not believe in government of any kind and complains bitterly to anyone who will listen about paying local rates and taxes. He has invented an early warning video system for his outer suburban property so he knows which and when government officials are visiting so he can take the necessary evasive actions.

Tom, a 45-year-old farmer, is married with three children under ten. Two years previously while working on a steep slope the tractor he was driving turned over and smashed both his legs. The crushed bones have not mended well and he has been in great pain and unable to walk without crutches or do his usual farm work. This incapacity has caused him a great deal of anxiety and depression even though the farm is big enough for others to do the work. Tom and his family live in a house some distance away from the big house where his father now lives alone after his mother died. Tom has never been close to his rigid yet financially successful father and since the accident he is more convinced than ever that his father was right to have called him a failure when he was young. One day Tom manages to drive the truck up into the hills and in a secluded spot in the forest he stops and fixes a hosepipe on the end of the exhaust and puts the other end in the cabin. He sits quietly listening to the hum of the motor as the fumes get thicker and unconsciousness slowly overtakes him.

These profiles are meant to be random examples aimed at illustrating the several levels of intensity associated with ego seeing. They are not meant to be prescriptive or regulatory but simply images of the various intensities of ego thought and seeing built from increasingly complex patterns of identification.

* * *

In Freudian psychoanalysis, the processes of identification are seen as the means by which the personality is constituted. 'It is not simply one psychical mechanism among others, but the operation itself whereby the human subject is constituted' (Laplanche & Pontalis 1973: 206). In terms of Meaning, identification is only one process in the three-step learning cycle of *identification, differentiation and integration* and so must constitute just one of the functions of the mind.

The ego is a formation created by patterns of identification that weld together a range of sensations, ideas and social expectations. Welded into this formation is the identification of self with the physical body so as to produce the understanding 'I am this body'. This amalgam represents a complex constellation of memories of emotional and physical experience that the psychiatrist Stanislav Grof (1993: 24) has called a COEX, for 'systems of condensed experience'.

Grof says that his 'research experience with COEX systems has convinced me that they serve to organize not only the individual unconscious, but the entire human psyche' (1993: 25). Growing up in a family of strong egos tends to produce in offspring this same system of condensed experiences. The ego is also nurtured by competitive social behaviour where winning is the whole point of the exercise. Any activity in which the body represents a central feature, whether for pleasure or pain, is an activity that reinforces the ego. This is the case because at the centre of the ego is the materialistic thought 'I am this body'. As we can love or hate our body, so the ego can be positive or negative. Each of the experiences of pain, shame, embarrassment and guilt are sensations that can buttress a strongly negative ego.

Because the three shadow ways of seeing (ego, tribe and separation) are closely interrelated, a tertiary education does not rid us of the ego. Rather, in many cases this training in symbolic abstractions only increases the intensity of the ego. Hence it is not unusual to see academics acting in highly competitive ways perhaps similar to schoolyard behaviour. In addition, honours and awards and especially the Nobel Prize are often pursued by scientists in ways that would fit well within the competitive culture of international football. In finance and commerce, the connection between symbolic use and ego is well established in the free-market salesman and his belief that 'greed is good'.

The ego represents the false self. The true self is the implicit potentials of the 'I' – that 'I' which is a feature of the universal Self (capital S). The difference between 'I' and 'ego' is the difference between the mind's essence (*Implicit-to-Implicit* exchanges) on the one hand and a set of identification (*Implicit-to-explicit*) patterns constructed by the ordinary mind. Once constructed, the ego of whatever intensity necessarily produces a sense of isolation from others, the community and the environment, and from the foundation source of the mind. This sense of separation comes from a false sense of autonomy, freedom and agency that the individual actually does not possess. Belief in the false self automatically creates an inherent sense of separation, which is painful but false.

Some Western psychologists do not agree that the ego is the

false self. They believe that many of us have weak or wounded egos and that this situation has come about through the results of some kind of trauma or suffering. The apparent remedy for a weak ego is doing such things as engineering our social environment to support our desires or involving ourselves in competitive activity. I suggest such beliefs misconstrue the COEX of the ego.

A so-called weak or damaged ego is usually a very strong but covert system. The person who is shy, fearful, shameful or guilty or who indulges in deliberate acts of self-harm has a strong ego in the sense that the COEX is buttressed by a series of defence mechanisms and then reinforced by a set of social expectations associated with these feelings. Guilt and fear rest on a presumed separate, autonomous identity that the individual believes to be their true self, albeit damaged or threatened. In contrast, a truly weak ego comes from the confidence of a healthy mature mind and this becomes manifest when we let go of control of our defence mechanisms as well as of our desires and let the flow of life take its course.

* * *

Learning through identification is the difficult process of learning by trial and error. This process represents the normal path of learning anything at any age but it is an especially dominant feature during the first twenty-five years of life. It is dominant because it is the first learning step in a three-step process and in this period we have a lot of new things to learn. As a consequence, the formation of an ego with its desires is a usual feature of life for those younger than twenty-five.

The ego represents our first take on who we are. Yet because of the pervasive dominance of our materialistic culture, for many it will also be the last take on who they are. In other words, for many people their first learning step of ego seeing will last their entire lives. But because identification is the first learning step in a three-step learning arc, in order to mature we need to progress beyond the concealments of this house by subjecting the ego and its desires to some critical enquiry.

The mechanism of identification combines two processes: attraction and exclusion. Attraction is an inherent connecting feature of *Implicit-to-Implicit* exchanges. In contrast, exclusion is the inherent feature of the way explicit differences work. In terms of relations, the attraction of *Implicit-to-Implicit* connections represents symmetrical relationships, while exclusion comes with the formation of non-symmetrical relationships. In this form, they represent discrete distinctions that gain their difference and distinctiveness from the contrast with other distinctions but also from the implicit background out of which they have arisen.

Like first sight, the mechanisms of identification (attraction and exclusion) are not open to conscious deliberation. These mechanisms, involving the three relations of symmetry, non-symmetry and asymmetry, are the key relational features of One Consciousness and thus are not created by the individual's conscious mind, even though they produce the important conscious first learning step of identification and recognition. In other words, these mechanisms are subliminal, that is, they operate below the level of the conscious mind. Yet these subterranean structures are the base upon which deliberation, reason and reflection rest. Thus, through these innate processes of identification an infant begins to recognise and identify objects as well as to create speech out of its expressive movements and babblings.

The same attraction/exclusion (symmetrical/non-symmetrical) processes operate in normal speech identification. For example, we recognise and identify speech first through the interconnecting frequency waves that our autonomic nervous system registers and then divides up into distinct units of sound.

These units combine to form speech patterns. Hearing speech is, therefore, a double autonomic process. First, there is a process of attraction inherent in the connecting, overlapping and oscillating waves of various frequencies. Second, hearing involves an excluding process that leads to divisions within the interconnecting spectrum of vibrations so that units of sound are constituted.

The attraction/exclusion mechanisms of identification, whether for the eye or the ear, are provided by One Consciousness. These mechanisms and their relationships are absolutely essential for any perceptual recognition to occur, and also for undertaking more complex conscious deliberation involving learning or relearning. However, difficulties begin to arise from these mechanisms of identification when our learning does not progress beyond the point of identification. When this happens, we find comfort in the sense and feel of identification and in so doing habitually repeat its processes over and over again, which then form large, hidden knots or syndromes of identification. This is what happens when the ego and its desires are created and then when we fall in love with them.

The attraction/exclusion mechanism can be best understood as the symmetric logic of identification. Traditional Aristotelian logic (discussed in Chapter 16) is asymmetric logic, while the logic of identification is symmetric. The meaning transformations that give rise to the processes of identification are the transformation of *Implicit-to-explicit* meaning, and with this change human speech begins. This beginning of speech involves recognition and identification processes which occur when a set of signifiers are joined together with a symbol or concept (signified) – that is, when an infant's expressive movements and babblings turn into some form of rudimentary speech pattern.

Thus human speech begins with the creation of signs. While this learning to create speech is an integral part of human growth and development, it carries with it the problem seeds of symmetric logic.[18] Symmetric logic says that A is B, that is, in this logic there is no conscious distinction made between A and B. What is constructed, however, is a meaningful unity (or set) that has both A and B features. To translate this logic into the sign structure we have a set of signifiers (A) that become signifieds (B). For instance, for an infant the signifiers of a visual image together with feelings of connection (A) become the signified 'Mum' (B), while another image and feeling (signifiers) become the signified 'Dad'. Hence, the speech patterns 'Mum' and 'Dad' becomes a unity of image, feeling and sound, rather than just formal abstractions of language.

These simple examples of symmetric logic hide a complex weaving of relationships involving the specific language spoken by parents as well as the culture in which the speech occurs. In addition, when claims of beingness and identity are added into the mix, as so often happens, symmetric logic increases in thickness and depth. This happens when the body of the individual together with a name, a location and a country become 'my' identity. Then I have become A and B and C and D in a complex unity of meaning where these individual distinctions are fused together into an identification pattern that cannot be expressed in any meaningful way except as the unity of 'me'.

Additions to these four basic distinctions (A, B, C, D) can be many and varied, but they will have something to do with childhood trust or mistrust, parental love or lack of it, and the negatives of pain and anxiety. Taking these into account the symmetric structure of 'me' could be as complex as A, B, C, D, E, F and G, where E, F and G could be a sense of insecurity, mistrust and failure associated with parents, school and society. Such is the basic symmetric logic of the ego that grows out of *Implicit-to-explicit* transformations and that is so different from the *Implicit-to-Implicit* exchanges of the true Self.

In his book *The Unconscious as Infinite Sets*, the Chilean psychiatrist I. Matte Blanco (1975) describes symmetric logic as the logic of the Freudian unconscious. I agree with his thesis;

however, symmetric logic represents the metaphysical framework of all identification patterns, and while that includes the Freudian repressed unconscious it also includes the construction of the ego and its desires along with the initial processes involved in human speech development. The important point about symmetric logic is its level of complexity. When my identity becomes an unconscious complexity of A, B, C, D, E, F, G and so on I will most likely be exhibiting some pathological behaviour that is intense, neurotic or perhaps psychotic. As a general comment, symmetric logic can be discovered in many subliminal and unconscious areas in the human mind and not simply in the repressed unconscious.

The ego and its desires are located beyond the curtain of the conscious mind that comes into operation at around 8 Hz (see Appendix A). As a consequence, when these subliminal processes form habitual patterns through reinforcements and repetitions there will be an accompanying tendency to perpetuate a hidden longing full of the wants of desire that are associated with these formations. Thus, as we are not aware of the processes of symmetric logic, we will also not be acutely aware of the make-up of our desires and wants. Desires are created when the normal grasping by the infant transforms into an unexpressed longing in adolescence: a longing that often finds expression in sexual behaviour.

Desire involves the knots of striving (grasping, clinging, wanting) after the lost paradise of connection, love and security. In this sense, desire is an attempt to substitute the open connecting love of our true Self with an exclusive, defensive and false identity (the ego) that appears to separate us from others. The attraction/exclusion tragedy of desire is that it is like a kind of second-order puppetry undertaken by the ego puppet. As such the desires of the ego can never be satisfied because the ego continually points towards a lack and a separation that actually does not exist. Along with this sense of lack and separation is the need for defensive protection.

The attraction that is evident in sexual desire is not so much love for another as the need for connection, a bridge across the gap constructed by the ego. Desire's main preoccupation is not with giving but with taking through the process of identifying with another body. This kind of attraction/exclusion does not create peace and fulfilment so much as disorder. Caught in the whirlwind of desire we start to believe that we need – and have to have in order to survive – an intense bond with another body. Such desires awaken feelings of isolation and loneliness, while the gravitational pull of attraction that answers to the aloneness is always offset by the excluding sense of a separate self. The confusion and tumult created by this mode of thought comes from the impossibility of it ever being satisfied.

Life assessments based upon ego and/or desire are always two-valued and involve the cardinal dualities of pain/pleasure, subject/object and inner/outer. The direction that desire points us in is always outward and it is the basis of a materialism that will disorder our life. Jacques Lacan (1985) wrote that all desire is the 'desire of the Other'. The other does not have to be a sexual object, although this is common after puberty. In general, our desires falsely appear to expand our sense of self while actually reducing our world. By desiring consumer goods or other people these objects seem to become part of 'my identity'. When we possess or own something the object rightfully becomes part of my ego and, therefore, 'mine'. In this way, I can believe that I own my wife and children as well as my car, camel and goats. This sense of ownership is built directly from a sense of ego autonomy replete with its conviction of personal control and doer-ship.

Desires are tricky because they reinforce our belief in the false self and then when our desires are not fulfilled we are stuck with the belief that our whole being has failed. This sense of failure does not readily recognise that the failed ego is actually an inauthentic self. The sense of failure created by identification patterns can at times become so extreme that this feeling turns into various forms of self-harm. Self-harm, whether from depression, family disruptions, razorblades, chains or suicide bombings, is an activity that reinforces the ego structure. The irony of desire is that we forget who we truly are and as a consequence neglect our welfare and long-term interests. This happens even though we may spend more time and energy on our desires than on anything else.

If we are to learn to grow and mature with the unfolding nature of our maturation, our young should learn to consciously experience the necessary dreams of their ego. These are the ordinary chimeras of youth that make us all fallible. In a maturing person, these should gradually slip away into a more mature and empathic response. When the young adult finally begins to enjoy the routine of helping others we know that this behaviour signals the next evolving step beyond the imprisonment that the ego and desires can create. In the first twenty-five years of life we will normally pass through the three learning and developmental steps of *identification, differentiation and integration* many times and hence will develop an expertise in a variety of areas, but especially in body movement.

We will be able to run faster, jump higher and have greater flexibility than at any other time in our lives. Some of us will develop an expertise in social areas, that is, we will know our preferences and be able to articulate our views of the world and still retain friends and group allegiances. In this period, most of us will therefore have some appreciation of what it feels like to have an expertise and mastery in some areas. Yet in the first twenty-five years most of us will also have the common learning experience of being stuck in some patterns of identification related to who we think we are.

These are the ordinary manifestations of an ego seeing that fits neatly into the norms of a globalised neoliberal culture where anxiety, depression and obsessional thought patterns are considered normal responses. This is where we find the common cultural assumption that everyone has a separate identity (the doctrine of many minds) and where celebrities are considered to be icons with super-identities. Yet when most adults become parents and the shadows of ego seeing begin at last to be thrust aside many will finally turn, because of maternal necessity, into the light of compassion and empathy.

15

Tribal Seeing

Like ego seeing, the system of condensed experience (COEX) that produces *tribal seeing* has three levels of intensity: *normal, neurotic and extreme*. These levels directly express various complex patterns of identification that connect the ego with a group. As such these three levels reveal our sense of vulnerability and how the threatened ego is protected and bolstered by tribal membership. One example of *normal tribal seeing* could be something like the following:

> The life of this family revolves around the Collingwood football club. Tracy and Bill work as volunteers for the Club and spend long hours raising funds standing behind stalls at the weekly matches selling a range of the club's memorabilia. Every year they buy season tickets and attend every match even when Collingwood is not playing at home. Walt, their 8-year-old son, is part of the Collingwood junior team and sometimes gets a game during the half-time interval. Tracy and Bill know many of the league players personally and treat all of them as if they were members of their extended family. During the season, their conversation is mostly about football and the Ladder, who is on top and how Collingwood one day will get there.

In contrast, a *neurotic tribal seeing* could be something like the following.

Diane and Keith have six children and live in a small Australian rural community. The family belongs to a Christian sect called the Bible Temple. Their eldest daughter is eighteen and has recently shown a romantic interest in a local farm boy the same age but who is not a member of the sect. This is a problem for Diane and Keith because marriage partners are always chosen for sect members and they cannot marry outsiders. If they do marry outsiders they are excommunicated from the sect. If this happened Diane and Keith would never be able to speak to their daughter ever again. Members of the Bible Temple do not vote at state and federal elections on grounds of religious belief, but the church elders have a program for members to be covertly involved in election campaigns against progressive politicians, conservationists and those who promote gay rights. The elders believe that the separation of church and state is part of a secular conspiracy and therefore covert political activities are essential to bring God's word back to the broader community.

A final example of *extreme tribal seeing* was the horror story of Jonestown, which is well known:

The American religious organisation called the Peoples Temple Agricultural Project under the leadership of the Reverend Jim Jones had settled in a commune in Guyana. Members were expected to work a 12-hour day, six days a week and after work to attend discussion groups where Jones would interrogate them individually on the implications of what they said and thought. Children called Jones 'Dad' and would see their own parents only briefly at night. Jones became increasingly paranoid about the Guyana authorities, the CIA and generally about the capitalist system, all of which he said were trying to destroy their commune. He would create emergency situations and the whole group would then practice 'revolutionary suicide'. They would drink a small glass of red liquid that Jones told them was poison. Afterwards Jones said that it was just a loyalty test. However, the loyalty test became real. On 18 November 1978 over 900 of this community died in mass suicides and murder. Self-administered cyanide was drunk, which caused most of the deaths, although some people who tried to escape were shot.

Tribal seeing represents the common practice of seeing splits, separations and divisions in an otherwise interconnected community. The difference between tribal seeing and ego seeing is marginal as the ego plays a dominant role in both. The predisposition of the ego is to continually point towards its own alienation and need for protection, and as a consequence, becoming a member of a like-minded tribe represents one way to ameliorate this kind of discomfort. This happens to those who find a special security in belonging to a religious, political, economic or social tribe.

Within tribal regimes the individual's sense of who they think they are becomes reinforced and buttressed by bonding with a group. In this manner, tribal membership and the individual's ego are fused together so they seem as one. The defence mechanisms of the ego are then fully available to use in a range of strategies for protecting the tribe, and by extension, protecting the ego. Yet not all groups are tribes and so this statement raises the question, when does a group become a tribe?

A group can be joined voluntarily, as in most school, peer, and sporting or recreational groups. Or a person may be born into a particular class or a caste system. Class and caste systems are usually tribal in the sense that their patterns of identification are wrapped up in compulsory requirements for individual members, patterns that often relate to work or gender roles. For example, tribes tend to divide up work between the genders so that women and men's work are separate and strictly prescribed. The separation of gender roles reflects a central feature of tribal life, which has a binary 'them' and 'us' mentality. The outward results of tribal identifications are usually immediately obvious through dress, manner, accent and speech content.

When voluntary groups become tribes, they put up borders that prevent people from coming or going. In this prescriptive manner tribes are predisposed to value internal tribal unity over external foreign differences. This valuation of unity over difference reflects the structure of the ego in which the unity of self-interest assumes priority over the interests of all others. The same ethic occurs when the unity of the tribe takes precedence over the interests of others, or internally within a tribe, when men take precedence over women. Hence modern tribal patterns of identification arise from the predisposition to see a separation between (male or tribe) unity and the differences of others (female or foreigner). Yet such patterns of identification are always unreliable because they reverse Meaning's inherent order while creating barriers that prevent an openness that allows further learning.

Tribal regimes can be ancient or modern, religious, secular or adolescent. The differences between these ancient and modern tribes involve the question of how closely the tribal culture reflects either the mnemonic resonance of *Implicit-to-Implicit* exchanges (the foundations of the mind) or the *explicit to explicit* exchanges that language tends to produce in separation seeing. Ancient tribes seem to be closer to the mnemonic resonance of clairvoyant seeing, while in contrast the modern exclusive private club or school or religion creates tribal boundaries with separating symbols, rules, protocols and rituals that contain the black-and-white morality of an either/or mind.

We find evidence of the mnemonic resonance of tribal life in The Dreaming, the sacred world of the ancient nations among the Australian Aborigines. Such groups tend to have a culture in which their common patterns of identification are closely associated with the implicitness of a here-and-now spirit world. In terms of Meaning, the spirit world of The Dreaming is the world of primary perception, that is, of clairvoyant seeing, a world created and given by *Implicit-to-Implicit* exchanges that involve a reliance on intuitions and clairvoyance. This spirit world of The Dreaming is usually overlayed by other cultural and tribal norms and patterns of behaviour.

According to W.E.H. Stanner (2009: 57), the 'central meaning of The Dreaming is that of a sacred, heroic time long ago when man and nature came to be as they are'. Yet neither time nor history, as we understand them, is involved in The Dreaming. The Dreaming cannot be fixed in time because it is also here and now. It is a truly nonlocal sensibility. As Stanner suggests, The Dreaming is a kind of *logos* or principle of order transcending everything mundane or significant. This principle of order also provides a narrative for tribal people to know who they are and to understand things that once happened and are still happening.

For an Aboriginal person, The Dreaming is a complex set of meanings that embrace modes of thought such as intuition and cultural identification patterns. The connections of these two modes create unities in places that can astound the modern mind. For example, as Stanner points out, an Aboriginal may see as a unity 'two persons, such as two siblings or a grandparent and a grandchild, or a living man and something inanimate, as when he tells you that, say, the woollybutt tree, a totem, is his wife's brother' (2009: 59).

These unifying connections that come from a combination of clairvoyant seeing and identification patterns create a cosmology that answers the questions of how the universe became a moral system and what life is and what it can be. Its narratives set out the norms of behaviour for marriage, exogamy, sister exchange, initiation and breaches of custom. As for the identity of individual members, these are formed by fully living this implicit yet identifying philosophy within the existing cultural matrix of the tribe.

Stanner goes on to tell us that 'the Aborigines have no gods, just or unjust, to adjudicate the world' (2009: 64). For gods to play a role in this ancient tribal regime there would have to be incorporated into their culture a substantial role for abstract symbolic representations, such as the written word. If writing were to be introduced as an integral part of The Dreaming it would change this ancient oral culture into a regime of meaning that would be sympathetic to separation seeing, which in turn would be detrimental to the intuitive tribal interconnections of The Dreaming.

In contrast to the tribal interconnections of The Dreaming there are modern tribes. In the current globalised community, a tribe can be a private school, a religious group, a motorcycle club, a corporation or a nation-state. The foreign policies of most nation-states are based on the tribal ideology of 'border protection' and 'national security' and 'national interest'. Communities in industrialised nations in times of peace, however, usually do not openly act towards their neighbours in a tribal manner. Yet the two valued either/or reactions that emanate from tribal defences and desire are never far below the surface in any modern community. This is because there are many institutions and political organisations that see private gains extending and perpetuating tribal and adolescent fears within the community.

Most religions are tribal or have tribal elements. The religious tribe combines patterns of identification with the use of the symbolic and hence they are able to produce complex scriptures and thus the signified: God. The modern religious tribe perpetuates itself with a set of border exclusions that are based upon the binary morality of the inner elect and the foreign other. Such exclusions create the sectarian. These exclusions are heightened in relation to other religions and take the form of 'my religion is superior to other sects – infidels, pagans or heretics'. Tribal exclusions can also occur within a religion and these are usually in relation to the sort of official positions and work that is barred to women and homosexuals. But fortunately not all religious organisations are tribal; some are ecumenical.

In *Bowling Alone*, Robert Putnam (2001: 22) writes about how social capital involves two broad forms of relationships: bridging and inclusive connections, and bonding and exclusive interactions. He tells us that bonding social capital is a kind of sociological superglue. I would prefer to call it the social glue of a tribe. In contrast, bridging social capital tends to be outward-looking and to 'encompass people across diverse social cleavages', such as 'the civil rights movement, many youth service groups, and ecumenical religious organisations'.

The distinction between bonding and bridging social capital is an important one in terms of sociology, but it is also important in terms of Meaning. The meaning generated by bonding social capital is of a very different nature from that produced by bridging interactions. In its extreme forms bonding social capital can produce sectarianism, ethnocentrism and wars between nations. On the other hand, bridging social capital can produce civic-minded actions, social harmony, peace, community health and goodwill.

Perhaps sympathy is the most virtuous response that can be generated by bonding patterns of identification. Sympathy is a bonding response that reaches out from a base of identification to include someone else within the normally closed circle of the ego, and that reaching can also include the circle of the tribe. Sympathy is not, however, an empathic bridging response that connects and integrates different beliefs, lifestyles, opinions or ethnicities. Sympathy is an emotional and sentimental response to those people who can be embraced by 'my tribe'.

For a person or a community to evolve beyond ego or tribal responses, that person or community has to develop a critical sense or an investigative discourse about their own ego and/or their group's patterns of identifications. As these patterns contain a degree of cultural and individual amnesia it means that learning about one's ego or cultural patterns of identification will be difficult. However, this difficult learning is absolutely necessary in order to evolve so that we are more able to understand who we are and to hear and appreciate some of the consequences of our actions.

16

Separation Seeing

Separation seeing is a product of the second step of learning, one that involves complex patterns of differential thought. These thoughts are produced by *explicit-to-explicit* exchanges of meaning and provide all the detailed forms that make up every abstract representational system. These are the meanings of intellectual or cognitive thought, constructed by and through the use of symbols, especially language, mathematics and the tokens of money. Like the first learning step of identification we can become fixated on these kinds of exchanges of meaning; when this happens we begin to see the world through a fragmented reference frame. Such a view represents the shadows of separation seeing.

The meaning-making activities of the intellect (cognition) represent not the apex or the end point in thinking but only a transitional stage in the circle of learning. The intellect sits midpoint in the circle of learning and it is this relative location that marks an important but provisional station in lifelong learning, as well as in the evolution of consciousness. The intellect's provisional status comes from lying between ego and tribal identifications on the one hand and the integrations of empathy on the other. This location is relative, and therefore conditional on the first as well as the last learning steps. The relativity of this location automatically makes the intellect a servant of either the ego or empathy as the following figure demonstrates:

The circle of learning

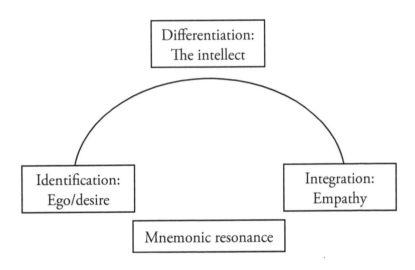

Because of this mid-location the intellect has the inbuilt tendency to continually direct us either forward to empathy or backward to the ego or tribe. As a servant of empathy or ego the intellect enables us to see a world either as an integrated whole or one full of divisions and separations. The one thing the (servant) intellect is unable to do is to work on its own behalf (as a master), for example to be more intellectual or rational. When this kind of meaning-making is attempted it always turns out to be activity on behalf of the ego. For example, people who continually display their intelligence do so to demonstrate their so-called superior social status. The intellect is, therefore, always acting, not on its own behalf because that is impossible, but in the service of one of the two magnetic poles of learning.

The reader will recall that ego and tribal seeing have three levels of intensity (*normal, neurotic* and *extreme*). The intellect also has three levels of intensity (*normal, neurotic* and *extreme*) and these relate to its mid-point location within the circle of learning. For example, when the intellect underpins empathy it creates the structures, arguments and character of a larger holistic empathic vision. This kind of empathic seeing supported by intelligent meaning-making I call *normal* because empathy represents the final and mature results of learning as well as the foundation sensibility for all social interaction. I discuss the *normal* of empathy in the next chapter.

In contrast, when the intellect acts in the service of the ego or tribe it will construct logical justifications for selfish or tribal behaviour through rationalisations based on norms that are generated from behaviour that is most commonly displayed in a community. This level of intellectual intensity I call *neurotic*, but in most societies it would be called 'realistic' or 'normal' behaviour. It is this second *neurotic* level of intellectual intensity that I intend to focus on in this chapter, because the separation seeing that it produces is largely hidden by the comforts of mainstream or orthodox assumptions that are very common in contemporary society but not so extreme as to stand out like a mental illness.

The third level of intensity (*extreme*) occurs when *explicit-to-explicit* exchanges act in concert with complex patterns of ego identifications to produce a potent mixture of logical argument charged with high emotion. The *extreme* level of psychic energy in this mixture can produce a psychotic world in which the individual loses contact with the stable and secure grounding of first sight. Locked into this insecure but hermetically sealed cell of emotions and symbols, the individual may experience paranoid and/or schizoid fears and visions. Similar *extreme* levels of intense thoughts can also produce a surplus of false and or disconnected facts that can constitute factitious syndromes characteristic of Munchausen disease. A related syndrome, more appropriately called 'factitious', is also evident with severe cases of anorexia nervosa. These *extreme* forms of meaning-making do not so much produce separation seeing as complete splits within the mind.

* * *

The metaphysics of mainstream Western culture are those of *neurotic* separation seeing. Within the orthodoxies of Judaism, Christianity and Islam we find the metaphysics of separation seeing: separate people are separated from God. The mirror image of this formula is found in the secular, Western scientific mainstream where separate people are seen to be separate from nature. In both Western religion and science there is a common adherence to the doctrine of many minds, together with an inability to take account of broader implicit, contextual meaning.

When the intellect is in the neurotic mode and serving the ego, it falls in love with its ability to use the distinctions and differences that have been created by *explicit-to-explicit* exchanges. This can lead to a neurotic level of intellectual intensity and to separation seeing. When this happens, we take on the doctrine of many minds and begin to see God or the physical world as an independent reality separate from our subjectivity.

Separation seeing is created when distinctions and differences become valued in their own right – as ends. This is a strategy where differences become overvalued to the extent that the underlying contextual meaning from which they have arisen is erased, devalued or ignored. When this happens we create barriers, splits or gaps that divide the world up into separate little boxes. David Bohm attempted to challenge this orthodoxy by introducing a broader context into physics with his implicate and explicate orders, but among his colleagues over the last three-quarters of a century the implicate order in particular has remained largely a mystery.

The deletion or erasure of contextual meaning is pervasive in mainstream Western culture and is exemplified by the protocols of reductive mechanical science, the medical model of medicine and psychiatry and the dictates of rational economics, as well as by Western religions. The protocols of these orthodoxies have little room for the contexts of culture, language, mind, consciousness or meaning. This modern separating culture hollows out religion on the one hand, while promoting a secular set of assumptions on the other. Religions become a series of 'dos' and 'don'ts', while science constructs the fiction of the ideal human as an autonomous agent capable of self-control and doer-ship. The impossible logic of separation seeing promotes the ego and its desires in both the religious and the secular individual and thus condemns them to a life of misery and so-called meaninglessness. This is because it is impossible to live on a diet of explicit meaning.

A feature of separation seeing is the belief and trust in the expert: an individual who has an unbiased and objective mind that is above the entanglements of self-interest, political expediency or predispositions. This idealised man (not woman) is supposed to have evolved from the cocoon of five or six years of tertiary training to emerge with a fully grown and properly trained reasoning mind. The 'expert', along with the ideal of a reasonable man, represents a central belief held by Western law courts when weighing up evidence in hearings. The ideal of a reasonable man has been born from a culture that prizes the intellect's love of *explicit-to-explicit* differences and then elevates this capacity into Reason with a capital R, thus raising the intellect's status to near infallibility, a rank once reserved for the Holy Scriptures.

The metaphysics of Western separation seeing has given us the rationality of Aristotelian logic. This kind of logic fits a binary and mechanical world and is derived from the cultural fondness that values differences so much that they become barriers and exclusions. The three laws of this classic logic are absolute and hold unconditionally. These three laws are the law of identity, the law of contradiction, and the law of the excluded middle.

The Aristotelian view goes something like this: an identity is nothing but an identity and is either so or not, while contradictions always exclude each other. With the strict application of this logic there is no middle ground and everything is ordered in black/white, either/or terms. The separations of Aristotelian logic have been the metaphysical foundation for mainstream Western culture and religion for almost two thousand years. A very different form of logic is the logic of empathy, which has much in common with quantum logic of complementarity (discussed in the next chapter).

The Aristotelian culture of separation seeing produced a Tower-of-Babel world where gaps, splits and separations are its most common features. In the hands of sceptics, separation seeing is hardened into a 'realist' ideology. Intolerance of implicit contextual meaning is a feature of those professional sceptics who create the illusion of certainty by constantly doubting anything. The card-carrying sceptic will deny a whole raft of implicit contexts such as One Consciousness, extrasensory perception, telepathy, the memory of water, and everything else that seems to challenge the dogmas of a mechanical, explicitly defined clockwork universe. Historically, the critics of any orthodoxy were treated harshly. Once they were burnt at the stake or condemned as heretics. Now, under the active influence of the professional sceptics, many simply have their reputations undermined.

A key feature of the rational materialism that dominates mechanical science is its general intolerance for the uncertainty inherent in all implicit meaning. This intolerance is accompanied by an added value given to graspable, explicit and differential forms that feature prominently in 'the machine'. Yet uncertainty arises naturally from contextual implicit meaning and it is this kind of ungraspable meaning with which the rational materialist has most difficulty.

Our uneasiness with uncertainty is a situation that the philosopher-theologian Nicholas of Cusa (1401–64) termed *learned ignorance* (Milne 2001). Learned ignorance is a state of the intellect when it *knows it does not know*. When the intellect is confronted by the uncertainties of implicit meaning it has two options: i) it can either accept the ungraspable, non-explicit nature of implicit contextual meaning and realise that such holistic systems can never be fully known explicitly, or ii) it can simply reject or delete implicit contextual meaning from its repertoires and then attempt to proclaim itself in a fully explicit language of Reason.

When the intellect works in the service of ego or tribe it will adhere to the doctrine of many minds while reconstituting some orthodoxy. This *neurotic* doctrinal separation seeing divides the world between the trustworthy of orthodox and the untrustworthy of the subjective. The main strategy for this way of seeing is to use language in ways that produce splits, separations and divisions where there is actually unity, interconnection and participation (see Appendix B).

Such a fragmented worldview was summed up succinctly by one old Australian Aboriginal man who spoke to W.E.H. Stanner (2009: 57) as though he were speaking in verse:

White man got no dreaming
Him go 'nother way
White man, him got different.
Him go road belong himself.

This old man was right; the materialist white man has no God and he travels a fragmented road of *heterogeneity without a context* (Jameson 1991). This is the road that says explicit particulars can exist independently without the need of a context. This is the Western scientific, commercial and economic focus that splits, divides, fragments and excludes the mind and the environment, and often society, in its worldview. This view can translate into personal terms so that most of us will work hard to achieve success through detailed, explicit and competitive methods without the benefit of a larger picture.

This is what many of us will do in our mid-twenties when we rationally organise our life into the compartments of work, love life, family and society. This is especially the case for those of us who are workaholics. Such people are especially prone to those rationally walled worlds of work, study or the corporation that split head from heart in order to provide logical proof, justification and reasoned financial argument for almost everything. Quite often this kind of devotion to the rationality of work, corporation, tribe or personal wealth will create an emotional crisis where life suddenly seems to lack meaning, and then the individual will fall into depression.

The parameters of life for materialistic men and women are limited because the intellect can become disoriented by a narrow rational and/or technological view of the world, a view that is often supported by a prodigious use of language. In addition, a prodigious use of language often comes with an outpouring of words that can easily disorient us, especially when we finally come to realise that the explicit certainties created by skeleton symbols actually fail to live up to the promise they hold out to us (see Appendix B).

When the intellect is serving ego or tribe the negative and *neurotic* effects are several: i) we become distanced from One Consciousness; ii) we become stressed and disorganised; and iii) our capacity to transform through learning is severely inhibited. These separating predispositions contain a blindness that is difficult to overcome. Of course, not everyone works hard at overcoming their blindness and quite often individuals, corporations, political parties and the media will wilfully celebrate the ignorance of separation seeing. In addition, vested interests can demonstrate their wilful ignorance through tribal decree or neo-liberal policies involving social exclusions and inequalities that are conveyed to the general public by appeals that stimulate fear and paranoid emotions. Such individuals often find it impossible to be empathic and then condemn those who are by calling them 'soft', 'wet' or 'politically correct'.

* * *

I now want to turn to depression as a negative, neurotic response produced by separation seeing, in contrast to the categorisation it often carries as a mental illness. The French writer and philosopher Albert Camus (1913–60) wrote a great deal about the absurd. In his philosophical essay *The Myth of Sisyphus* (2005), Camus undertakes to answer the only philosophical question he considers matters: 'There is but one truly serious philosophical problem and that is suicide.'

His essay describes how the world is unreasonable; how we live as if not knowing about the certainty of death; how rationality fails us and how science is unable to explain the world. According to Camus, when the human need for understanding meets a world that is unreasonable, the contradiction of the absurd must then be acknowledged, lived through and constantly confronted. Yet Camus' answer to his question of suicide is to say that suicide, as the philosophical answer to the absurd, should be rejected.

Camus' view of the absurd is a harsh philosophy to live by and in its recognition of the limits to the logic of reason it has some affinity with the current view that Reason carries a virus that denies the importance of implicit meaning. Unlike the current approach, however, Camus' sense of the absurd comes from what he describes as a life that appears to be without meaning, as told in *The Myth of Sisyphus*. But a life without meaning is a statement that needs examining. Camus' statement of a life without meaning does not address the question of how we make meaning in this life, nor does it say anything about how the meaning of an absurd world is made. Rather, his absurd and unreasonable world appears to represent the single meaning of an objective rational statement without qualification.

We know that objective statements are essentially false because they rest on a single meaning. Camus' view is that of an Enlightenment man who has already awarded reason an infallible and unconditional authority. Such a view produces the objective argument that life has failed on its own terms to be reasonable and therefore it is logically absurd. But this kind of internally consistent argument has itself failed to take account of the provisional position that the intellect holds within learning and, in addition, it fails to consider the possibility that the world is unreasonable because we think it so. Finally, this rational argument erases the constant underlying mnemonic field of implicit meaning that supports and hosts the ordinary mind and that provides the means of escaping the rational absurd.

While Camus rightly rejects suicide as a philosophical response to the failure of reason, the less philosophical among us, when faced with a crisis that has been made solely by the unreasonable terms of a strictly rational mind, may experience a sense of meaninglessness and as a consequence may take that path of suicide. I would suggest that successful suicide represents a selfish and final act of aggression against others and self. What is denied in suicide is the possibility of learning and transforming the painful explicit details of what may appear to be an intolerable situation into something that can retain a glimmer of hope for a better future.

In terms of learning, the depression that brings about suicidal thoughts can sometimes play a positive bridging role from identification through the intellect to the more ordered harmony of empathy. We become depressed when life seems meaningless, when what we have valued or held dear suddenly disappears or when pressing problems seem to have no solution. A sense of meaninglessness arises from an undue reliance on *explicit-to-explicit* meaning to solve our problems. Hence when the world seems unreasonable or to lack meaning it is because the intellect tells us this miserable story. Yet what it does not tell us is that this story has arisen because the intellect is working in the service of ego and not in the service of empathy.

Meaninglessness and a sense of the absurd is never due to a lack of implicit meaning, for this *nous* is always present and continues to exist while not depending on any human conscious thought. The mind of *Implicit-to-Implicit* meaning represents the cosmic mind of One Consciousness and this context invades and surrounds the ordinary conscious mind via the autonomic systems of the body. These *Implicit-to-Implicit* exchanges represent a universal resource or full bank account of meaningfulness, a continuous reserve of well-being that only has to be tapped into.

Depression represents the second last stage in Elisabeth Kübler-Ross' five stages of dying. The stage after depression is acceptance. The place of depression in these five stages tells us something about the nature of depression. It tells us that depression is a stopover station on the pathway to something else. In terms of Meaning, depression is the black-hole station in which we are forced to stop in order to come to terms with the bankruptcy of the values and trust we had put in rational, analytical practices, thoughts and behaviour. When the body is sick or when finances fail or when our love leaves or when we feel socially isolated and excluded we can become demoralised, and then our faith in a rational world suffers. It is then we have to deal with the sense of failure through the experience of depression.

Some of us will have to experience despair and misery in order to grow, which means that depression is not a mental illness so much as a feature of internal growth that needs to be worked through. A feature of internal growth represents a feature of learning. The learning situation of depression may in some instances be helped by the short-term use of drugs. But the limitation of antidepressant drugs is that these drugs cannot change meaning or help us achieve a sense of meaningfulness. Rather, the learning that is necessarily involved in depression is a change that brings to light the meaningfulness of the individual's own lived, implicit context.

This context of One Consciousness is discoverable whenever we set out to learn about the continuing consciousness that underpins our ordinary conscious mind. It is then that we can begin to let go of the all the discrete nonsense that armours the false self (the ego) and find a replacement for it within the inherent and implicit joy of Self. This evolving readjustment cannot be brought about by rational argument or by material objects meant to reinforce the ego's defences. Thus all prior learning patterns are redundant when it comes to moving from an analytical 'head' process through depression to the heart feelings of empathy.

The learning transformation from intellect into empathy is facilitated by the recognition that when taken to its logical conclusion, logical, rational arguments are always unreasonable. In practical terms this means recognising the limitations of using symbols as a method of bolstering the ego. If we rely upon this strategy to give us certainty or truth or understanding, at some point we will find that we have been led astray. An uncompromising reliance on the differential exchange values of symbols will always create an explicit world that is full of contradictions.

To move beyond the explicate order we have to recognise the non-explicit metaphysical nature of our being. This requires a felt appreciation (not a rational argument) of empathy, unity and participation (interpenetration). The very best that the intellect is able to achieve here is to employ a language that points us in the general direction of empathy and towards *Implicit-to-Implicit* exchanges. Yet this 'very best' is always a conditional state of knowing, for we cannot know everything explicitly. Within this state of mind language exists as nothing more than a set of provisional signposts that point to a contextual and implicit understanding beyond the rational and symbolic.

Settling on a daily spiritual practice can help the learning that will ease our way through the black hole of depression and take us beyond the unreasonableness of the absurd. This boat ride across the sea of negativity is the natural progression in becoming an evolved and mature person. The learning potentials of this spiritual path may only become apparent when the hollowed out individual finally admits in the depths of his depression that the light that leads him out of this cave comes from his own spiritual awakening.

In conclusion, separation seeing has become the fashion in our modern world. In David Bohm's view, many of the problems of society as well as of science come from us breaking things up that are not really separate. He suggests that this tendency to break things up creates a sense of social and personal fragmentation. Bohm's answer to this modern culture of alienation and disconnection was the suggestion that we should start dialogue groups that would over time transforms the relationships between people, but also the nature of consciousness in which these relationships arise (2006: xvii).

Separation seeing is the modern mind virus that has, since the seventeenth century, spread like a pandemic across the globe. Within this Trojan horse hides the destructive potentials that split mind from body and subject from nature while isolating individuals from each other as well as from their environment and their larger Self, or the wholeness of One Consciousness. Through the orthodoxy of separation seeing almost any polarity or dualism is subjected to the distortion of becoming a binary pair whose principles are in opposition to each other. This happens because separation seeing prizes binary opposites along with the single meaning of constituents while disdaining the uncertainty of broader and deeper implicit contexts. The extraordinary division of wealth in the world today between the several hundred super-rich and the rest is practical proof of how pervasive and influential this viral, distorted way of seeing has become. The illness spread by this limited and partial view is manifest in widespread alienation, fragmentation, hopelessness and depression.

17

Empathic Seeing

Empathic seeing is the final mode of thought and learning of the ordinary mind. The potentials of this way of seeing are often buried beneath desperate knots of desire and all the arguments, scepticism and justifications of reason. The potentials of empathy have been there all the time, often hidden from view but nevertheless exerting a benign influence on the way we think and see the world and act towards others. The closer empathy is to the surface of our awareness the more we see empathically and the more we allow ourselves to act compassionately as our brother/sister's keeper. When we can see empathically the world is no longer desperate or absurd but full of love, connection and Meaning.

Empathy is integrated thought. It is the mode of thought that integrates the distinctions and differences of meaning into larger contextual frameworks or wholes. Empathy is a reflection of the holographic structure of One Consciousness by seeing the many within the one and the one within the many. Hence the order that is constructed by empathic seeing is the order of love where there are no separations; where the transient or the discrete represent local features of the infinite, eternal and unified. While the eternal and the transient are clearly distinct, empathic seeing orders them into integrated wholes.

Rather than emphasising differences and separations, as is the bias of separation seeing, empathic seeing pays attention to what is common to all organisms and what ties all people together into communities. Specifically, empathic seeing involves the intellect (*explicit-*) when it works in the service of compassion (*to-Implicit*). It is only within this transformation from *explicit to Implicit* that the general gestalt of mind (of constituent and context) is recognised as a natural synthesis of Meaning and is applied as such.

As a consequence of this broader and deeper perspective, knowledge will be seen to come in wholes, while every discrete detail will represent a part of that ultimate whole of Meaning. It is well known that a context always gives most of the meaning to any set of details, and it is this contextualising process that is the hallmark of empathic seeing and action. Empathy produces more meaning than the thoughts of separation seeing, and therefore it produces meaningfulness, which is a state that includes a sense of happiness. The sum total of empathic seeing is thus a life of happiness and meaningfulness.

With the three shadow ways of seeing, what is considered to be the outer world represents the only causal reality, while the inner world tends to be reduced to a distrusted place that is ignored or belittled. Hence the outward-looking individual feels justified in blaming others and at times this exclusively outward view produces acrimonious debates, like those around the demarcation of science and non-science.

In contrast, empathetic seeing takes a non-oppositional viewpoint, one in which outer details are always compromised by inner contexts and vice versa. The logic of empathy is akin to the complementarity principle of quantum physics that was first enunciated by the Danish physicist Niels Bohr (1885–1962) in the early part of last century. Quantum logic tells us that opposites are complementary and that they fit within larger wholes. So when we use the terms 'particle' and 'wave' in exclusive, mechanical ways we become convinced that it is impossible for an object to be both of them at the same time. This impossibility comes from the Aristotelian logic of separation seeing.

However, when we use quantum logic and begin to understand that opposites are complementary, a particle and a wave simply become distinctions within a large whole. That whole is the whole of consciousness and this context is entirely relevant to the question of what kind of measuring device scientists decide to use in quantum physics. This is a crucial question for quantum physics because it has been confirmed time and again that the kind of measurements used determine the results of the experiment; in other words, the mind of the scientist has become part of the experimental equipment.

A more everyday example of quantum/empathic logic is found in the biblical story of King Solomon who ruled on the claim by two women who said each was the mother of the same child. The King called for a sword to cut the baby in half, so each woman would could have a part of the child. One woman did not argue with this ruling, saying if she could not have the baby then neither of them could. The other pleaded for the child's life saying, 'give him to her'. Solomon the wise pronounced that this was the true mother. The contradictory logic of a mother who wants her child but is willing to give him up so he could live displays how these opposites feelings are complementary when seen within a larger whole. That whole was the mother's love and empathy for her child.

In terms of mechanical science where inner versus outer views, the Aristotelian logic of this binary pair represent two separate worlds of objectivity and subjectivity. But the complementary logic of empathy tells us there is no such thing as a truly outer, objective or empirical viewpoint, practice or world. All practices, observations and ways of seeing have a combination of outer and inner features. This complementary mixture will attend all observations, and the differences between observations will depend on which set of inner or outer features we decide to value and emphasise.

This quantum/empathic logic of complementarity means that there is no scientific practice, theory or observation that is separate from consciousness. In terms of emotions it means that blame, revenge and hatred are unacceptable and inappropriate responses to disagreements that arise from different ways of seeing. Using empathic logic, we can say that the underlying state of implicit wholeness represents the basis of every scientific experiment, theory or way of seeing, for this kind of Meaning is always the larger part of every image, thought or discourse.

Empathic seeing comes with the capacity for self-reflection. Self-reflection has a 'vertical' structure in that *explicit-to-Implicit* exchanges occur between the conscious mind and One Consciousness. This occurs in discourses about spirit, love, meaning and soul. In addition to the capacity for self-reflection, empathic seeing is at home with the ability to read and comprehend several levels of meaning at once. This is the ability to recognise, read and appreciate parables, allegories, metaphors, satire and ironies. It is the ability to read and understand the subtexts within any message, but in particular the subtext within the trinity of being that is evident in an embodied Self. As a consequence of this heightened receptivity to multi-levels of meaning, empathic seeing can recognise the spiritual possibilities and metaphysical principles within any aspect of the universe.

The idea of multi-layered meaning is ancient. Origen (202 CE), the Christian theologian, wrote that the Holy Scriptures had three levels of meaning: the literal, the moral and the allegorical. These three levels were not seen as possible alternative readings that we might like to choose, but as multi-layers that existed within every scripture.

From the perspective of the meaning of Meaning, there are at least four levels of meaning within every text, discourse and communication. These are associated with various ways of seeing in the following manner: i) an ego reading where the literal, single meaning is prized above all else; ii) a tribal reading where binary morals motivates an exclusive sense of us; iii) a separation reading in which symbols become the concrete realities and therefore our idols; and iv) an empathic reading where multi-levels of meaning exist together within an essentially spiritual vision of the world. While I can agree with Origen that every text and discourse has multi-levels of meaning, this complexity of meaning does not register with the three shadow ways of seeing and reading. In other words, our reading of the scriptures of religion or science is a result of how far we have transcended the hidden mountains of identification that make up our shadow way of seeing the world.

* * *

I have already suggested that empathic seeing represents the *normal* and by extension the healthy level of intensity for the concept (signifieds) we form and use. There are, however, some distinctions within the normal range of empathic responses and these relate i) to the amount of time and energy spent down the cave of the mind seeing through veils of identification, and ii) the amount of time and energy spent in serving others. The first takes us back to the shadows of the cave and the second takes us out of the cave into the light towards a Self seeing. Sometimes both these paths occur within the same person so that they have the contradictions of an empathic life entangled with negative behaviour.

Empathy is commonly understood as the *ability to imagine oneself in another's place and understand the other's feelings, desires, ideas and actions.* While some would understand this definition to include sympathy, empathy is very different from sympathy. That difference relates to the degree of knotted identification we have associated with expressions of love. With sympathy love is narrowed by our desires. In contrast, love is expanded by empathy. However, empathy can reduce to sympathy when our desires are activated.

Empathic seeing can evolve into a spiritual path that points to the innocent love (*Implicit-to-Implicit*) inherent within the mnemonic resonance of the foundations to our mind. Yet this path of empathy has many traps. When we experience a sudden connection to one who enlivens us we can often fall into the trap of transforming that person into the object of our desire. When this happens, our perception narrows into ego seeing, and hence the experience of a new love can easily stimulate hidden and unfulfilled desires. Yet empathy and desire are worlds apart. Unlike desire, the love within an empathic response has no end point or object that is seen to be the source or cause of love. The source of love within an empathic response is the universal mnemonic resonance in which we live. As a yogi once said, 'Love the One Love in all of us' (Yogananda 1994: 197).

When we desire another the feelings of attraction become restricted by identification processes. These processes fuse together two or more objects as if they were one. This fusing process represents a narrowing of vision that is halfway between the implicitness of insight and a full conscious differentiation. Desires have subliminal patterns of narrowed attraction that create the internal dynamics of wanting and demanding. These are the common core experiences in infancy, childhood and adolescence. The love of desire is, therefore, a love that wants to cling to and holds on to the objects of desire. In the classical world of the Greeks, this kind of love in adults was generally understood to be a kind of madness.

In contrast, the love that develops with empathy is the kind of attraction that comes innately and implicitly from the underlying resonance of implicit meaning. The love within empathy is a reflection of the attraction and connection of One Consciousness, which is the foundation of the mind. In other words, empathy is the ordinary mind's attempt to mirror what lies close beneath it, and this is the unconditional love of the *Implicit-to-Implicit* foundation of mind. The natural attraction within implicit meaning means there is no need to hold on or cling to others, so there are few if any conditions or qualifications that restrict empathic love.

With empathic seeing there is simply the fullness and recognition of interconnection that carries its own reward, which is joy. The love within empathy is perhaps close to what Socrates said about *agape*, which he defined as selfless love with a longing for wholeness. With empathy, there is a taste of the wholeness of the Self, but empathy is still an ordinary mind mode of thought and so this taste of the Self's completeness remains a savoured yet unrealised reality. A sense of peace and completeness usually only comes from years of daily spiritual practice.

When people arrive at mid-life or when they have children, empathy begins to develop in most of us. When this happens, we start to become disentangled from our desires but also to disengage somewhat from the complex defences of our ego. Such detachment is unlike the scientist's idea of objective non-participation; rather it may involve a studied self-reflection in which the internal knots of our desires and ego begin to untangle in the face of time constraints or a critical learning. As empathy develops our sense of personal hurt, injustice and failure diminishes, while our sense of connection and participation enlarges and becomes real. Empathic seeing can be said to represent a wisdom that views the self not as a separate entity like the ego but rather as the eternal spiritual essence that is the central vital feature in their being as well as in seeing.

When the intellect works in the service of the ego it can produce a highly expert technical knowledge that is narrow in focus and devoid of broader contexts. In contrast, the intelligence of empathic seeing produces a wisdom that comes from integrating the discrete differences and distinctions of technical knowledge into broader contexts that ultimately involve consciousness and Meaning. With the wisdom of empathy, we automatically seek out and value links, similarities and isomorphic connections, whereas with rational materialism or the politics of neoliberalism differences are valued as ends. 'Similarity' is an important word for the development of empathic seeing. Similarity carries a meaning that begins with differences and then reduces their individual values by locating them within broader systems and contexts. This kind of understanding of similarity embodies the contradiction that objects are always *discrete but unified into larger wholes.*

* * *

C.S. Lewis' classic book *The Allegory of Love* was an influential treatment of love in the Middle Ages. Lewis writes that humanity does not pass through phases like a train passing through stations: 'being alive, it has the privilege of always moving yet never leaving anything behind. Whatever we have been, in some sort we are still' (Fulweiler 1993: 9). This is an apt description for the learning path into empathic seeing. Empathy may seem like the end 'station' in the cycle of learning yet it includes the core of what has gone before. What has existed in the ego, desires and the intellect in some manner exists also in empathy. This is because empathy incorporates and expresses the main features of these ways of seeing in complex, holistic and loving sensibilities that do not simply mirror the earlier modes but create something that is entirely new.

For most of us who arrive at the age of empathy (around mid-life) we are not suddenly born again or transformed into mature saints. At mid-life, most of us arrive with the baggage of our past modes of thought and hence tend to deploy the personal habits we brought with us rather than use what is always free and given in this station. The circle of learning indicates that life in a human body is a spiritual journey taken by everyone, no matter their class, creed or tribe. The end of this evolutionary journey is a spiritual place that at first looks similar to where we began, which is the resonance and joy of implicit love. This similarity occurs because empathy is a reflection of joy and innocent love, yet it comes with the mature awareness of a seasoned traveller.

A society based upon empathy does not return to some kind of rural innocence or a tribal paradise. Similarly, a 50-year-old who feels the tension of mid-life cannot turn the clock back to adolescence or childhood innocence. Many may try to return to the identifications of their youth through cosmetic surgery or drugs, yet these attempts amount to a failure to recognise the nature of the cosmic change that has already occurred and continues to occur in their bodies. Empathic seeing is, therefore, not a turning back but rather a moving forward through healing and learning that relies upon intuition, curiosity and letting go of those old habits of mind.

Except for those fortunate few individuals who seemed to have come into this world fully mature, for most of us the path that will expand empathic capacities will be slow and difficult. As each of us is unique this pathway will also be unique in the sense that it will fit the character and circumstances of the individual. In a more generic sense this pathway means changing our high-energy, competitive ego anxieties and defence mechanisms along with those fully charged political distinctions and exclusions into lower-energy expansive concerns for others. It will also mean giving up the rhetoric of reason and letting go of orthodoxies and settling instead for the small daily joys of a routine and imprecise life.

The master narratives of religion or science do not dominate the vision of those who see empathically, even though such narratives can exert influence on the way we think and act. We may call ourselves Christian, Buddhist, Hindu, Muslim, scientist or rational atheist, but for the person of empathy these labels do not represent an insignia that denotes membership of a tribe that separates *us* from *them*. Rather, these labels are the fallible route maps that provide a set of expectations and a direction and purpose for our action. Empathic seeing and action are post-rational, post-desire, post-nationalistic and largely post-ego. Yet this non-dualist mode of seeing and thinking does not obliterate reason, nation, ego or desire, but values them less than the connections of community, compassion, love, joy and spiritual growth.

* * *

Empathic seeing represents the only path of virtue. There is no other path of virtue so innocent and unconditional. There are no rational, patriotic or tribal paths that are not mean, bitter and contradicted, and there is little virtue in our desires or ego. Only the compassion of empathic seeing stands as continuously virtuous under all conditions. When asked which is the greatest commandment, Jesus said, 'Thou shalt love the Lord thy God with all thy heart and with all thy soul and with all thy mind'; and the second, 'love thy neighbour as thyself' (Matthew 22: 36–40).

The combination of these two loves represents the virtue of empathic seeing. Empathy involves knowing the Self in order to love your neighbour as yourself. It is impossible to love your neighbour as yourself if you are ignorant of your true spiritual nature. One must begin where Jesus said to begin, by knowing and loving the Lord, which is your true Self. Knowing your Self always involves knowing the difference between the ordinary transient mind and the constant, eternal cosmic foundation of that mind.

Compassion grows with the growth of self-knowledge. This is the integrated wisdom that comes with a fourfold vision; it is the wisdom of the 'heart' that comes from knowing the three deliberate steps of learning. Compassion does not grow from expert or technical knowledge of the scriptures or from a specialised knowledge of mechanics, sociology, politics or technology.

Publicly performing these various kinds of technical knowledge can afford us some celebrity status, but this acclaim does not make us wise or virtuous and nor does it make us more able to love our neighbour as our own true Self. Only self-knowledge can do this, while a holistic understanding can provide us with the force and momentum to continue down this path of virtue.

Empathic seeing is, therefore, not the result of rational knowledge and neither is it 'emotional intelligence'. Having intelligence about emotions may simply be the result of diplomatic training, such as the businessman receives before he visits a foreign country. In such situations, this training does not obliterate the businessman's desires or self-interest; rather, it often augments it. Training to identify emotions is like studying comparative religions, an exercise that does not necessarily make students more tolerant or empathic.

In addition to virtue, empathic seeing represents the only valid and sane response to the world. 'Sane' and 'sanity' have been much used terms over the last century, but their use has generally lacked any systematic context beyond the vague idea of adjusting individual needs to the norms of society – the approach taken by the American Psychiatric Association, or in Erich Fromm's case, of 'adjusting society to the needs of man' (2002: 70). As a consequence, these relative and cultural concepts of sanity have become unqualified states that are blind to their own cultural underpinnings.

In contrast and from the point of view of Meaning, the idea of sanity is related to how well the individual appreciates their connections to the implicit Meaning of One Consciousness. By this I mean how aware individuals are of their secondary and infallible nature as well as how aware they are of the presence of the universe's awareness. With ego, tribal and separation seeing there is little appreciation of these holographic connections, and so these meanings largely remain hidden or rejected. Holographic connections begin to be realised in the love that is empathic seeing. Hence empathic seeing is virtuous as well as sane. The sanity of empathy is the realisation that our true nature is love and that this foundation connects every one of us to each other and to the rest of the universe. This realisation gives us the wisdom that our ordinary mind is not autonomous but rather a unique part of the collective mind of One Consciousness.

Empathic seeing will often produce voluntary and spontaneous social interactions that create bridging connections and a caring concern for others. These kinds of selfless actions are usually undertaken in friendship for the welfare of others without thought of reward. They are the unplanned acts of kindness and love that come directly from our most basic implicit and connective Self. Such positive social actions happen spontaneously in the present moment.

In conclusion, a relatively sane and mature person will respond overwhelmingly to the world with empathy and understanding, but such a person is also capable on occasion of reverting to shadow seeing. Such individuals tend to have tolerance for others and a mature appreciation of their own and other's fallibility. The learning path through empathy is essentially a spiritual one and it leads towards those practices that will evolve the individual's mind so that he or she can spend less time in the cave of shadows and more time involved in spontaneous acts of love, kindness and generosity. Such practices also contain the innate purpose of discovering who we really are.

18

Clairvoyant Seeing

Clairvoyant seeing arises within us from One Consciousness. The communications involved in this kind of seeing have a structure that comes from *Implicit-to-Implicit* exchanges of Meaning.

Clairvoyant forms of communication are actively at work in the ordinary conscious mind and are usually called insight, understanding, comprehension, implication, inference, connotation and so on. Clairvoyant seeing also operates between people as extrasensory perception, and many experiments in parapsychology have time and again confirmed their existence. A further area in which *Implicit-to-Implicit* exchanges occur is between the universe of One Consciousness and the perceptual mind of the individual. These holographic forms of communication also occur in intuition, conscience, realisation, creative insight and revelation.

Clairvoyant *Implicit-to-Implicit* exchanges represent the 'readiness potential' for any and all thoughts to emerge into explicit existence (see footnote 4). These exchanges operate at the pre-reflective level of mind and are carried out by the autonomic systems of the body, but more generally they can be called the communication exchanges of One Consciousness.

We should note that while *Implicit-to-Implicit* exchanges are metaphysical they are active and carry a charge. They have a mnemonic resonance that interpenetrates and underpins each

of the three steps of learning and all the activity of the conscious mind. These exchanges have four active features: i) they
have being; ii) they contain the light of illumination, which is
the awareness within the sight of seeing; iii) they contain the
joy and bliss of innocent love; iv) the extent and scope of these
exchanges are infinite and eternal. These four features represent
our underlying nature and one could say, our true Self.

These four composite features are represented by the ancient
Indian term *satchitananda*. This Sanskrit word is described by
Stanislav Grof (1998: 117) as consisting of three words brought
together: '*sat* meaning existence or being; *chit*, which translates
as awareness; and *ananda*, which signifies bliss'. *Satchitananda*,
or being, awareness and bliss, represents the features of one
infinite consciousness and therefore of the implicit awareness
inherent within, between and surrounding all people and particles and which includes photons of light.

It needs to be stressed that the conditions of *satchitananda*
are not explicit features of the conscious mind but the foundation to that mind. This is the character of the 'no-mind' mind.
By this I mean that within the non-explicit field of this consciousness there is no ego, no desire, no rational thoughts, no
expressions made through exchanges of signs or language. The
joy and innocent love of One Consciousness represent the experience of our constant, extended communal and universal mind,
which is an infinite ocean full of being, awareness and bliss.

The mnemonic resonance of *satchitananda* is thus empty of
all ordinary mind functions and operations but full of Meaning. This is a universal holographic field where every local point
in the universe is at the same time nonlocal. Since this mode
of consciousness underpins and supports every function of the
ordinary mind, the mnemonic resonance of *satchitananda* could
be called the place of ordinary mind emptiness. Yet its permanent presence informs us that every thought or concept we create does not have an independent stand-alone existence. Rather,

every local feature and effect of the ordinary mind floats in and is dependent on the mnemonic resonance of this ground state of *satchitananda*.

The *Implicit-to-Implicit* exchanges of *satchitananda* also represent how we implicitly know things. Implicit knowing is usually called intuition, insight or revelation. This kind of knowing is not unconscious or repressed but is an active feature of knowing anything and everything. In addition, *Implicit-to-Implicit* exchanges represent the concealed character of contextual meaning associated with every transaction of the ordinary mind, whether in the modes of ego, tribe, separation or empathy. But these ordinary ways of seeing are not equal when it comes to the *Implicit-to-Implicit* exchanges of meaning.

The three shadow ways of seeing constructed by complex patterns of identification tend to resist, erase or ignore implicit exchanges through their overfocus and near-sightedness on a limited number of details. In contrast, the broader and deeper thought processes of empathy acknowledge and engage with the implicit meaning of contexts as well as acknowledging the intuitive exchanges with One Consciousness.

When *Implicit-to-Implicit* exchanges operate between people it is commonly called extrasensory perception. Such exchanges are called 'extra'-sensory because normal perceptions as well as communication derive from using the body's five senses and will always contain some form or detail or explicit differential meaning common to signs and language. In contrast, *Implicit-to-Implicit* exchanges of intuitive perceptions between people do not rely on mechanical, technological, physical methods or sensory pathways. As a consequence, what facilitates extrasensory communication is for those involved to refrain from negative thoughts or the use of differential language; these actions reduce the effectiveness of extrasensory communication.

In his book *Clairvoyant Reality*, Lawrence LeShan argues the case for ESP involving precognition, telepathy and clairvoyance.

He maintains that ESP, which he calls a clairvoyant reality, is a different way of seeing from our ordinary everyday sensory perception. ESP has been dismissed by many mainstream scientists. Why should the idea of ESP be so detested? One answer is that separation seeing excludes the possibility of clairvoyant communication because acceptance of it opens the door to the possibility that mind and consciousness are not caused by brain activity and that they can operate outside or beyond the body.

Under the influences of reductive materialism, *Implicit-to-Implicit* exchanges are non-standard and could be called 'extra'. A general resistance to implicit knowing is also promoted by organisations such as the US based Committee for Sceptical Inquiry. This organisation is dedicated to expunging what it considers to be fake science, and especially science that deals with the 'paranormal'. Yet what is normal for a science that deletes consideration of meaning, culture, language, consciousness, mind from its studies?

Implicit contextual knowing is not a knowing that is added on, 'para' or 'extra' to the normal, explicit meanings generated (as signifiers) through the five senses, or deliberately by the conscious mind using concepts (signifieds). Rather, this kind of innate knowing is always prior to any sequences of distinctions and, in addition, it represents the sight awareness within first sight. Because of this order we should more accurately call this kind of perception *primary perception*. It is primary because it belongs to the foundation of our normal conscious mind and the Meaning exchanged always precedes the explicit meaning contained in sensory perceptions.

In *The Secret Life of Your Cells*, Robert Stone (1989) uses the term 'primary perception' to describe the connection between humans and animals, humans and plants or humans and cells. In contrast to ESP, *primary perception* implies a range of perceptions that runs from the sight of One Consciousness, which is the sight of our first sight, and then on to the inner sight of concept formation (signifieds), and then to the possibilities of imagination, and finally to the light of insight, intuition and revelation. Such a range more accurately describes a broad spectrum of perception where clairvoyant seeing represents the means of communicating without reference to sensory or physical means.

In this book I have used the term 'clairvoyant seeing' rather than 'primary perception', even though both refer to a seeing that is nonsensory. Clairvoyant seeing is primary perception and its intuitive knowing comes from within the patterns of *Implicit-to-Implicit* exchanges rather than focusing on, or desiring to know, an object or a set of forms. Clairvoyant seeing operates without any consideration of locality or time, or any other distinction.

* * *

The term 'mnemonic resonance' used to describe *Implicit-to-Implicit* exchanges has a similar meaning to the terms Rupert Sheldrake uses to describe the organisational field related to the creation of biological forms. Sheldrake has become well known for his theories of morphic resonance, a concept that suggests memory is inherent in all of nature. This is a controversial idea for many mainstream biologists. From the point of view of Meaning, Sheldrake's theories are pertinent to the current discussion on ways of seeing for they point to an organised consciousness that is inherent in all of nature.

As a biochemist Sheldrake was interested in morphogenesis, that is, the processes that create an organism's architectural shape and form. For almost a hundred years some biologists have thought that in living organisms morphogenesis is organised by fields which can be described as non-material regions of influence. Sheldrake takes up this approach to morphogenesis by investigating the nature of these fields. He states that 'the

structure of the fields depends upon what has happened before'
(Sheldrake 1988b: 108). In other words, the structure of these
metaphysical fields comes from a resonance that involves memory, which Sheldrake calls 'morphic resonance'.

Sheldrake tells us that morphic resonance 'takes place on
the basis of similarity' (1988b: 108) and similarity is referred
to specifically as 'like upon like' (1993: 89). Hence these fields
of memory and organisation are seen to surround and permeate
each organism or form and they also have a resonant structure
that comes from the vibrations of *like upon like*. The phrase 'like
upon like' is almost identical to the phrase used in this book that
describes *Implicit-to-Implicit* exchanges of meaning.

Criticism of Sheldrake's approach has come mainly from
those working within the traditions of reductive materialism; for
example, see the Appendix of his *A New Science of Life* (Sheldrake
1988a). Yet from the point of view of this study of consciousness, I consider that Sheldrake does not go far enough outside
traditional boundaries. For example, morphic resonance and his
hypothesis of formative causation are primarily concerned with a
contextual organisational agency that is essentially metaphysical
and beyond the actual constituent form of organisms. It seems
to me that here is the organisational field of One Consciousness.

It is my contention that Sheldrake's theories of morphic resonance would be more complete if they went further outside
reductive materialism and were to admit the concept of a universal consciousness. For example, what is it that is transferred
through morphic resonance from one generation to the next? It
can only be meaning that is transferred between generations and
that meaning comes from *Implicit-to-Implicit* (*like-upon-like*)
exchanges. Here the use of the terminology of 'information',
which Sheldrake relies on, simply causes ambiguity and confusion. In addition, I prefer to call these resonances 'mnemonic'
rather than 'morphic' because the term 'mnemonic' is explicitly associated with memory and memory is a key feature in

the reproduction of all forms as well as consciousness. The term 'morphic' is associated with the creation of forms and, interestingly, forms are a central feature of explicit meaning that creates the conscious mind. The differences between 'mnemonic' and 'morphic' reflect the difference in my focus to the metaphysics of Meaning and Sheldrake's biological approach.

I believe, however, that Sheldrake's work in biology clearly indicates how the mnemonic resonance of *Implicit-to-Implicit* exchanges operates within the area of biology and also how a collective memory operates for every member of every species. A collective memory is the community 'us' feature of One Consciousness. In general, Sheldrake's work implies that the same structures and processes of One Consciousness are operating in physics and biology as they are within the ordinary mind of individuals. These are the structures and processes of *satchitananda* and they operate as the implicit bridge between an individual's explicit (conscious) mind and the explicit (conscious) mind of other individuals. However, this permanent implicit bridge or field also acts as the resource reservoir that is available to every organism in order for it to receive and create communications and to exchange meaning across local space and time.

In other words, it would be impossible to communicate between individuals or organisms across space and through time if there was no permanent background reservoir or field of implicit Meaning. This field contains all the potentials needed for communication and for the exchange of meaning and as a consequence, all the potentials for morphogenesis. The concept of One Consciousness makes it possible to comprehend how it is that organic and inorganic forms are perpetuated over time and through generations. By taking into account the background field of One Consciousness we can also understand how it is possible to exchange meanings between individuals of a species and also between different species because every form is always already an organised part of the universal structure of Meaning.

* * *

Stanislav Grof makes an important distinction between religion and spirituality. He writes that 'organized religion, bereft of its experiential component, has largely lost the connection to its deep spiritual source and as a result has become empty, meaningless, and increasingly irrelevant to our life' (Grof 1998: 245–6). For Grof, lived spirituality has been replaced in many religions by 'dogmatism, ritualism, and moralism'. I would add that many organised religions have become tribal and thus their orthodox ways of seeing the world are essentially exclusive and often irrelevant to the important political concerns in contemporary society, such as AIDS, sexual preferences and women's right to ministry. Many religions promote a partisan stance that insists on literal beliefs and dogmatic scriptural understandings wrapped up in a way of seeing that is essentially tribal.

Grof is equally critical of scientism, which is the tribal response of many scientists: 'many scientists use the conceptual framework of contemporary science in a way that resembles a fundamentalist religion more than it does science' (1998: 247). When tribes of science collide with tribes of religion the usual result is much confusion and misunderstanding about both science and religion, but there will be a great deal of fuss made about how deluded and wrong the other side is. The tribes of science and religion are mirror images of each other: both argue from within the same sleep of the single vision (see Appendix A).

Spiritual knowledge is experiential knowledge and this particular experience comes in the form of *Implicit-to-Implicit* exchanges. As a general attribute this kind of knowing represents the certainty of intuited knowledge. Such knowledge contrasts with the uncertain knowledge or, at least, the hoped-for certainty that arises from ordinary mind expressions that rely upon language and signs. The certain knowledge of intuition and insight comes upon us before the reflective mind can think, and therefore it operates pre-reflectively before deliberate choices or judgments. It may arise silently when we look at a new moon on a clear night and feel joy, awe, wonder and a unifying connection to the wider world. This implicit knowing also produces realisations, revelations, the 'aha' reaction and the spiritual knowing of Blake's fourfold vision. Such exchanges can even be generated when a closely held view is suddenly enlarged and we are able to distinguish the details of the trees but still perceive the contextual generality of the forest.

The mnemonic resonance of *Implicit-to-Implicit* knowing is essentially a spiritual knowing. This is the knowing expressed sometimes as faith and felt in spiritual insight and joyful feelings of cosmic unity. Implicit interconnections can also represent those swells of tacit and inferential energy that move us from one perspective to the next and provide us with that upward shift of lightness that brings joy. In their deeper and quieter movements, the resonance of *Implicit-to-Implicit* knowing can become the celestial floods of spiritual harmony, inspiration and unconditional love. As consciousness is a singular unity the structure of this knowing (*Implicit-to-Implicit*) is the same for everyone, hence the everyday sharing of non-verbal activities is an effortless and harmonious way of making implicit connections with others. These kinds of connections are the natural basis of community and they exist within all cultures and every society.

19

Presence

In *The Marriage of Heaven and Hell* William Blake reflected on the nature of infinity by writing 'If the doors of perception were cleansed everything would appear to man as it is, infinite. For man has closed himself up till he sees all things thro' narrow chinks of his cavern.'

Blake was using Bishop Berkeley's (1685–1753) argument that if our senses had infinite acuteness we would perceive not more of the material world but infinity (Raine 1968: Part VI). The infinite world of *satchitananda* represents the permanent presence of One Consciousness with its symmetric structure of *Implicit-to-Implicit* connections and an awareness that is also implicit. This invariant presence of One Consciousness gives rise to our sense of communion, unity and love as well as our ability to communicate with other people and to have spiritual connections to the natural environment and to 'That' – One Consciousness.

The eternal and persistent presence of *Implicit-to-Implicit* connections does not announce itself to our conscious mind in any explicit way, but comes to us quietly, often through the influences of nature or in the form of synchronicities, intuitions, revelations, epiphanies, insights and so on. It is only after the tacit influence of this spiritual presence that we are then able to represent some small feature of this infinity with expressions such as *satchitananda*, or One Consciousness, or the meaning of Meaning, or the Self. Without the felt experience of the Spirit that is the life of *Implicit-to-Implicit* exchanges we would have no will or vocabulary to represent it.

Teilhard de Chardin has a handy description of this elusive presence: 'What you see gliding past, like a world, behind the song and behind the colour and behind the eyes' glance does not exist just here and there but is a Presence existing equally everywhere' (de Chardin 1970: 79). He goes on to say that this Presence is not remote from us, but 'at every moment he awaits us in the activity, the work to be done, which every moment brings.' For de Chardin this Presence is 'at the point of my pen, my pick, my paint-brush, my needle – and my heart and my thought' (1970: 77).

This is the eternal presence of NOW. This background presence of mnemonic awareness is prior to our thoughts yet, as Les Murray writes in 'Equanimity', it is 'as attainable as gravity, it is a continuous recovering moment'. In our daily activities, most of us take the context of gravity for granted, yet its importance is beyond measure. The same can be said about the eternal presence of *Implicit-to-Implicit* exchanges, for we take these unmeasurable pulsations of Meaning for granted whenever we receive images through visual perception or make meaning through language, sign, thinking or behaviour. In the same poem Murray writes about those who miss the presence he calls equanimity: 'Pity the high madness/that misses it continually, ranging without rest between/assertion and unconsciousness.'

The rest of this chapter is taken up with some examples of how this eternal presence operates at every moment 'in the activity, the work to be done'. These are moments where *Implicit-to-Implicit* connections are evident to those who are not suffering from some high, separating madness. What I find interesting about these examples is the breadth of activity that de Chardin suggests: 'at the point of my pen, my pick, my paint-brush, my needle – and my heart and my thought' there we find intimations of *Implicit-to-Implicit* awareness and connections. It will be noted that these examples do not reiterate the many thousands of successful experiments in ESP, for these have been written about many times before. Rather, these moments tend to show how common, mundane and normal are our spiritual experiences.

* * *

If we are lucky we may become aware of the infinite and continual presence of *Implicit-to-Implicit* connections through a synchronicity. Jung coined the term 'synchronicity' to indicate a physical event that is meaningful to the individual at a particular time. A synchronicity, or what is sometimes called an 'acausal connection', occurs beyond the individual's control and involves non-personal, implicit exchanges of meaning that are highly significant to the individual. Jung's most famous story was about the time a scarab beetle, the Egyptian symbol for rebirth, tapped at the window of his surgery at the precise time his patient was telling him of a dream she had about a scarab:

> My example concerns a young woman patient who, in spite of efforts made on both sides, proved to be psychologically inaccessible. The difficulty lay in the fact that she always knew better about everything. Her excellent education had provided her with a weapon ideally suited to this purpose, namely a highly polished Cartesian rationalism with an impeccably 'geometrical' idea of reality. After several fruitless attempts to sweeten her rationalism with a somewhat more human understanding, I had to confine myself to the hope that something unexpected and irrational would turn up, something that would burst the intellectual retort into which she had sealed herself.

Well I was sitting opposite her one day, with my back to the window, listening to her flow of rhetoric. She had had an impressive dream the night before, in which someone had given her a golden scarab – a costly piece of jewelry. While she was still telling me this dream, I heard something behind me gently tapping on the window. I turned around and saw that it was a fairly large flying insect that was knocking against the windowpane from outside in the obvious effort to get into the dark room. This seemed to me very strange. I opened the window immediately and caught the insect in the air as it flew in. It was a scarabaeid beetle, or common rose-chafer (Cetonia aurata), whose gold-green colour most nearly resembles that of the golden scarab. I handed the beetle to my patient with these words, "Here is your scarab." This experience punctured the desired hole in her rationalism and broke the ice of her intellectual resistance. The treatment could now continue with satisfactory results. (Jung 1973: 109–10)

Another example of how the mnemonic resonance of *Implicit-to-Implicit* connections operates is seen in the tendency for fertile women living in close proximity to each other to synchronise their menstrual cycles. The mainstream scientific rationale for this common phenomenon is the claim that this synchronisation is due to sensory cues that come from chemicals produced in the armpits of the women. This is highly unconvincing as there are all kinds of bodily variables that could accompany this kind of synchronisation and none of them seem to indicate a causal or connecting link. In addition, if our scientific approach to this question automatically deletes the study of consciousness and meaning, there has to be only one answer left, and that is physical.

In terms of Meaning, the cause of the synchronisation of women's menstrual cycles is not to be found in the sense perception of bodily chemical reactions but is more likely to be found in the *Implicit-to-Implicit* resonance within the community mind generated by the behaviour of the group. This resonance has an implicit organisational potential that operates below the level of the conscious mind of any individual and therefore beyond the conscious control of anyone in the group. The organisational resonance of *Implicit-to-Implicit* exchanges has a bias towards harmony and interconnection and therefore towards synchronisation. Given this permanent, persistent background influence towards connection and harmony, it is little wonder that this unifying force will, in a few short months, exert an influence on the group's mind and then on the bodies of fertile women living in close proximity to each other so that their menstrual cycles are harmonised.

Implicit and intuitive knowing created by *Implicit-to-Implicit* exchanges are part of everyday life for most of us. Perhaps the earliest and most common experience of them is in the wordless and repetitive exchanges of joy and innocent love most of us have experienced between mother and child. At birth our mind is largely filled with implicit feelings, a vast intuitive field connecting us to our mother and to the background context of One Consciousness. This field of comprehension is the foundation for a set of developmental processes that gradually unfolds and transforms, and then in later life becomes a stable set of features we call character.

The first six months in an infant's life are thus a significant region of influence that affects later growth and development. This region of influence represents the implicit field of mother, child and the Self. This field is not the 'blank slate' that Thomas Aquinas and later John Locke formulated, rather it is the infinite field full of implicit exchanges that carry the primary potentials of a yet to be developed character. Although separate from each other in space, it is natural for both mother and child to form a symbiotic whole: a single unified field of implicit love and coherence.

With his psychoanalytic approach to child development, Erik Erikson called this first phase a time when the infant develops a sense of trust or mistrust. In the cognitive theory of Jean Piaget the first two years of life represent the sensory motor phase of child development (Maier 1965). In terms of Meaning the first six months in an infant's life are dominated by the mnemonic resonance of *Implicit-to-Implicit* feelings and intuitions. This structure has a natural organisational bias in favour of love, connection and dependency. We could say that trust is created when this natural bias for love is supported. Mistrust can develop when this implicit structure is unsupported. These tendencies for trust and mistrust occur because they are the natural outcomes of an already existing field of implicit interconnections involving exchanges of joy and love between mother and child.

The infant's capacity to learn during this early period results in exchanges of meaning that occur within the loving and joyful resonance of this field. These exchanges are overwhelmingly implicit, but over the first six months there will be a growing number of identifications and recognitions associated with sensory motor activity such as vocal intonations, body movements and what child psychiatrists call 'mental cueing'.

The organisation of this field of mother and child will therefore gradually change as these developments are tied to the child's increased capacity for greater levels of identification, and then of differentiation and specialisation. These developmental processes create an ever-changing balance between the child's inherent tendency for interconnection and love and its growing tendency towards autonomy associated with greater levels of specialisation and differentiation. A child's physical mastery over itself and its environment therefore rests firmly on this inherent field of implicit exchange which the child shares with its mother.

In the first six months, there are massive exchanges of meaning occurring in this field. These exchanges will largely flow from the implicit meaning of the mother, and the immediate parental environment (usually involving other parental figures), through the implicit field of One Consciousness to register as implicit understandings in the child. Some portion (depending on the family structure) of these exchanges can be negative. For example, the desires and predispositions of the mother are made from patterns of identification that are largely concealed. In addition, the mother's attitudes at times can be associated with an agitation that arises from unfulfilled desires and/or an overactive and perhaps frustrated intellect. These attitudes and responses, which inherently arise from submerged patterns, can be subliminally (implicitly) transferred across this field to the infant to affect its understanding and comprehension of the world. In this manner, an infant can take on the subliminal predispositions and attitudes of its parents without any conscious effort or thought by either parent or child.

Out of the initial structure of feeling there grows, though the seeds of sensory identification, the capacity for the child to locate itself as distinct from its mother and as somewhat physically autonomous. At around six months of age the normal infant can differentiate sufficiently so as to assertively create and recognise the boundaries of its own body image in a mirror and recognise this as distinct from its mother's image. When this level of identification and differentiation is reached, the implicit unity of the mother and child field is not broken but is instead the beginning of a more complex developmental stage. Between some mothers and children this implicit field of love is never broken and continues on permanently as a background resonance throughout life.

In Donald Winnicott's view the learning objective of the child is that it is in search of reality, not engaged in an attempt to escape from it (Phillips 1988: 68). From the viewpoint of Meaning, this is correct. The child is in search of the reality that the learning processes present, that is, finding the joy of unfolding all the implications of its growth. This discovery activity is associated with everything it experiences. The resonant field of mother and child will thus gradually transform over the years, and with that change the child's capacity to use explicit meaning will increase and become more specialised in a range of areas. Gradually the child will employ more and more complex systems of the ordinary mind such as a language and a repertoire of behaviours that can convey a diverse range of meanings. However, children differ widely in their capacity to learn, and each child will set its own pace through its ability to handle and comprehend wider areas and more complex, explicit differentiation. This means that some children will want to be kept immersed in the implicit vibrational field of mother and child for longer periods than others.

This unity of mother and child is an echo of the cosmic implicit unity we all experience at varying degrees, even though many of us will be totally unaware of it. The role of the mother in this mnemonic resonant field is that of a surrogate for the cosmic Host: the Self. The mother is the infant's host. She provides the resting and holding context in which the infant can grow and develop. This context of support is not a primary state to which we regress, as Freud suggests in his *Civilization and Its Discontents*, rather it is a secondary self-similar replication of the universal Host's support that holds all of us within a cosmic embrace in order for us to develop spiritually. The 'mother unity' is the child's initial bodily experiences of joyful wholeness: a wholeness that is created through the mother's unplanned and unintended exchanges of *Implicit-to-Implicit* meaning.

Historically, the presence of this universal field of intelligibility has at times been spoken about as the place between heaven and earth. In Plato's *Symposium* Socrates describes this particular world as populated by immaterial beings that act as the envoys and interpreters between heaven and earth; these envoys fly upwards to heaven with our prayers and worship and then descend with the heavenly answers and commandments (Voss 2011).

For William Blake, this field of intelligibility was eternity, and those beings who populate this field he called the eternals. In *The First Book of Urizen* Blake created several woodcut images that show the Eternals looking into 'this abominable Void', a reference to the philosophical themes of John Locke, who wrote at great length on the dark voidness of space and time (Raine 1968 vol. 2: 135). These mystical views of Plato and Blake have little philosophical or scientific currency today, and while the terms of this debate have changed somewhat it is interesting to note that space is no longer considered to be a void, but rather full of hidden energy, something more akin to Plato and Blake's mystical views than to the dark empiricism of John Locke.

It is also interesting to note that some of us have experienced first-hand the force and power of this intermediary, eternal domain. This happened to me when in 2012 I was trekking to the source of the holy Indian River Ganga. The Ganga is the sacred river that flows from the ice shelves of the Indian Hima-layas over two thousand kilometres into the Bay of Bengal. For most Indians Mother Ganga is no ordinary river but represents a Goddess who is said to be the vehicle of ascent from earth to heaven. My experience began with our small party of five reaching the source of the river at a place called Gaumouk. At an altitude of about four thousand metres I took off my boots, socks and trousers and bathed in the icy waters of the Ganga at the edge of the ice shelf that gives birth to this river. Bathing in this holy river is supposed to wash away one's sins, so I thought I should take up this once-in-a lifetime opportunity.

Afterwards, as the others left the glacier, I sat down to say a prayer of thanks for the trek. I began by intoning the sacred Sanskrit syllable OM three times. This is a part of my normal daily meditation practice, yet here in the valley of Gaumouk the sounds were different. They seemed to happen by themselves in an infinite universe that was here but not here, a universe in which I was not a separate being but a part of the landscape. In that moment, I felt enlarged; my being was in reverberating harmony with the environment and with all other beings. This experience of unity and interconnection happened in a dimension that was not physically locatable but was both physically here and yet not here. It was as if the background to my observing the world had suddenly become the foreground of my understanding. In spite of the fact that I meditate daily, this experience of unrestricted unity was a shock to my mind, a mind that is generally busily attuned to the material domain of everyday life. To realise the unity of the universe is a revelation, an epiphany; it is the realisation of an essential spiritual truth that cannot be denied or held in abeyance.

In a state of mindless serenity, I caught up to the others who had stopped to have a blessing from a sadhu who lived for most of the year in a small rock enclosure about a kilometre from the ice shelf of Gaumouk. While one of the party was receiving a blessing from the sadhu the rest stood around in mutual silence. I sat close by on a granite rock made smooth by the ancient work of the moving glacier, content just to be there. Then, quite suddenly, I was being pulled skyward by an attraction that felt like the force of a huge magnet. It was not the pull of someone tugging at my sleeve; it was a swirling force of attraction that I had never felt before and it was pulling not my body, even though I felt the force in my body, but my whole being. It was a sublime force of attraction on my whole being.

To actually experience Ganga's potency and heavenly Spirit was so astonishing and bewildering that I resisted – fool that I was. I thought I would die if I gave myself up to this force. The overwhelming thought that immediately came into my mind over and over was: 'I can't go, I can't die now. I have duties and responsibilities to attend to'. This extraordinary experience lasted no more than thirty seconds to a minute and left me feeling extremely disoriented and groggy. It took several kilometres of walking to regain my normal sense of being located on earth and not halfway to heaven.

A few years earlier in 2005, I had a different kind of experience of this implicit intermediary domain. It happened when my daughter Cleo and I were eating in the Western canteen of an ashram that sits on the Arabian coast of Kerala in southern India. We had been at the ashram for several days and being a vegetarian I was feeling much in need of some protein so had ordered an egg sandwich. It was lunchtime and the two of us had found a table inside the large pavilion. The building had no side or front walls and many of the local birds flew about picking up food scraps that were left or dropped on the floor. There were also two bronze eagles that presided over the other birds and sometimes they would steal food off the table while people were sitting having a meal.

Before our meal arrived, I noticed one of the eagles sitting high up on a post that supported the building. He was looking down on the diners. The bird must have been about fifteen metres (50 feet) away from our table. When my sandwich finally arrived, I was slow to pick it up, but when I did it was halfway to my mouth when the eagle struck, grabbing the sandwich with such precision that his razor-sharp claws never touched my fingers. And his wings, which stretched for almost two metres, touched neither my daughter nor me even though we were sitting only an arm's length apart. Robbed of my sandwich in a flash! It was such a shock, and afterwards, a delight, and I learned something about animal clairvoyance.

It would have been physically impossible for the eagle to take off from his perch the moment he saw me pick up the sandwich and then fly the distance in the time it took to raise the sandwich halfway to my mouth. The eagle had fantastic timing but also something else. He knew when I was going to pick it up. He read the pre-reflective 'readiness potentials' of my mind. Rupert Sheldrake notes in his book *Dogs That Know When Their Owners Are Coming Home* (2000) that animals have abilities which humans rarely use in a deliberate manner. If Sheldrake is right and dogs know when their masters are coming home then dogs know this implicitly. As dogs do not express themselves symbolically they are incapable of knowing about their masters coming home explicitly, symbolically or rationally.

Before I consciously decided to pick up my sandwich the eagle intuitively knew what I was going to do. He knew this implicitly, and knowing implicitly is a superior and faster way of knowing. *Implicit-to-Implicit* exchanges represent that universal background resonance of our ordinary minds, but perhaps not so background for dogs and eagles. The eternal presence of the mnemonic resonance of *Implicit-to-Implicit* exchanges is the unmediated and unconditional ground for all ordinary mind activity, and this is what we share with each other and with all other creatures. (A further example of *Implicit-to-Implicit* exchanges taken from neurological studies is discussed in Appendix C.)

20

Self Seeing

Self seeing is the process of becoming aware that our awareness is part of the awareness of the universe. The universe's awareness is the sight within implicit meaning – the sight within our seeing. To be aware of the sight and space of seeing is to be aware of no external thing but rather to be aware of the metaphysics of order, purpose, Meaning and our destiny, which is inherent in cosmic consciousness or what can be called the Self. For most people *Self seeing* is impossible to achieve without long practice. Fortunately, there are a whole host of helpful *Implicit-to-Implicit* steps along the way such as prayer, ritual, repetition, reflective self-alignment and meditation.

Historically in the West, *Self seeing* has been called self-knowledge. 'Know thyself' was inscribed in the forecourt of the Temple of Apollo at Delphi, which dates back to the fourth century BC. 'Know thyself' was a maxim Plato used extensively to refer to the need for philosophical wisdom. Ralph Waldo Emerson once wrote a poem called 'Know thyself' on the theme of the God within. Ramana Maharshi, the Indian spiritual leader who died in the 1950s, continually urged his disciples to pursue self-enquiry by asking 'who am I?'

In India, the phrase 'know thyself' has been widely understood to mean God realisation. In his opening speech to the 1920 International Congress of Religious Liberals in Boston,

Yogi Paramahansa Yogananda told the assembly that 'In reality, God and man are one, and the separation is only apparent' (Goldberg 2010: 113). But in the West in the last century knowing yourself, whichever way it is interpreted, has not been a favoured maxim even among those who make a living from psychology.

Behind the practices of psychoanalysis that began over a hundred years ago was the aphorism 'analyst, teach me about myself' and this was to be achieved with a therapist through the talking cure. Throughout history and in many countries, there have been a large number of voices raised urging us towards greater self-knowledge, yet in this technological age in the West we largely remain an enigma to ourselves. This is because three shadow ways of seeing makes self-knowledge the hardest knowledge of all to obtain. We have landed on the moon, found cures for a whole host of physical illnesses, created computers, robots and the Internet, yet most of us resist the path of self-enquiry.

For Freudians, the self does not exist except as a de-centred sum total of the individual's psychic activity that is represented by the functions of the id, ego and superego. While holding to the doctrine of many minds, Freud was not so much interested in the self as he was in neurosis. His method for identifying the neurotic symptom was to 'take as our starting point the contrast that distinguishes the patient from his environment' (Freud 1961: 91). I think Freud was correct in his impulse to compare the individual with his background environment. The problem was that he chose an unstable and ever-changing cultural background, which was the social norms of Freud's European community.

The only background for the individual that is stable and constant is the background of the universal One Consciousness – the Self. The benefits of this transcendent background relate to the infinite and eternal stability of the Self and to its transcultural application that relates equally to every person, whatever his or her age, colour, tribe, ethnicity or gender. In terms of Meaning, our true nature is the implicit Meaning of *satchitananda*: being, awareness and bliss. These are the characteristics of this universal field of implicit Meaning that resides everywhere: in the spaces between our thoughts; in subliminal sensory consciousness; and in the physical space we mistakenly attribute to the outside universe. These spaces are always full of implicit Meaning that provides a coherent order to the universe and to our sensory perception of it.

In *What is Life* Erwin Schrödinger wrote about how orderly life was. 'Life seems to be [the] orderly and lawful behaviour of matter, not based exclusively on its tendency to go over from order to disorder, but based partly on existing order that is kept up' (Schrödinger 1993: 68). How do we not go over into disorder but keep up the existing order? Schrödinger gives us a clue. He describes the 'astonishing gift' the organism has when it is '"drinking orderliness" from a suitable environment', and also when it is able to 'concentrate a "stream of order" on itself' (1993: 77). In other words, as organisms we maintain and can increase our internal order by 'drinking' order from the environment. What can it mean to 'drink order' from our environment?

We drink orderliness from the environment first by eating fresh fruit and vegetables and by not eating meat and potatoes that have antibiotics or pesticides in them. We drink orderliness by drinking fresh unpolluted water and not eating copious quantities of sugar, or breathing fresh air and not smog. We drink in this kind of order to keep the body healthy, but perhaps more importantly, we can also drink in the meanings of cultural order or disorder.

We drink in cultural order from empathic seeing and from being in the presence of compassionate and empathic people. We drink in disorder from anger, blame and depression and with experience of, and exchanges with, the three shadow ways of seeing: *ego, tribal and separation seeing*. If a person's life and work is mostly dominated by *ego, tribal* or *separation seeing* they will tend to spread disorder like a pervasive fog wherever they go. Unfortunately, the shadows of disorder are dominant themes in today's alienating culture where untruth is considered necessary to maintain a raft of inequalities in a society, where the celebrity ego is worshipped and where the abstractions of the economy are seen to have more legitimacy than the rights of individuals.

Within this dark culture, 'drinking orderliness' becomes a necessary therapy for most of us. Most practices undertaken to 'know thyself' are practices aimed at drinking in order, and when they are successful they are mentally and physically therapeutic. What do I mean by 'therapeutic'? In terms of Meaning, practices are therapeutic that help bring order, balance, harmony, equilibrium, homeostasis, beauty and peace to our thoughts, actions and behaviour. Practices are therapeutic if they increase relaxation, well-being and feelings of joy while reducing stress and anxiety. Therapeutic practices should also increase the coherence between the order of our thoughts and the order inherent in One Consciousness.

'Drinking order' is both therapeutically uplifting and affects both body and mind since they are partners in the life of an organism; what affects the body will also affect the mind and vice versa. We are mind-body organisms and within this dualism there is a hierarchy that begins with mind, which has primary agency, and the body comes second with its secondary forms of agency. This is the order inherent in Meaning and it is an order that is reversed whenever we award the body a primary place. When this happens, mind is immediately reduced to a secondary symptom of the body. This is the disorder inherent in a great deal of mechanical science as well as economic and commercial activity.

Healing the mind by 'drinking order' can be a complicated process because the disorder and confusion of our thoughts tend to get in the way of the healing process. Such confusion comes with strong beliefs, intense emotions, forceful doctrines, and the prosecution of dogmas or official orthodoxies. Similar impediments to reordering the mind come from the stress and anxiety of traumatic memories. When thoughts and memories are intense, high levels of anxiety, stress, fear, depression and/or paranoia usually accompany them.

The order inherent in the love of empathy represents an integrated meaning where what is thought, seen and distinguished is always contained within a more meaningful context of implicit sensibility. This is not the kind of love that comes from owning things or people and also not the love of lust and desire. These are the drinks of disorder. The order of empathy comes from drinking in compassion from spontaneous acts of kindness, generosity and reciprocity. The word 'order' is sometimes used by public officials to suppress or repress political expressions that are critical of the ruling establishment. Such an ordering does not produce the long-term order of compassion but is more likely to produce short-term social disorder.

The order of love has several layers of feelings, predispositions, pre-conscious autonomic responses and the implicitness of One Consciousness. In terms of brainwaves the order within love involves the ability of an individual to use the whole range of brainwaves from 0 to 50 Hz without being fixed into the grooves of any one bandwidth (see Appendix A). In contrast, contemporary cultural predispositions tend to mandate thinking processes within the *beta* band of 22–38 Hz. In this bandwidth, we replay the well-worn tracks of familiar, fixed narratives that have us overvaluing those distinctions and differences associated with commonsense justifications for not changing our behaviour, or citing official doctrines and orthodoxies against change. These are the hallmarks of separation seeing.

The difficulty of a therapy based upon 'the talking cure', that is, a practice that involves *beta* brainwaves in the 22–38 bandwidths, is that it is difficult to find a release in the client from their prison house of language simply by using language itself. Like the overintellectual patient in Jung's example of synchronicity, there are a million ways we can invent to justify why we should not go beyond logical discussion. The impetus needed to break out of this language prison house is the kind of irrational shock that Jung's client received with the beetle that resembled the golden scarab (Chapter 19).

However, the problem of language when used as a therapeutic tool is not, I suggest, in the content of what is said, but in the level of intensity of the thoughts and feelings contained within the language used. This is to say that thoughts and feelings have various levels of intensity, in the same way that brainwaves have different frequencies. The thoughts that are most intense are those that rest on hidden identification patterns of which we are unaware. Thoughts that are least intense rest on known contexts. Hence it is a normal transformation that as we grow older and become more mature our thoughts and memories of an earlier time are often drained of some of their intensity. Growing older we may find that we have become overfamiliar with our earlier patterns of understanding and now see that they do not work as well as previously. In this neutral state, these thoughts become what they actually are, secondary representations containing less value.

When thoughts and memories are recognised as shadowy veils and not as the pillars that hold up our identity, we can develop the capacity to intuit the concealed outlines of the Self. By having thoughts and memories that are open and qualified we can make many mistakes and hence we are already on the open road to learning new ways, new thoughts and new behaviour.

There are at least four conditions in which our thoughts will not stand in the way of drinking in the order of love from our environment. These are when thoughts and memories

   i.   have a broad perspective

   ii. contain a clear gestalt structure where explicit details are always modified by their implicit background contexts

iii. are of low intensity, that is, we recognise them as secondary maps of other more meaningful realities

iv. have an order that copies the natural order of Meaning.

When these four conditions are put into practice they produce a loving, ordered and balanced state of mind in which happiness is not a foreign territory and the path to realising our true
nature appears before us. The problem is that by just reading
about these conditions very few can actually put them into practice. We cannot do it because almost everyone has a long history
of developing predispositions that will disorganise us and put
our mind in opposition to these four conditions.

What are the practices that can go some way to assist drinking in love from the environment? By necessity they will have to
be open, integrating and balancing practices that can reinforce
the natural variety of meaning that flows back and forth within
the trinity of 'I', 'us' and 'That'. This is the approach to healing
the mind by working with the body to enhance and stimulate
the senses and by these methods to stimulate the implicit nature
of One Consciousness. How this is achieved relates to the general aim of the exercise. The therapeutic aim when addressing
the implicit nature of One Consciousness is to establish balance
between form and context; or, I could say, between detail and
overview; or the present moment and persistent thoughts; or
sensory perception and conception. All of these different terms
refer to essentially the same set of meaning-making processes,
which I will refer to as the ordered balance between heart and
mind.

This means that any therapeutic balance within the conscious
mind requires not a focus on the intellect or cogitative processes
or even rational dialogue and more accurate and informed
thinking. Rather, a therapeutic and ordered balance will be
one that comes from a greater stimulation of the senses. Direct

mechanical stimulation from devices like the PoNS machine does not overload the senses with anxiety but instead produces a calm and peaceful sensation (see Appendix C). This balance represents a 'vertical' balance between sensory stimulation and thinking; in terms of visual perception that means a balance between signifier and signified: sensing the world and thinking about it. This vertical balance is distinct from the 'horizontal' relationships that come from thinking about thinking or speaking about thinking or past actions.

In studying sensory processes, we see that they operate implicitly below the level of explicit and deliberate thought and through the autonomic systems of the body. In neuroscience, a distinction is often made here between the brain and the mind, and this is usually seen as the vertical separation between the brain's lower subcortical areas and its higher cortical functions. Within this model the brain's cortical functions are said to produce conscious and wilful decisions and choices, while the subcortical areas involve autonomic brain and nervous system functions. In the vocabulary of neuroscience these non-conscious, sensory autonomic functions of the nervous system are classified as brain functions. In effect, this classification by neuroscience makes use of a materialistic order in that it awards agency to the brain and then reduces the mind to a secondary symptom of the brain.

In contrast to this kind of *separation seeing* and in terms of Meaning, every sensory and autonomic system of the body functions as part of the mind. Both the sympathetic (fight-or-flight system) as well as the parasympathetic (rest-digest-repair system) have predictable and ordered mind operations that function implicitly below the level of the conscious and deliberate mind. These systems are concealed from the conscious mind but that does not make them physical; rather this concealment means these mind operations are implicit and subliminal and very much part of the foundation state out of which the conscious and explicit mind arises. It is simply a traditional habit of *separation seeing* that limits the human mind to its explicit operations, conventionally seen to be produced by higher cortical functions. As I have argued, this materialistic view is inadequate to explain visual perception or sensory processing.

Studying visual perception, we find that implicit and autonomic processes have produced the images we know as the environment. These images are signifiers for they carry the meanings of the immediate environment and they are produced without our conscious consent, explicit control or effort. The relationship of these uncontrolled signifiers to controlled conscious thought represents the relationship of signifier to signifieds. This dualist relationship is not binary or separate. As stated earlier, this is a unified and symmetrical relationship within the sign structure; in other words, the symmetric logic of the sign.

Returning to the balance of senses and thoughts, when thoughts, memories or theories are intense, obsessional and/or habitual and they occur over long periods they are often accompanied by anxiety, stress, anger, fear, depression or paranoia; intense thoughts closely held usually produce negative effects. This coincidence suggests that intense, habitual and obsessional thoughts tend to produce an imbalance between perception and conception by drawing energy away from sensory and perceptual processes while intensifying the energy around cognitive and conceptual processes. This vertical imbalance is like the imbalances created by severe sensory deprivation in that both produce unbalanced judgments and thinking that is detrimental to the individual's wellbeing. In addition, this kind of imbalance between perception and conception reverses the order inherent in Meaning and in doing so puts us at war with ourselves.

The therapeutic practice needed to help reverse the imbalance created by intensely held thoughts, memories or theories will thus have a focus on sensory and intuitive processes. A range of practices can achieve this rebalancing without attempting in any way to change the content of these thoughts, memories or theories. The aim of such practices is to realign the energetic intensity of both sensory sensations (signifiers) with conceptual thought (signifieds) so that there is a flowing balance involving both. In theoretical terms this is the gestalt balance between foreground constituents within the conscious mind and the background implicit contexts in which these details arise. When this gestalt is out of balance the implicit and sensory background context is always discarded.

My experience with such rebalancing practices dates from the early 1960s when I worked as a psychological counsellor in clinics in Sydney and Melbourne. These clinics were unusual at the time and would be so today if they existed. In those clinics counselling involved applying a range of repetitive techniques that were aimed at continually bringing the attention of the client back to the present moment over some extended period, often for an hour. This approach was very different from psychoanalysis, where clients are supposed to understand the 'right' psychological interpretation of their personal narratives. We were not much concerned with the content of personal narratives as with reducing the influence and intensity of them.

To give one example drawn from a number of years with hundreds of clients, I recall a young woman who had for many years suffered from anorexia nervosa and who when she saw me on this particular day was experiencing an intense panic attack. I sat her down in a chair, sat beside her and took her had in mine for a short moment and said, 'thank you'. Putting her hand down again I then repeated the process over and over for approximately forty minutes. At the end of this time the anxiety of the panic attack had subsided and she was in a more buoyant frame of mind. One session with this process did not cure her long-term tendency for panic attacks or her anorexia, but it was a non-toxic, learning process that had no side effects and could be repeated at any time with similar results.

Any repetitive practices that continually bring the client's attention back to the present moment automatically produce *Implicit-to-Implicit* exchanges. These exchanges occur, to some degree, with any repetitive learning actions, but when the repetitions involve some socially acceptable physical (sensory) contact that is focused on the present moment (visual perception) and are also accompanied by an empathic person, then together these largely implicit features produce a resonant climate in which it becomes possible for the client to begin to tune into the mnemonic foundation resonances of her own mind. When this happens the individual feels relief, an absence of anxiety and some equanimity. While it may take years for most people to directly and fully appreciate the subtle depth and fecundity of their astonishing implicit mind, any tuning in to it for even a short time has some beneficial and healing effects. This happens even when the idea of a holographic Self is totally unrecognised by the client.

I am reminded that within the Indian philosophy of Advaita Vedanta there are four yoga paths that can lead one to realise the true nature of the Self. These four paths have the same overall therapeutic objective as the psychological counselling I used to balance heart and head. These four paths are i) Karma yoga, which is the yoga of action involving selfless practices and the surrender of the fruits of one's action to the Self; ii) Bhakti yoga, which is the path of love, devotion, prayer, worship and formal rituals; iii) Raja yoga, which involves mainly meditation practices; and iv) Jnana yoga, which is concerned with the intellectual enquiry into one's own nature. While these four paths emphasise different types of practices, each is essentially a spiritual path and is thus concerned with the importance of the Implicit Self. In addition, each of these paths works in ways that reduce the intensity of thoughts, memories and orthodoxies by restoring and stimulating sensory and implicit connections with the Self.

In my experience, mantra meditation can reduce the intensity of thinking in subtle ways. Not everyone can or should undertake mantra meditation, but for those who are able it is both highly efficient and beneficial. Meditation brings order to the scattered and disordered mind with a one-pointed focus on an object such as the breath or a mantra. The key to meditation is repetition because repetition creates *Implicit-to-Implicit* exchanges, which are the non-conscious exchanges within the implicit foundations of the mind that are so important for all learning. Most people find doing a repetitive job boring, yet repetition is the key to learning the piano, or tennis, or anything else for that matter, and it is certainly the key to learning the depths of the Self.

While meditating the mind will naturally wander onto something that worries or fascinates it. The wandering or scattered mind is full of ideas, concepts and memories, and these have a force and level of intensity that creates those circular obsessional habits of thinking that are associated with stress, fear and anxiety. The focus on an object through repetitive actions establishes beneficial conditions whereby an individual will in time become aware of thoughts as distractions and so be able to return to the object of meditation. The wandering mind is not a failure of meditation; rather, it is the actual process that reduces the intensity and force of thoughts, thereby healing the mind.

A final word about that great and noble enterprise, *Self-seeing*. Perhaps it is the most difficult enterprise anyone can ever undertake. The Self is both local and universal: the seer and the seen. This is the holographic Self and it emerges from a holographic seeing. The wise say that Self-seeing is a state of everything and nothing: a feeling of unity with everything and the realisation that we are nothing separate. Whatever path we consciously take and whatever practices we use, this journey into the luminous heart of the Self will eventually be undertaken by every human being and each of us will end in the same place, which is the loving, meaningful bliss of One Consciousness.

Appendix A

Brainwaves

The measurement of brainwaves was not the focus of this book, but the periodic rhythms of brainwaves do have some interesting correlations with the five-step cycle of Meaning described in Chapters 4 and 11. Brainwaves are typically measured by placing sensors on the scalp and recording the synchronised electrical impulses from brain cells (neurons) with a machine called an electroencephalograph (EEG). These waves or rhythms are measured in cycles per second (Hertz) in four to six wave patterns: *Infra-low, delta, theta, alpha, beta* and *gamma*.[19]

The causal relationship between brainwaves and Meaning is not a simple directional-linear movement but rather, this relationship is circular and in two directions: Meaning to physical, and physical to Meaning. Hence brain damage in the form of disease, strokes, accidents or neurological changes due to drugs directly affect the functions of meaning-making (mind). However, the underlying order of this circular relationship is always hierarchical in that Meaning provides the causal foundation for normal brainwave changes. In other words, the transformations of Meaning produce change in brainwaves (electrical impulses per second). Thus brainwaves are caused by the kind of meaning that is being made, so brainwaves change their frequency according to what we are doing, thinking, feeling and learning. Learning is a set of processes that change our meaning-making and is therefore an important factor in changing brainwaves. The five steps within the learning cycle (0, 1, 2, 3, 0) are important factors in what some neurologists have called 'neuroplasticity'.

The conventional interpretation of brainwaves comes from a belief in the doctrine of many minds and as a consequence these waves are usually thought of as measurements from that isolated and private world of the individual. From the holographic point of view, the private world of the individual is an illusion. Instead, to a larger or lesser degree, what brainwaves measure are the vibrational effects of mind interacting with One Consciousness on the brain. In all holographic systems the whole inheres within every part. As the brain is a part of the whole universe it can never be fully understood when seen as a separate entity divorced from the rest of the functions of the universal system.

In addition, as the brain and nervous system are made of the same physical stuff as the rest of the universe, the brain's rhythms represent a feature of the universe's vibrations, and in the same way the individual's mind is part of the larger mind of One Consciousness. These two categories of 'One Consciousness' and 'mind' represent Bohm's categories of the implicate and explicate orders and their complex interrelationship is contained within the five transformations detailed described in Chapter 4 as 0, 1, 2, 3, 0.

Given this complex interconnection of Implicit Meaning with mind (implicit and explicit meaning), we should expect to see some of the fingerprints of this relationship in the various bandwidths of brainwaves.

The six bandwidths of brainwaves and their associated functions are described as follows:

Infra-low (<.1 – .5 Hz)	slow mysterious rhythms that appear to be linked to nervous system coordination
Delta waves (0.5 – 3 Hz)	very slow cycles produced by deep meditation and dreamless sleep

Theta waves (3 – 8 Hz)	produced by twilight states where we drift in and out of sleep
Alpha waves (8 – 12 Hz)	occur with quiet flowing thoughts
Beta waves (12 – 38 Hz)	produced when we are alert, attentive and engaged in problem-solving
Gamma waves (38 – 42 Hz)	produced by a sense of universal love, altruism and feelings of spiritual enlargement.

How do these six brainwaves correlate with the five-step cycle of Meaning? I will begin with a description of *Implicit-to-Implicit* exchanges.

0 – Implicit to Implicit – no brainwaves – 0 – .1 Hz.

Implicit-to-Implicit exchange patterns can be understood as a set of implicit relationships that are self-connecting. The term 'relationship' is an interesting one because it raises the question, 'what is a relationship? As these *Implicit-to-Implicit* exchanges contain an intrinsic awareness we can say that they will have the vital agency of Meaning and as such they represent the eternal patterns of intelligibility: the intelligence of One Consciousness.

Hence, *Implicit-to-Implicit* relations represent an eternal and infinite field of intelligibility that cannot be measured. Implicit relations cannot be measured because they are empty; empty of any explicit object like a cycle or a rhythm. In the sense of being empty, both implicit and explicit relations of Meaning are quintessentially metaphysical or, I can say, they exist prior to the physical vibrations of brainwaves and, in addition, prior to physical objects of perception and symbolic forms of measurement. Relations have no mass and no measurable energy; they are entirely metaphysical and they stand as the universal mental forces of mind and consciousness and they are represented in terms of brainwaves as: 0 - Hz.

In essence, all relations have holographic properties because they represent the basic units as well as the whole of consciousness. It is impossible for scientists not to mention or specify some relations in their work in medicine, physics, neuroscience, biology, chemistry, mathematics or cosmology, and by so doing they necessarily introduce some metaphysical quality into their focus on physical objects. We can say that relations are the fingerprints of consciousness in the universe. Scientists have the option to accept relations as the evidence of one holographic consciousness in their work or to simply ignore it, which is the usual response.

In contrast to the unmeasurable *Implicit-to-Implicit* world of One Consciousness, for the individual a highly diverse environment filled with moving objects, (Bohm's explicit order) slowly begins to come into existence. This is the second of the exchange patterns of Meaning where there is a transformation from *Implicit-to-explicit* meaning.

1. Implicit to explicit (conscious mind arising) <.1–8 Hz

The three bandwidths that measure between <.1 and 8 Hz reflect two functions of the conscious mind: i) a slow arising from its foundation of Implicit Meaning; and ii) its ability to suspend external awareness and dive deeply into the Implicitness of One Consciousness through meditative and empathetic practices.

In regard to the conscious mind slowly arising from Implicit Meaning, it comes into existence at around 8 Hz when there is sufficient explicit meaning to construct its complexity. Within the three measurement bands of *infra-low*, *delta* and *theta* the number of vibrations gradually increase (from <.1 to 8 Hz), and this increase in the number of vibrations (cycles per second) is a reflection of the underlying and increasing number of explicit differences and distinctions that have arisen from the Implicit background of One Consciousness. Explicit differences and distinctions represent the meaning content of the conscious mind. Yet within this range (<.1–8 Hz) there is a yet 'un-risen' conscious mind which means that it is not fully active or 'here'.

Within the first of these three bandwidths, *infra-low* (<.1–.5 Hz) the vibrations are slow and difficult to detect and measure. They are sometimes known as Slow Cortical Potentials. The mind at this level is mostly a non-conscious awareness. This general state of implicitness is not 'unconsciousness' in the sense of repressed desires, but simply a non-conscious state below the level of fear, desire or perception. The slow brainwave vibrations tell us that there are few explicit distinctions being created within the underpinning level of mind. Hence the conscious mind cannot yet be constructed because there are not enough intense distinctions (reflected in the kind of vibrations) occurring. In terms of brainwaves (<.1–.5 Hz), neuroscientists know very little about them except that they appear to be related to the important organising roles of timing, modulation and coordination within the nervous system. These are some of the functions of the autonomic nervous system.

In the next band of brainwaves, *delta* (.5–3 Hz), the number of vibrations slowly increases. These slow, loud vibrations are reported to be like a deeply penetrating drumbeat within the nervous system. The autonomic systems of the body also function within this band of brainwaves, in particular the parasympathetic nervous system that produces the healing, regeneration and restoration of body and mind. Within this bandwidth is the state of mind that occurs mostly in dreamless sleep. Those who have long experience in meditative practices may be able to reach this deep, penetrating state of mind through meditation. However, in terms of the conscious mind arising from its foundation of Implicit Meaning, within this bandwidth the conscious mind still does not exist as the number of explicit distinctions (vibrations) that occur around 3 Hz are not enough to produce the complexity of an awakened conscious mind.

Within the next bandwidth of *theta* (3–8 Hz) the conscious mind begins to stir through dreams, nightmares, fears and imagery. This is the twilight state that we often experience as we drift in and out of sleep. This is the state of mind that spans the borders between the Implicit, autonomic functions of the nervous system and our conscious and deliberate intentions. The mental state of this bandwidth can also occur when we perform some task that is automatic, or nearly so, like dressing, driving a car, or washing ourselves. In this state, our sense perception of the external world is not alert and our conscious mind, such as it is, is not fully active and attentive but is mostly dealing with sensations and feelings and often with fears or intuitions. The *theta* world can be understood as the world of ego illusion; of underworld figures where fears, troubled histories and feeling of guilt are usually kept locked away and defended. These non-conscious stirrings are the knots of meaning that create our predispositions towards ourselves and the world, and which in turn influence our conscious and logical decisions.

2. explicit to explicit (deliberative acts) 8–38 Hz

The conscious mind finally arises within the next bandwidth of *alpha* waves (8–12 Hz). *Alpha* waves are recorded mostly in conjunction with quiet flowing thoughts and meditative states when the eyes are closed. In this state, the conscious mind is awake, at rest, integrated and calm. *Alpha* waves are reduced when the cycles per second go up or down. This happens when the eyes are opened and faster *beta* waves take over. *Alpha* waves are also reduced when the individual is drowsy or when they are meditating, and then the cycles per second reduces.

The calm alertness of the conscious mind within the *alpha* bandwidth (8–12 Hz) also provides a fertile ground for learning, which is a set of processes that needs open and contextual meaning-making exchanges. I have referred to these kinds of exchanges as *explicit-to-Implicit*. Such exchanges are associated with feelings of empathy, love and compassion. Within the *alpha* band the *explicit-to-explicit* exchanges of meaning (exchanges that have created the conscious mind) appear to be influenced by an open and calming underlay that is typical of *explicit-to-Implicit* empathetic exchanges.

This mental underlay of implicitness represents the foundations of the conscious mind, which is the implicitness of One Consciousness. As *theta* waves are largely produced from exchanges of implicit meaning it is understandable that this implicit influence will continue on into the next *alpha* bandwidth.

However, while the transformations of Meaning as outlined in Chapter 4 follow a particular order (0, 1, 2, 3, 0), this is not a simple linear order. Rather, these numbers indicate a series of transformations within a permanent background ocean of Implicitness (0). This means that every set of transformations 1, 2, and 3 will take place within the context of 0: Implicit Meaning. Hence within the calmness of the *alpha* mind the implicit background context will be highly influential.

The next bandwidth produced by *explicit-to-explicit* exchanges of meaning is the *beta* waves of 12–38 Hz. This large bandwidth can be subdivided into three sub-bands: *beta* 1: 12–15 Hz; *beta* 2: 15–22 Hz; and *beta* 3: 22–38 Hz. All beta waves are produced by an awake, conscious mind and the three sub-bands within this bandwidth of 12–38 Hz reflect changes going on within the conscious mind.

When we open our eyes, there is an increase in frequency of brainwaves. Why this is so has puzzled researchers for many years. The conventional neuroscience approach is to largely ignore mental aspects when studying the brain. This approach has led to the mystery of why when we open our eyes brainwaves change from *alpha* to *beta*. However, this puzzle is solved when we understand that underlying changes of Meaning have produced the changes in brainwaves.

When we open our eyes the processes of visual perception begin to operate and the mind is suddenly flooded with differences and distinctions of perceptual Meaning. These relate to the awareness of space and the distinctions of light intensity, forms, colours and tones. This inflow suddenly increases the number of distinctions and differences of Meaning and as a result there is a corresponding increase in the number of brainwave cycles per second. This change from *alpha* to *beta* simply reflects what is happening within the conscious mind of the individual when the eyes are opened.

Within the *beta* 1 sub-band of 12–15 Hz the individual is thus awake and the environment is being perceived. In a quiet and slow-running manner the five senses begin to apprehend the suchness of the environment NOW. In this state, the conscious mind is involved in a kind of musing without commitment to a particular set of concepts, vocabulary or interpretation of what is seen. This is a healthy state of mind

In this sub-band of 12–15 Hz the visual perceptions of the physical world involving space, movement, objects and colours arise not through an individual's creative abilities or their intended purposes, or even through their imagination. Each of these possibilities is implied when we separate the observer from the observed and rely on the misleading doctrine of many minds. Rather, the physical world, which includes the measurements of brainwaves, arises within the processes of normal sensory perception at about sub-band *beta* 1. This means that both the physical world and sensory perceptions arise together as the result of the natural ordering potentials of One Consciousness, and this happens when it transforms itself from its primary state of Implicitness into the secondary *explicit-to-explicit* meanings of visual perception.

However, if we interpret the statement that the physical world arises simultaneously with visual sensory perception from the standpoint of many minds we will soon be arguing about trees that fall in the forest when no one is there to observe them. This traditional criticism of the proposal that the world arises in observation is premised on the belief in an independent physical world that is separate from local, subjective minds.

The sub-band of *beta* 2: 15–22 Hz is produced by a conscious mind involved with interpreting what it is that is seen. In other words, these are the exchange patterns mainly related to human conceptual thinking (signifieds) and this involves the use of language and symbols. Abstract symbols can be called language, mathematics, money and a range of other terms. But language and symbols are not innocent or neutral mediums. (see Appendix B).

The use of symbols falls into two broad categories of understanding: light seeing and shadow seeing. Light seeing creates integrated and holistic conceptual systems where abstract symbolic representations are anchored into the territory they seek to map. This is the kind of conceptual work that values background contexts while placing foreground distinctions and differences within those contexts as integrated features. Social and historical narratives along with empathic discourses produce this kind of mix and this kind of integrated thinking appears to produce the sub-band of *beta* 2.

The high number of cycles per second within *beta* 3: 22–38 Hz is caused by very complex, abstract thought along with high levels of anxiety and/or excitement. This kind of conceptual work produces what in this book is called the shadows of separation seeing. Separation seeing occurs when the marks of explicit meaning (the differences of *explicit-to-explicit* exchanges) are over-valued to the degree that they become separations or divisions in thinking and seeing. It is only within this narrow band of brainwaves (*beta* 3: 22–38 Hz) that the hallowed ground of Reason (with a capital R) is produced. We can note that separation seeing represents the darkness of the shadows of Plato's cave.

3. explicit to Implicit: empathy – low and high Hz

The enfoldment of explicit meaning into Implicit Meaning is a function of the conscious mind when it is in the mode of empathy. Empathy involves love and compassion and the possibility of a transcendent self-understanding. These feelings arise from meaning exchange where the connections of implicit meaning have become primary and dominant and where explicit meaning in the form of differences and distinctions has a secondary or derivative role. Empathy is a mode of thought that integrates these distinctions and differences of meaning into larger contextual frameworks or wholes.

This kind of mental work, with its emphasis on Implicit Meaning, is seen in a variety of brainwave bandwidths. For example, within *delta* brainwaves there is an emphasis on Implicit Meaning that incorporates a range of explicit distinctions (vibrations) as secondary contextual features. This is exactly the combination of Meaning exchanges that produces feelings of empathy. Empathy thus is one of the mental factors that can produce *delta* brainwaves.

The other bandwidth where we can find empathy is within the *alpha* wave. I have already referred to the *alpha* band were the *explicit-to-explicit* exchanges of meaning are influenced by an open and calming underlay that is typical of *explicit-to-Implicit* empathic exchanges. Here the empathic mind produces *alpha* brainwaves. Finally, empathy is a major factor in producing *gamma* brainwaves of 38–42 Hz.

Gamma waves are the fastest brainwaves and thus have the

highest frequency (like a flute). Neuroscientists believe that *gamma* brainwaves relate to a set of synthesising processes involving a wide range of brain areas. But these brainwaves are a mystery to neuroscientists because their frequency is above the possibilities of normal neuronal activity, which means that they must be caused by factors that are not physical. *Gamma* waves relate to peak performances, lucid dreaming and expansion of the mind, and have been recorded during mystical, spiritual and transpersonal experiences.

Synthesising meaning is a complex process; a great deal of meaning is made very quickly by synthesising the distinctions (vibrations) that come from many areas of the brain. Synthesised meaning is empathic meaning; it is the meaning of the big picture, of the broader perspective, the far horizon and the spiritual experience. This is the kind of meaning-making in which we accept that we are our brother and sister's keeper. In terms of implicit and explicit meaning, this is the exchange combination where details and distinctions take a back seat to the broader holographic context that involves us.

When our thinking and seeing is dominated by *explicit-to-Implicit* exchanges we will have the freedom to think and see ourselves as essential and integrated features of the whole cosmic fabric. The freedom we have with integrated seeing expresses itself intuitively and empathically in a process whereby individuals accept being part of the politics of eternity, an evolving and learning cycle that involves their own development and maturation. This freedom is associated with feelings of joy, happiness, bliss and a sense of a transcendent self-awareness.

I want to reiterate that the five movements within the singular domain of One Consciousness, 0, 1, 2, 3, 0, give us an understanding of the natural, coherent order of the universe; a teleology that is at work within every part of the universe. This discussion of the correlations between the movements of One Consciousness and brainwaves may need further refinement with further research. However, those refinements will only come from researchers who are able see in an integrated and holistic manner. They will not come from separation seeing; from neuroscientists who believe in the doctrine of many minds, or who think that minds are the by-products of brains.

The coherent politics of One Consciousness (0) has local and secondary features (1, 2, 3) that constructs the local conscious mind of individuals and produces a range of brainwave bandwidths. Given that these five movements of Meaning (0, 1, 2, 3, 0) are also closely associated with patterns of learning and maturation, the primary purpose of One Consciousness appears to be something like cosmic self-revelation.

Appendix B

Language

I want to discuss some of the internal contradictions of language. The more proficient we become at using the differences (*explicit-to-explicit* exchanges) of language the more capable is the intellect. Yet proficiency in using the symbols of language or mathematics does not necessarily mean that the meanings we make will mirror the actual structures of language we use, or resonate with the internal order inherent in Meaning. For that to occur we need to have some appreciation of the nature of language.

Every symbol we use has a relative agency in that the meanings it carries are simultaneously both hidden and revealed. This contradictory function comes into operation whenever we speak, write, use symbols to communicate or build imaginary castles in the sky. The existence of this paradox tells us that in every expression, measurement or signal we communicate, something is revealed, while at the same time some accompanying meaning is hidden.

This contradictory agency of language makes it impossible to express a concise, clear, logical and certain statement without ambiguity or uncertainty. In other words, every statement will always be provisional and thus contain ambiguities and uncertainties. This is the case even for the axiomatic statements of science, mathematics or logic. The failure of language generally to produce a totally closed and certain system is due to its representational status and role. Symbols have a reality that is secondary and derivative because they are always representatives of something else. Like a democratically elected parliamentary representative, symbols are stand-ins for a broader and deeper constituency. Hence symbols have a pointing role that directs our attention to events beyond the symbolic. The only time this is not the case is when we use language to point at itself (as I am doing here).

As a consequence of this paradox, all discourse, every piece of data, measurement, logical conclusion or story will be provisional and open to the vagaries of different interpretations, as well to cultural changes and emphasis. Open-ended uncertainty is, therefore, the reality of all language and all symbols. And I might add that the acceptance of uncertainty is the basis of humility. For the scientist who disagrees and says that the periodic table has complete certainty and represents a set of axiomatic truths, one may reply that science is never finalised and that even the periodic table is provisional as it contains the possibility of further modification.

Most of us in our daily life, however, choose to ignore how the discourses we use simultaneously reveal as well as conceal meaning. A common attitude towards language is to treat it as if it were a simple reflection in a mirror, or sometimes even to see language as having no agency at all, as if it were neutral in respect to the way we express ourselves, or how our mind works, or how the world is.

Such trust leads to a sense of pride that comes with the illusion of certainty. This happens because we believe in the truth of the single meaning. Whenever we want to create the illusion of certainty we resort to the use of the single meaning, which is created by a closed and seemingly unambiguous statement. Such statements are especially addictive to the ego. The illusion of certainty generated by closed statements represents what

William Blake called the sleep of single vision: the outward signs of ignorance, arrogance or pride:

> *Now I a fourfold vision see*
> *And a fourfold vision is given to me*
> *Tis fourfold in my supreme delight*
> *And three-fold in soft Beulah's night*
> *And twofold Always.*
> *May God us keep*
> *From single vision & Newton's sleep.*

To reinterpret Blake's verse in terms of Meaning, I assume that his fourfold vision represents the kind of seeing we have in an epiphany where the universe is experienced as one interconnected whole. The threefold vision can be understood as the everyday unreflected view we have of a three-dimensional spatial world about us. 'Twofold' is always the beginning of the problems of separation seeing and this happens with binary oppositions that split and separate. Finally, Blake reserves his most damning criticism for the single, literal vision of Newtonian science.

The sleep of the single meaning comes from literal and surface understandings, or from the rendering of a text – whether scientific, religious, ethnic, commercial or monetary – in such a manner as to delete its implicit contexts. Statements that hide their contexts do not focus on revealing meaning; instead they increase the concealment of meaning. In other words, the categorical imperative, the rhetorical oration or the axiomatic statement operate in a manner that hides more meanings than they reveal. In order to reveal meanings, we have to include those implicit contexts so they are at least part of the larger picture, with a gestalt relationship clearly operating between the discrete foreground details of discourse and their implicit background contexts.

Yet if all this sounds too hard and we decide to ignore the traps of language we will end up being dominated by them; that is, we will unintentionally give the language of someone else control over our thoughts. This is also the case for technology, for technology represents a symbolic tool that has been created through the representations of measurement and computation. If we become dominated by someone else's language our thought patterns will become rigid and fixed, so much so that at times it will appear as if we are asleep in a prison-house of the status quo.

When we are out of tune with the reality of language and of Meaning we can easily be lulled by spin, influenced by rhetoric or advertising, or swayed by the authoritative voice of some orthodoxy. To be out of tune with the structure of language is to believe in a single or twofold vision; that it is possible for language to have a single meaning, or that the physical world is separate from us. When we see the world through these kinds of glasses it becomes very limited and narrow. In the words of the Zen Master Yoka Daishi (665–713), we should not belittle the sky by looking through a pipe.

Perhaps a productive way to discuss the paradox of language is through the use of metaphor. Here language can be seen to be like a house. In this contemporary globalised world education is generally thought of as necessary. I agree with this, so we could say that everyone should become literate and be able to live in the house of language and use this abstract level of mind with some proficiency. If we live illiterate lives by being only a visitor to the house of language then most likely we will suffer from the harsh weather conditions of an inhospitable social climate as well from as a lack of individual fulfilment.

On the other hand, if we become fascinated by the differential wonders of sign, symbol or financial token we may find we are unable to move outside this house. If this happens, the symbols we use will use us, and in this manner they will become our prison-house. In the prison-house of language there are few clear views beyond the stress and tension provided by mountains of abstract differences. Without the courage to challenge the trust we gave to the single meaning of money, or black-letter rules, norms and orthodoxies, the shadows of this prison-house close in upon us.

Thus it is essential for our well-being to come and go freely from the house of language whenever we wish. But how are we to leave? We do not leave by simply denying that this level of mind exists or that it has no force. This is the ploy used by materialists who simply delete any reference to language, mind or meaning in their investigations. Yet living in rags in a cave or taking a vow of silence in a monastery does not guarantee an escape from the prison-house of language. Such practices offer a range of practical spiritual benefits but do not always lead to an escape from our domination by language and thought.

Rather, my preferred method is to leave this house through the doorways offered to us by knowing something about the role and status of language. This means having the receptive ability to read sub-text, context, metaphor, irony and parable. These are the practical multi-meaning passports to a freedom of empathy beyond the self-enclosed walls of pride and the single or binary vision. These are the escape passages that can lead into the light of a larger and perhaps fourfold vision, a vision that comes from the non-symbolic depths of Meaning.

Metaphors are used to express a depth of meaning. A depth of meaning also implies multi-levels of mind. We therefore need to employ a depth of meaning in order to escape from the prison-house of the single meaning. One current example is to use the metaphor of a cartographer's toolbox to speak about symbols. A cartographer is a mapmaker and in this sense, we are all cartographers, for symbols are a map-making (representational) mode of thought. Symbols provide us with maps of, and for, other territories. Map-making is itself a metaphor that highlights the important distinction between signifier and signified, that is, between the given images of the environment and our constructed interpretations of the seen.

There can be many maps of the same territory and usually the more maps the more meaning that is revealed. This suggests that no single map is ever complete, unconditional or has an absolute and closed value. Maps are always works-in-progress. Even the axiomatic and factual maps of science that deal with particles, atoms or molecules represent maps that are incomplete and open to continual reinterpretation. This also applies to the sacred maps of Holy Scripture and to the 'word of God', for such scriptures and words have to be read and then understood by ordinary fallible minds. Hence the truths we create by using language and symbols cannot ever be anything other than interim, provisional and incomplete.

Appendix C

Brain Studies

I want to add some comments to Chapter 19 regarding the Implicit presence of One Consciousness with an example taken from brain studies. The language of this example is a long way from those used in Chapter 19 and the philosophy of Advaita Vedanta, Mother Ganga, eagles or dogs. However, while neurological experiments are normally framed within a technical language and an objective (separating) perspective and do not include any reference to consciousness, the results are always open to interpretations, specifically in terms of *Implicit-to-Implicit* exchanges.

To introduce this neurological example, I use a quotation from Thomas Merton's *Zen and the Birds of Appetite*. These lines are from a dialogue with D.T. Suzuki and Merton and they come specifically from Suzuki.

'A Zen Master was once asked: What is Tao? (We may take Tao as meaning the ultimate truth or reality).
A: It is one's everyday mind.
Q: What is one's everyday mind?
A: When tired you sleep, when hungry you eat' (Merton 1968: 134).

The largest proportion of our everyday mind involves the hidden functions of the autonomic nervous system. This is the mind I want to discuss and the example comes from some new developments in sensory technology. The extraordinary results that have been reported draw our attention to the powerful and beneficial effects that can result from simple sensory stimulation of the tongue. This is an important example of the everyday mind and how its implicit consciousness orders and organises the autonomic functions of the body. It also tells us that these ordering functions of consciousness are not fixed but can be improved in those people who have some form of brain damage or nervous system disorder. Improving mental functions by physical means should be no surprise to anyone who exercises for health and well-being.

The University of Wisconsin-Madison Tactile Communication and Neurorehabilitation Laboratory (TCNL) have developed this technology. In the last few years TCNL has created an all-purpose brain stimulating devise called a PoNS. The PoNS device is based on almost forty years of research in neuromodulation, an area involved with changing and regulating the electrochemical structures of the brain. The technical term 'neuromodulation' refers to those activities that balance brain functions, or in terms of Meaning, these are the activities that order and organise brain functions.

The PoNS is a small pocket-sized device, part of which goes in the mouth and rests on the tongue while the other part is linked to a battery or energy source. The tongue unit has 144 electrodes that fire off patterns of electrical impulses (50–200 Hz) in a rhythm of three signals, pause, three signals, which activate only the sensory nerves in the tongue. The vibrations from the electrodes are said to produce a tingling sensation like drinking fizzy water. All that this device does is produce a variety of tiny vibrations that directly stimulate the sensory nerves of the tongue, which in turn stimulate the nerves of the brain stem.

The results of using the PoNS device have been dramatic. For example, after two weeks of using the device twenty minutes a day a woman immobilised by Parkinson's disease recovered her ability to speak and walk and her tremor was diminished. A stroke victim who could not speak, write or read found after therapy she could read anything she wanted. Eight MS patients who came twice a day for two weeks were given the device to take home for another twelve weeks. All seven of the patients who had come in on canes were 'now able to walk faster, longer, go up and down stairs not having to hold on to the rail' (Doidge 2015: 248). The researchers stated that 'Patients reported improved bladder control and improved ability to sleep ... These are things we were not treating, but they're changing'. As MS and Parkinson's are progressive and degenerative diseases these results are truly remarkable.

A significant feature of the PoNS device is what the authors call 'information-free stimulation' (Wildenberg et al. 2010). This means that the device does not attempt to relay any messages, codes, data or instruction through the stimulation of the tongue. In addition, the PoNS device is not involved in any classical conditioning programs that manipulate pain and pleasure sensations. Its stimulations are neutral in regard to pain or pleasure. Hence the device does not attempt to change thought or thinking processes; rather, I suggest, these and similar devices stimulate the no-thinking mind, that is, the autonomic *Implicit-to-Implicit* foundations of the conscious mind.

The artificial electrical stimulation from the PoNS device occurs only on the surface of the tongue and involves sensory neurons 300 microns deep. These neurons 'send their normal, natural signals via the cranial nerves into the brain stem and on throughout the whole functional network' (Doidge 2015: 272). Thus electricity from the device does not stimulate the whole of what Doidge calls the 'functional network' of the nervous system but only the surface sensory neurons of the tongue. And yet the whole functional network of the nervous system is clearly changed by this low-dose neutral stimulation.

What is going on to create these extraordinary breakthroughs in the rehabilitation of these degenerative diseases? The neuroscience explanation for these developments begins from the traditional medical position of *separation seeing*. From this standpoint, it is the physical brain (not the mind) that learns through what is called 'neuroplasticity' and so it is the brain that changes itself physically because the senses provide the direct and necessary avenues for the brain to rewire itself. This materialistic viewpoint is unable to say how or why the physical brain 'knows' about the blueprints for rewiring itself or the order inherent within the rewiring programs, or what constitutes a rewiring. All that this materialistic view can say is that the brain rewires itself because the senses have provided the avenues for the rewiring. This kind of explanation lacks causal linkages as well as coherence.

The other feature of the neuroscience interpretation that is relied on is the doctrine of many minds. This doctrine, which as we have seen is unsupported by any scientific evidence, declares that individuals have separate minds because they have separate brains and brains produce minds. From this perspective, the concepts of 'agency' and 'self-regulation' are entirely local events and are therefore limited to the activities of a specific nervous system. The local event of self-regulation is referred to as 'neuromodulation' and this is the general title given to the research undertaken by TCNL.

When formulating the reasons for these astonishing results the neuroscience vocabulary goes like this: 'the neurostimulation leads to improved homeostasis, or neuromodulation, which balances the network' (Doidge 2015: 275). Yet technical terms like 'neurostimulation', 'neurodifferentiation', 'neurorelaxation' and 'neuromodulation' do not provide a solid argument for the materialist doctrine of many minds or the truth of separation seeing. Simply applying the prefix 'neuro' to a whole range of ordinary terms does not give us evidence that brains produce minds and nor does it overcome the problem of how only minds learn, order, organise and self-regulate. Learning, and therefore plasticity and also differentiation, are functions, not of physical brains but only of minds – of consciousness.

Similar comments can be made about the results of Cranio-Electro Stimulation (CES) in which this kind of stimulation is described as a 'brain-calming technique. These techniques operate by sending small pulses of electrical current through the brain' (Siever 2014). CES devices deliver electrical stimulation through the skin to the brain and nervous system and they have been shown to have beneficial results on depression, anxiety and sleep. Siever writes that 'CES primarily modulates the brain via neurotransmitter production'. What then is the mental equivalent to 'neurotransmitter production'?

Neurotransmitters are the chemicals that make communication between the neurons possible. They are said to regulate (that is, order) moods, cravings, addictions, energy, libido and sleep. In terms of Meaning, here we are talking about exchanges of Meaning in communication, and with an increased production of neurotransmitters we are referring to an increase in the number of connections and exchanges of Meaning. An increase in 'neurotransmitter production', therefore, stands for an increase in exchanges of Meaning, and the kind of Meaning that is being exchanged will be largely Implicit.

In relation to Doidge's reference to 'the network balance', this general phrase can refer to mind functions as much as brain functions and this is because the balance of the whole nervous system entails agency, order and self-regulation. These are features of consciousness and are the key critical features necessary for all living organisms. In other words, the term 'network balance' is just a technical way of referring to the general attributes of the Implicit consciousness within the autonomic nervous system of all living organisms, so these features are not specific attributes of a local human brain.

In terms of Meaning, the organisational functions involved in self-regulation do not refer to a separate individual brain or mind. These functions are inherent features of the meaning of Meaning. Thus the 'self' within self-regulation is not a separate, isolated, individual unit such as the ego or the brain. The 'self' within self-regulation represents a local manifestation of the universal Self of One Consciousness. In other words, the agency by which self-regulation comes about does not come from a local agent (the brain), but represents the local expression of the universal agency of One Consciousness. That universal agency involved in self-regulation comes about because these circular functions are related to order and disorder that are universal qualities.

In other words, self-regulation comes about because order is restored to the system. What does that specifically mean to this network of nervous system interconnections? In terms of Meaning, it can only refer to an abundance of circular relationships and a rich reciprocity of interconnections. In other words, a nervous system restores itself to a well-balanced modulated system when there is an abundance of circular pathways available to provide the Implicit mental energy and freedom necessary to undertake new behaviour. These are the relationships inherent in learning. Leaning is not solely a function of separate minds even though exam results tend to imply this to be the case. Each of us learns according to the universal structure of the arc of learning and these principles apply to all organisms that learn.

Learning begins with the mnemonic resonance of *Implicit-to-Implicit* connections. These Implicit pathways provide the ordered foundation on which we build more abstract and specific symbolic exchanges. Given Schrödinger's principle of 'order-from-order', we can say that the order inherent in Meaning rests with an infinite variety of circular connections of the *Implicit-to-Implicit* variety, and therefore the order inherent in a nervous system that has a healthy self-regulating function comes from the freedom that is provided by high levels of reciprocal interconnections between neurons. As a consequence, what will inhibit such freedom to learn are old linear and separating habits that are deeply engrained and defended as well as having damaged or diseased neurons.

In terms of Meaning, the kind of sensory stimulation produced by the PoNS device is most interesting. It is stimulation that is called 'information-free'. This is the type of stimulation that produces *Implicit-to-Implicit* exchanges and does not contain *Implicit-to-explicit* exchanges; that is, the stimulation contains no coding, no conscious thought or discrimination, even those associated with pain or pleasure. Thus the kind of meaning exchanges that are stimulated by the PoNS device are sensory, non-thinking, *Implicit-to-Implicit* exchanges and these, as I have argued throughout this book, are the foundation features of One Consciousness and stand as the carriers of order.

What is intriguing and surprising about these new developments in sensory stimulation is that a low-dose neutral stimulation of the tongue can reorganise the physical apparatus of brain and nervous system to the extent that some individuals with degenerative diseases are able to function much better. These renewing developments indicate several things. First, these results show how physical stimulation can aid the *Implicit-to-Implicit* functions of One Consciousness so as to regenerate physical and biological forms within the brain and nervous system. According to Doidge (2015, 275–6), these developments involve changes to cell functions, or new and longer lasting synaptic connections, or changes directly to cells, or whole-of-system changes. Each of these physical changes is morphological, that is, they represent the creation of new or improved biological forms.

As stated previously, morphogenesis is the study of how physical forms are formed. As a result of low-dose neutral stimulation of the tongue, new physical and biological forms are formed and created in damaged nervous systems. This evidence indicates a prior causal role for consciousness as the non-physical agency for creating new biological forms through the mind processes of learning and relearning. The agency of One Consciousness is already inherent within the functions of the entire nervous system of every organism that is alive. I would argue that the neutral stimulation from the PoNS and similar devices increases the existing mnemonic resonance of the *Implicit-to-Implicit* exchanges and this increases the flow of Meaning within the whole network so that new and improved biological forms are created.

In this regard, it is worth noting that the physical changes in a nervous system that has had sensory stimulation by a PoNS device are not random, disorganised or chaotic. Rather, they have an order and organisation about them in so far as damaged neurons are reorganised so that the whole system is regulated to function close to its original healthy state. This kind of complex ordering and reorganisation does not fit the functions of a blind, mechanical, dead universe, which is the kind of universe that drives the materialistic interpretations of neuroscience in relation to the PoNS results. Rather, at work here are the organising potentials and purposes of an intelligent One Consciousness.

The extraordinary effects of neutral sensory stimulation are interesting to the therapeutic practitioner because they indicate a possible new habit-changing approach to therapy. Traditionally, the practice of meditation will over time stimulate the non-thinking implicit foundations of the conscious mind. Meditation does this through a repetitive focus on an object (breadth or mantra) so that the influence and intensity of thoughts are slowly reduced, allowing more energy and awareness to be available to the implicit and pre-reflective foundations of the mind. A similar kind of transference of energetic force appears to be happening with the PoNS and CES devices.

For many this direct method of neutral sensory stimulation

may be just what is needed for physiological, psychological and behavioural changes and improvements as well as for those who seek a spiritual evolution. Hence, while these new devices have brought extraordinary results to a range of patients with MS, Parkinson's, stroke and other neurological diseases, these or similar devices may also assist a much wider group of people who suffer from various illnesses. In addition, the benefits of the PoNS device may well extend to those who seek a functional rebalance to their way of thinking and seeing. I am suggesting, therefore, that the PoNS or similar devices may be beneficial not only to people who suffer degenerative neurological diseases but may also become useful to the psychologist, psychiatrist and social worker and as well to the seeker of the Self.

Notes and References

Introduction

1   In this book, I have not used Ken Wilber's ideas on levels of consciousness or referred to his transpersonal view of human evolution as described in his book *Up From Eden* (first published in 1981) and refined in his *Integral Spirituality* (2007). My reason for these omissions is that his levels of consciousness, while intriguing, are not based upon the underlying metaphysical structures and functions of meaning. Rather, they are based loosely on history, scriptures, colours, myth analysis and other writers who have similar theories and discourses. I would respectfully suggest that the structures and functions of meaning can provide a tighter, more definite and coherent set of evolutionary levels of consciousness than more descriptive approaches. The reason for this is the superior explanatory power of meaning, for meaning is inherent within experience, but it is also a subject matter that can be discussed in terms of its metaphysical structures and functions.

2   The Irish visionary poet and activist George William Russell (1867–1935) made the distinction between the politics of time and the politics of eternity in his short novel *The Interpreters*, first published in 1922. The philosophical narrative of this novel is set in the future and is concerned with the question of what constitutes an ideal society. Russell thought that politics was a profane science only because it had not yet discovered it has its roots in the sacred and the spiritual.

Chapter 1

3   For those psychiatrists who are somewhat sympathetic to the role of mind the situation is more complicated. For example, the psychiatrist Jeffrey Schwartz has written, 'The will, it has become clear, has the power to change the brain – in OCD, in stroke, in Tourette's, and now in depression' (Schwartz & Begley 2002: 250).

In giving some credence to the role of the mind, Schwartz goes on to write that 'the arrow of causation relating brain and mind must be bidirectional. Conscious, volitional decisions and changes in behavior alter the brain' (Schwartz & Begley 2002: 95). Schwartz is speaking here about the success of mindfulness treatments for conditions such as obsessive-compulsive disorders (OCD), but his comments are relevant to treatments for a range of neurological conditions.

For Schwartz, the mental force of the mind comes from conscious, wilful intentions. In terms of treatment for brain damage, this force can often activate neuronal circuits in parts of the brain responsible for habitual behaviour (such as the basal ganglia). When this happens, Schwartz says, 'the brain takes over' (Schwartz & Begley 2002: 95). The idea that the brain can take over from the conscious mind has become part of the mythology of neuroscience. It is inherent in the titles of the books by Norman Doidge, *The Brain that Changes Itself* (2010) and in his more recent *The Brain's Way of Healing*, (2015). The idea that the brain can take over from the mind comes from the neurological division in the brain between the subcortical brain that deals with autonomic functions which are said to be 'brain' functions, and a cortical brain that produces conscious attention and deliberate decisions.

In calling subcortical operations 'brain functions', neurological practitioners and researchers have created confusion. The confusion comes from the assertion that the brain's cortical organisation produces conscious wilful decisions while subcortical areas produce autonomic brain functions. In other words, the brain produces both mind functions and brain functions. How can this be possible if the arrow of causation relating brain and mind is bidirectional? Here is confusion about the force and nature of mind, and how bidirectional causation actually works. This ambiguity also raises many questions about the term 'neuroplasticity'.

I am conscious that with his emphasis on mind, Schwartz was challenging the scientific mainstream at the turn of this century. Inherent in that scientific mainstream was the tendency to pay lip service to mind while over-valuing the physical brain. While this imbalance may well have been due to the extent of research undertaken on the brain over the last fifty years in comparison to the work done on the mind, in terms of the question of bidirectional causality the weight that has been given to the brain is, in my view, excessive. I would go even further and suggest that the balance in bidirectional causality should be weighted very much in favour of the mind, not the brain.

In addition, the mind involves much more than just conscious, wilful decisions. Sigmund Freud made this basic observation over a hundred years ago. I would argue that the major part of the mind is non-conscious or pre-reflective and the functions of this part occur within all those operations of the autonomic systems in the body. The logic that develops from this unified view of the mind, which has both conscious and non-conscious parts, is that all the non-conscious autonomic functions of the nervous system have the capacity to learn or relearn simply because these are features of a mind and only a mind can learn and relearn. When non-conscious learning or relearning occurs these mental changes of habit produce the changes that neurological research has witnessed in brain pathways and this is what has been called neuroplasticity. Jeffery Schwartz makes a similar point when he writes, 'Our brain is marked by the life we lead and retains the footprints of the experiences we have had and the behaviours we have engaged in' (Schwartz & Begley 2002: 212).

4 Yet another feature of the neuroscience model of mind involves some interesting research that has detected what has been called the 'readiness potential'. Using the electroencephalograph (EEG), researchers in Germany in the 1960s discovered that between 0.4 and 4 seconds before a voluntary movement occurs (by hand or foot) there was related brain activity. This was interpreted as the brain's preparing to create a voluntary movement. The neuroscience question that came out of these experiments and also later ones in the United States by Ben Libet was how to accurately fix the moment when conscious will arises from the brain.

In this century, a further group of scientists led by Professor John-Dylan Haynes from the Max Planck Institute of Human Cognition and Brain Sciences set about to measure the readiness potential in order to demonstrate that there is an unconscious preparation for decision-making by the conscious mind. They found that this preparation, which is indicated by prior brain activity, might take as long as seven seconds before a free-choice decision is made. The term 'unconscious' was used by the Haynes team to describe this process rather than 'brain activity', and Schwartz has also used this term when discussing Libet's work on readiness potentials (Schwartz & Begley 2002: 306).

Research into the readiness potential suggests a prior context to conscious volition, yet the character of that prior context is confused for neuroscience. For example, is that context one of mind or brain? Within the neuroscience model of mind there is no 'unconscious', so the readiness potential context is brain activity. There are many drawbacks to this model along with its inability to tell us anything about how and why conscious volition arises from brain processes. It is also limited in that this model does not go beyond correlations in regard to the mind–brain relationship ('Unconscious Decisions in the Brain', *Nature Neuroscience*, 13 April 2008, www. physorg.com). I suggest that many of the problems of this model stem from its reliance on the doctrine of many minds with its inbuilt predisposition to see separations where there are none.

5   For Freud and most of his contemporaries the instinct of hunger and reproduction, with the latter's by-product of sexuality, were taken to be the basic motivations for human life. Under these primitive motivating regimes, it was deemed necessary for the civilized European to modify or control his or her instinctual drives in order to live somewhat harmoniously within a community. To accommodate this necessity, repressed desires became an important feature of Freud's complex model of mind. This was a three-part model that involved the systems of id, ego and superego.

The id represents the impulsive part of the mind that is immediately driven by the instincts of hunger, sex and aggression. In contrast, the Freudian ego was the realistic, rational part of the mind that mediates between the impulsive id and the environment. The superego incorporates the values and morals of parents and society and had a role in inhibiting the impulses of the id. In addition to the id, ego and superego Freud proposed various qualities of mind. These were the states of conscious, subconscious and unconscious mind. Freud named another category of mind, the un-repressed unconscious, and then hardly ever mentioned it. However, I have found this a useful term for describing some of the functions of meaning.

Freud assumed his tripartite model to be an archetype that exists beyond the cultural values of Europe or the nineteenth century. However, in challenging that view I would say Freud's model of mind reflects historical conditions in that it refined many of the then common ideas about rationality and irrationality. He also naturally drew on a nineteenth century vocabulary and understanding. His debt to Charles Darwin, for example, is apparent in his theories of child psychology and in the way he uses the term 'instincts'.

Chapter 2

6   In his paper, "Brains and Beyond: The Unfolding Vision of Health and Healing" published in *Being and Biology: Is Consciousness the Life Force*, (2017) Larry Dossey describes a vast number of scientific experiments that provide strong evidence for the individual's mind as a collective experience. One example, Dossey cites was a 2008 paper in the British Medical Journal titled, "Dynamic Spread of Happiness in a Large Social Network". The authors, James H. Fowler and Nicholas A. Christakis state, 'Your happiness depends not just on your choices and actions, but also on the choices and actions of people you don't even know who are one, two and three degrees removed from you . ...emotions have a collective existence - they are not just an individual phenomenon.' The authors of this study found that it was not only happiness that is contagious but so is depression, sadness, obesity, drinking and smoking habits, ill-health and a wide range of other things.

7   In her paper 'Green Symphonies: A call for studies on acoustic communication in plants', Monica Gagliano tells us that plants can communicate with their environment as well as with other plants. 'We have begun to appreciate that plants can warn each other of approaching insect attacks using an extensive vocabulary of chemical molecules' (Gagliano 2012).

Chapter 3

8   In this book meaning is viewed in a holistic sense that is more encompassing than a sense of significance or purpose and also broader than a social drive or personal motivation. Such views of meaning are common to the writings of Viktor Frankl (*The Will to Meaning*, 1988) who was the founder of the Viennese school of psychotherapy called logotherapy. A social psychological view of meaning as a drive or motivation is expressed in a range of papers that have been published in the last two decades. See for example, Heine, Proulx & Vohs 2006 and Van Tongeren & Green 2010.

9   This metaphor I have borrowed from Galen Moore, 'On the Nature of Spiritual Meaning', which was published on a website that no longer exists.

10 The Meaning Maintenance Model (MMM) developed by Heine, Proulx & Vohs (2006) proposes that we derive our sense of meaning from four drives or motivations: a sense of personal worth; resolving doubts and ambiguities; being part of something larger than ourselves; and leaving something of significance behind after death. What is taken for granted in this model is the doctrine of many minds and this situation is somewhat addressed with the idea of *fluid compensation* as an ego-defence mechanism. The concept of fluid compensation means that if one of the four drives for meaning is threatened the individual will seek compensation in extra meaning from the other three drives. For example, if reputation and self-esteem is threatened this may cause the individual to seek comfort in dogmatically reaffirming their view of reality.

From the current perspective that views meaning and consciousness as representing the same mental territory, a psychological discourse about ego-defences may be entertaining but will never enlighten us about the nature of meaning itself. In addition, while the MMM proposes that humans are inexhaustible meaning-makers it cannot describe the meaning-making forms that are available to humans beyond the idea of a lack of meaning that needs a corresponding compensation. Yet it is not from a lack of meaning that we suffer, rather from detrimental forms of meaning-making. For example, the so-called lack of meaning in the life of the individual who is depressed is not due to a 'lack' of meaning, but from knotted patterns of identification of meaning that needs to be unwound, disclosed and lived through. When this therapeutic process occurs, the individual begins to take on new forms of meaning-making that are beneficial and thus more in tune with the structure and functions of Meaning itself. Hence, therapeutic rehabilitation is possible simply because the forms of our meaning-making are tied to and have grown out of, not ego-defences but the broader domain of one universal consciousness.

11 In 1922 *The Meaning of Meaning* was first published. The authors, C.K. Ogden and A.I. Richards, came up with sixteen different definitions of meaning. The ambiguity of these competing definitions did not help to clarify the nature of meaning, its primary status or its relationship to

language and signs. Similarly, the famous 1930s Vienna Circle of logical positivist who emphasised reason, logic, science and technology failed to add to our knowledge about meaning because they were so concerned with proving the truth of empiricism they neglected to study the metaphysics of meaning.

Chapter 6

12   The term often used in scientific literature to describe a relationship of non-symmetry is 'broken symmetry'. This is a term that carries a great deal of confusion because it mixes the metaphysical (relations) with the physical (object). Physical objects can be broken but relations cannot as they can only be transformed. A broken symmetry is a term for a broken potential, which is most confusing. Conventionally, physics does not make distinctions about consciousness or mind, let alone about meaning, and as a consequence these important differences within metaphysics are simply lost in a vocabulary that privileges the material object.

Chapter 7

13   http://www.ctr4process.org/bibliobase/process-and-implicate-order-their-relevance-quantum-theory-and-mind

14   BBC News Technology, 2 December 2014,
      http://www.bbc.com/news/technology-30290540

Chapter 8

15   In *Languages and the Brain* (1981) Karl Pribram cites a series of experiments that show how the visual centres of the brain are surprisingly resistant to surgery. Referring to an experiment by Lashley in 1929, Pribram tells us that 80–90% of the visual cortex of rats were removed or interrupted 'without impairing their ability to discriminate patterns' (Pribram 1981: 119). In addition, Pribram's own experiments in the 1960s found similar results that were 'incompatible with the view that

a photographic-like image becomes projected onto the cortical surface'
(1981: 123).

16 Pribram argues this on the basis that the role of light in visual perception seems similar to its role in the hologram. In addition, he suggests
there is a similar interference occurring in brain activity where there
is an interaction with neighbourhood cell that produce similar kinds
of interference. His neurological investigations had a focus on physical
processes which he then compares with the interference patterns of the
hologram and which display 'many of the attributes of the neural process in perception and thus makes the brain's Imaging mechanism a little
easier to comprehend' (Pribram 1981: 145).

Chapter 13

17 Krishna Das uses this analogy in his DVD *One Life at a Time.*

Chapter 14

18 In his paper, "Complexity, Complementarity, Consciousness" Vasileios
Basios discusses the various features of three systems of logic: quantum
logic, classical Boolean/Aristotelian logic and symmetric logic, (*Being
and Biology: Is Consciousness the Life Force?* Ed., Brenda Dunn & Robert
Jahn, Princeton: ICRL Press, 2017). A system of logic is produced by a
set of implication and/or predispositions that in turn have been created
by the manner in which we perceive the world and make meaning of it.
Hence, symmetric logic is created by patterns of identification that also
create ego and tribal seeing. Aristotelian logic/Boolean logic is created
by the predispositions of separation seeing while quantum/empathic
logic is a feature of empathic seeing (discussed more fully in Chapters
16 and 17).

Appendix A

19 The six brainwaves that are referred to here come from a London-based neurofeedback clinic: brainworksneurotherapy.com Other organisations have indicated only four bandwidths: *delta, theta, alpha* and *beta*. For correlating the transformations of consciousness with brain waves six rather than four provides greater explanation and this is why I have used six here.

Bibliography

Augustine (1960). *The Confessions of St Augustine*, transl. J.K. Ryan. New York: Image Books.

Aurelius, M. (2004). *Meditations*. London: Penguin Books.

Barfield, O. (1988). *Saving the Appearances: A Study in Idolatry*. Middletown CN: Wesleyan University Press.

Being and Biology: Is Consciousness the Life Force? (2017). Ed., Brenda Dunn & Robert Jahn, Princeton: ICRL Press.

Benveniste, E. (1971). *Problems in General Linguistics*, transl. M.E. Meek. Florida: University of Miami Press.

Berger, J. (1972). *Ways of Seeing*. London: BBC and Penguin Books.

Blake, W. (1961). *The Poetical Works of William Blake*, ed. J. Sampson. London: Oxford University Press.

Bohm, D. (1983). *Wholeness and the Implicate Order*. London: Ark.

Bohm, D. (1994). *Unfolding Meaning*. London: Ark.

Bohm, D. (2006). *On Dialogue*. London: Routledge Classics.

Bohm, D. & Hiley, B. (1995). *The Undivided Universe*. London, Routledge.

Boyce, J. (2014). *Born Bad: Original Sin and the Making of the Western World*. Melbourne: Black Inc.

Camus, A. (2005). *The Myth of Sisyphus*, transl. J. O'Brien. London: Penguin.

Capra, F. (1982). *The Turning Point*. New York: Bantam.

Crick, F. (1994). *The Astonishing Hypothesis: The Scientific Search for the Soul.* London: Simon & Schuster.

De Chardin, T. (1970). *Hymn of the Universe.* London: Fontana.

Doidge, N. (2010). *The Brain That Changes Itself: Stories of Personal Triumph from the Frontiers of Brain Science.* Melbourne: Scribe.

Doidge, N. (2015). *The Brain's Way of Healing: Remarkable Discoveries and Recoveries from the Frontiers of Neuroplasticity.* Melbourne: Scribe.

Dennett, D. (1991). *Consciousness Explained.* London: Penguin Press.

Dossey, L. (2013). *One Mind: How our Individual Mind is Part of a Greater Consciousness and Why it Matters.* New York: Hay House.

Frankl, V. (1988). *The Will to Meaning: Foundations and Applications of Logotherapy.* New York: Meridian Books.

Fraser, P.H., Massey, H. & Wilcox, J.P. (2008). *Decoding the Human Body-Field: The New Science of Information as Medicine.* Rochester: Healing Arts Press.

Freud, S. (1961). *Civilization and its Discontents*, transl., J. Strachey. London: W.W. Norton.

Fromm, E. (2002). *The Sane Society.* London: Routledge.

Fulweiler, H. (1993). *'Here a Captive Heart Busted': Studies in the Sentimental Journey of Modern Literature.* New York: Fordham University Press.

Gagliano, M. (2012). 'Green Symphonies: A call for studies on acoustic communication in plants.' *Oxford Journals, Science and Mathematics, Behavioural Ecology* 24(4): 789–96.

Gilson, E. (2002). *God and Philosophy.* New Haven CN: Yale University Press.

Goldberg, P. (2010). *American Veda.* New York: Three Rivers Press.

Goswami, A. (1995). *The Self-Aware Universe: How Consciousness Creates the Material World.* New York: Penguin Putnam.

Grof, S. (1993). *The Holotropic Mind: the Three Levels of Human Consciousness and How they Shape our Lives.* New York: Harper San Francisco.

Grof, S. (1998). *The Cosmic Game: Explorations of the Frontiers of Human Consciousness.* Melbourne: Hill of Content.

Hauke, C. (2000). *Jung and the Postmodern: The Interpretation of Realities.* London: Routledge.

Heine, S.J., Proulx, T. & Vohs, K.D. (2006). The Meaning Maintenance Model: On the coherence of social motivations. *Personality and Social Psychology Review* 10: 88–110.

Hiley, B.J. (n.d.). Process and the Implicate Order: Their relevance to quantum theory and mind. *Theoretical Physics Research Unit, Birkbeck, University of London*, Malet Street, London. /www.ctr4process.org/publications/Articles/LSI05/Hiley%20paper.pdf

Hiley, B. & Peat, F., eds (1991). *Quantum Implications: Essays to Honour David Bohm.* London: Routledge.

Huxley, A. (1970). *The Perennial Philosophy.* New York: Harper & Row.

Jahn, R.G. & Dunne, B.J. (2011). *Consciousness and the Source of Reality: The PEAR Odyssey, Princeton.* New Jersey: ICRL Press, ebook.

Jameson, F. (1991). *Postmodernism, or, the Cultural Logic of Late Capitalism.* Durham NC: Duke University Press.

Jung, C. (1973). *Synchronicity: An Acausal Connecting Principle.* New York: Princeton University Press.

Koestler, A. (1974). *The Roots of Coincidence.* London: Picador.

Krauss, L. (2012). *A Universe from Nothing: Why There Is Something Rather Than Nothing.* New York: Free Press.

Kübler-Ross, E. (1997). On Death and Dying. New York: Touchstone Books.

Küng, H. (2008). The Beginning of All Things: Science and Religion. Cambridge: William B Eerdmans Publishing Co.

Lacan, J. (1985). *Écrits: A selection*, transl. A. Sheridan. New York: W.W. Norton.

Laplanche, J. & Pontalis, J.-B. (1973). The Language of Psychoanalysis, transl. D. Nicholson-Smith. New York: W.W. Norton.

Lao Tsu (1972). Tao Te Ching, transl. Gia-Fu Feng & J. English. New York: Vintage Books.

Laszlo, E. (2004). Science and the Akashic Field: An Integral Theory of Everything. Rochester: Inner Traditions.

Laszlo, E., Houston, J. & Dossey, L. (2016). *What is Consciousness: Three Sages Look Behind the Veil*. New York: SelectBooks Inc.

Le Shan, L. (1980). *Clairvoyant Reality: Towards a General Theory of the Paranormal*. Surrey, UK: Biddles Ltd.

Lohrey, A. (1997). *The Meaning of Consciousness*. Ann Arbor MI: University of Michigan Press.

McLynn, F. (1997). *Carl Gustav Jung: A Biography*. London: Black Swan.

Maier, H. (1965). *Three Theories of Child Development*. New York: Harper.

Massimo, P. (2016). https://aeon.co/essays/the-string-theory-wars-show-us-how-science-needs-philosophy

Matte Blanco, I. (1975). *The Unconscious as Infinite Sets: An Essay on Bi-logic*. London: Duckworth.

Merton, T. (1968). *Zen and the Birds of Appetite*. New York: New Directions.

Milne, J. (2001). 'Visions of the cosmos: Nicholas of Cusa and Giordano Bruno.' *Temenos Academy Review*: 80–93.

Morgart, E. (2014). 'The theory of Everything has Nine Dimensions.' *USA Today Magazine* January: 66–8.

Murray, L. (1994). *Collected Poems*. Melbourne: William Heinemann.

Nagel, T. (2012). *Mind and Cosmos: Why the Materialist Neo-Darwinian Conception of Nature is Almost Certainly False*. New York: Oxford University Press.

Neppe, V. & Close, E. (2015). 'How some conundrums of reality can be solved by applying a finite 9-D spinning model.' *IQNexus Journal* 7(2): 7–94.

Ogden, C.K. and Richards, I.A. (1985). *The Meaning of Meaning*. London: Ark.

Phillips, A. (1988). *Winnicott*. London: Fontana.

Plato (1986). *The Republic*. New York: Penguin Books.

Pribram, K. (1981). *Languages of the Brain: Experimental Paradoxes and Principles in Neuropsychology*. New York: Brandon House.

Prabhavananda (1983). *The Upanishads: Breath of the Eternal*, transl. Swami Prabhavananda & Frederick Manchester. Hollywood: Vedanta Press.

Putnam, R. (2001). *Bowling Alone: The Collapse and Revival of American Community*. New York: Simon & Schuster.

Radin, D. (2006). *Entangled Minds: Extrasensory Experiences in Quantum Reality*. New York: Parview Pocket Books.

Raine, K. (1968). *Blake and Tradition*, 2 vols. New York: Princeton University Press.

Saussure de, F. (1978). *Course in General Linguistics*, Intro. J. Culler, ed. C. Bally & A. Sechehaye, transl. W. Baskin. Glasgow: Fontana/Collins.

Schrödinger, E. (1993). *What is Life? The Physical Aspects of the Living Cell, with Mind and Matter, and Autobiographical Sketches.* Cambridge: Cambridge University Press.

Schwartz, J. & Begley, S. (2002). *The Mind and The Brain: Neuroplasticity and the Power of Mental Force.* New York: Regan Books.

Searle, J. (2015). *Seeing Things as They Are: A Theory of Perception.* Oxford: Oxford University Press.

Selected Letters of Romain Rolland, 1990, Ed., Francis Dore & Marie-Laure Prevost, Delhi: Oxford University Press.

Sheldrake, R. (1987). 'Part I – Mind, memory, and archetype morphic resonance and the collective unconscious.' *Psychological Perspectives* 18(1): 9–25.

Sheldrake, R. (1988a). *A New Science of Life: The Hypothesis of Formative Causation.* London: Paladin.

Sheldrake, R. (1988b). *Presence of the Past: Morphic Resonance and the Habits of Nature.* London: Collins.

Sheldrake, R. (1993). *The Rebirth of Nature.* London: Rider.

Sheldrake, R. (2000). *Dogs That Know When Their Owners Are Coming Home, and Other Unexplained Powers of Animals.* London: Arrow.

Siegel, S. (2011). *The Contents of Visual Experience,* ebook. Oxford: Oxford University Press.

Siever, D. (2014). 'Two earclips, wires, a little box and presto – the wonderful world of cranio-electro stimulation.' *Mind Alive*: https://mindalive.com

Spencer-Brown, G.S. (1977). *Laws of Form.* New York: Dutton Paperbacks.

Stanner, W.E.H. (2009). *The Dreaming and Other Essays.* Melbourne: Black Inc.

Stapp, H. (1971). 'S-Matrix interpretation of quantum theory.' *Physical Review D3*: 1303–20.

Stone, R. (1989). *The Secret Life of Your Cells*. Atglen: Whitford Press.

Storr, A. (1983). *Jung: Selected Writings*. London: Fontana.

Talbot, M. (1991), *The Holographic Universe*. London: Grafton Books.

Thich Nhat Hanh (1974). *Zen Keys*. New York: Anchor Books.

Tononi, G. (2012). *Phi: A Voyage From the Brain to the Soul*. New York: Pantheon Books.

Uexküll von, J. (2010). *A Foray into the Worlds of Animals and Humans: With a Theory of Meaning*, transl. D. O'Neil. Minneapolis MI: University of Minnesota Press.

Van Tongeren, D.R. & Green, J.D. (2010). Combatting meaninglessness: On the automatic defense of meaning. *Personality and Social Psychology Bulletin* 36: 1375–84.

Voss, A. (2011). 'God or the Daemon? Platonic astrology in the Christian cosmos. *Temenos Academy Review* 14: 96–116.

Vygotsky, L. (1981). *Thought and Language*, transl. E. Hanfmann & G. Vakar. Cambridge MA: MIT Press.

Watts, A. (1975). *TAO: The Watercourse Way*. New York: Pantheon.

Whorf, B. (1979). *Language, Thought and Reality*, ed. J. Carroll. Cambridge MA: MIT Press.

Wilber, K. (ed.) (1984). *Quantum Questions: Mystical Writings of the World's Great Physicists*. Boston: Shambhala.

Wilber, K. (1996). *Up From Eden: A Transpersonal View of Human Evolution*. Wheaton IL: Adyar Books.

Andrew Lohrey

Wilber, K. (2007). *Integral Spirituality: A Startling New Role for Religion in the Modern and Postmodern World*. Boston: Integral Books.

Wildenberg, J.C., Tyler, M.E., Danilov, Y.P., Kaczmarek, K.A. & Meyerand, M.E (2010). 'Sustained cortical and subcortical neuromodulation induced by electrical tongue stimulation'. *Brain Imaging and Behavior* 4: 199–211.

Yogananda, Paramahansa (1994). *Wine of the Mystic: The Rubaiyat of Omar Khayyam*, transl., E. Fitzgerald. Los Angeles: Self-Realization Fellowship.

Young, A. (1999). *The Reflexive Universe*. Cambria CA: Anodos Foundation.

Acknowledgments

This book has had a long history, going back to the 1970s. I was then a member of the International Society of General Semantics where I was trying to come to a workable appreciation of Alfred Korzybski's tome: *Science and Sanity*. This is a difficult but extraordinary book written by a very creative thinker. I struggled for years over the myth of identity as captured by the verb 'to be', yet many of the pegs that mark out this current book have come from *Science and Sanity*. Overall, Korzybski's work provided me with a framework for a depth of appreciation of the idea that meaning has multiple levels.

Korzybski's many references to 'semantic reactions' had me continually pondering the question: 'what was a semantic reaction'? This query broadened in the 1980s when I began studying semiotics and applied linguistics and undertook my PhD at the University of Technology, Sydney. During that research I discovered that Korzybski's 'semantic reactions' could be discussed in terms of implicit and explicit meaning and these in turn were complemented by David Bohm's theory of the implicate and explicate orders. That series of connections led to the structure and function of consciousness as described in this book.

Korzybski wrote about meaning not as a by-product of the interaction of signs, which is the standard approach. Rather, he conceived and wrote about meaning as a primary and vital force, a lived experience that involves the ways in which we respond to the world. It was this empathic view from the inside of meaning that inevitably led me to map consciousness with the implicit/explicit structure of meaning.

Over the years this book has changed a great deal and gone through many drafts. I do not regard what is written here as a finished work but more a work-in-progress. I am now getting old and feel this writing journey needs a publishing rest at a place that is above the drafting valley, beyond the foothills of endless thought where on clear days the elevation and fullness of the mountain may be glimpsed through the fog.

The spiritual pole-star of this writing about science and consciousness has come from the long, deep silence of my guru, Amma. Perhaps it would be more generally acceptable to also acknowledge that the works of William Blake have influenced me greatly. My appreciation of Blake and the cultural context in which he lived and wrote has been broadened and deepened by the reading of his work offered by the visionary poet Kathleen Raine. Her two volumes of *Blake and Tradition* are a masterpiece of illumination.

I am indebted to a range of people who have assisted me in producing this book. I thank Venetia Somerset for her empathic and critical editing and her useful suggestions about where I should insert my own experience into the text. I am also grateful to James Boyce who read a recent draft and made some constructive structural suggestions that I have implemented. My thanks also go to Professor Bruce Boreham who read the manuscript and was kind enough to write some supportive comments from the viewpoint of a physicist.

My sincere appreciation also goes to the distinguished United States physician and author, Larry Dossey whom I have never met but who has been so supportive of my work over several years. Finally, I would like to thank the long-ago supervisor of my PhD dissertation, Professor Stephen Muecke who was good enough to read the manuscript and write the Preface to this book.

I also acknowledge my debt to my daughter Cleo who has been a critical friend in this endeavour and to my gifted wife Amanda, who has been my harshest and best critic. Thanks also to Michelle Lovi for her early designs and layout. Finally, my appreciation goes to Brenda Dunne and the production team at ICRL who have published this book and have worked so quickly and positively on the final product.